RED INC.

RED INC.

Dictatorship and the Development of Capitalism in China, 1949 to the Present

Robert K. Schaeffer

Paradigm Publishers
Boulder • London

Published in the United States by Paradigm Publishers, 2845 Wilderness Place, Boulder, Colorado 80301 USA.

Paradigm Publishers is the trade name of Birkenkamp & Company, LLC, Dean Birkenkamp, President and Publisher.

Library of Congress Cataloging-in-Publication Data

Schaeffer, Robert K.
Red inc. : dictatorship and the development of capitalism in China, 1949 to the present / Robert K. Schaeffer.
p. cm.
Includes bibliographical references and index.
ISBN 978-1-59451-711-2 (hardcover : alk. paper)
ISBN 978-1-59451-712-9 (pbk. : alk. paper)
1. China—Economic policy—2000–. 2. Capitalism—Political aspects—China.
3. Dictatorship—China. I. Title.

HC427.95.S33 2011
330.951—dc22

2011008494

Printed and bound in the United States of America on acid-free paper that meets the standards of the American National Standard for Permanence of Paper for Printed Library Materials.

Designed and Typeset by Straight Creek Bookmakers.

16 15 14 13 12 5 4 3 2 1

Contents

Preface

> "Some books present fresh evidence; others make arguments that urge the reader to see old problems in a new light. This work is decidedly of the latter sort."
>
> *Theda Skocpol, States and Social Revolutions*[1]

This book takes as its subject the development of capitalism in China. Like Skocpol's, it urges the reader to see old problems in a new light. The central problem is how to understand economic and political developments in China since 1949. I take 1949 as a starting point because developments in the 1950s and 1960s shaped policies and practices in subsequent years. Thus, contemporary events can be understood only by taking a close look at China in the early years.

Many scholars have argued that Chinese history since the revolution should be divided into two parts: a Maoist period (1949–1978), when the Chinese Communist Party promoted "socialism," and a reformist period (1978 to the present) when Deng and his successors promoted "capitalism." This approach emphasizes the economic *dis*continuity between the two periods regardless that the reforms adopted by Chinese leaders in the 1980s were first introduced by Mao in the 1950s and that the Communist Party held political power throughout the entire postrevolutionary period. In my view, this approach creates several problems.

First, it requires the reader to assume that the regime under Mao practiced "socialism." This is difficult to sustain. As Maurice Meisner has argued, "There was little that was socialist in Chinese Communist policies during the early years of the People's Republic. The accomplishments of the mid-1950s essentially amounted to a capitalist or bourgeois revolution, albeit with only marginal participation of what remained of the bourgeoisie."[2] I would go further. There was *nothing* socialist about the regime's policies. It was socialist only if one defines the term in an extremely cynical and impoverished way. From the outset, the regime worked furiously to accumulate the capital it needed to finance rapid industrialization and provide wealth for the new ruling class. This ongoing project promoted the development of *capitalism,* not socialism, in China.

Second, this approach means that because the regime remained in power during *both* periods, it must have changed in some fundamental way from a party led by "socialist revolutionaries" to a party led by "capitalist roaders." This requires the reader to assume, as many scholars do, that the class character of the regime changed dramatically from one period to the next. However, this argument is difficult to sustain empirically because the ruling class that came to power in 1949 remains in power today, and central political figures like Deng Xiaoping provided leadership during both periods.

Third, this approach urges readers to adopt what is essentially a Maoist interpretation of events. This is extremely problematic given the fact that Mao adopted disastrous economic and political policies, repeatedly changed his positions, and always provided a self-serving justification for his actions and retractions. In my view, the lingering nostalgia for Mao, which finds expression in the emphasis on the *dis*continuities between Mao and his successors, undermines serious scholarship and should be abandoned.

Conversely, this book sees the problem of periodization in a different way. First, it sees *continuity* where others see *dis*continuity. In my view, the regime in both periods promoted capitalist development, a goal that the regime shared in common with many other developmentalist dictatorships during the postwar period. Around the world, dictatorships in both "capitalist" and "communist" spheres promoted capitalist development as a way to industrialize their economies, modernize their societies, and catch up with urban, industrialized countries in the West. Second, the regime in China did *not* fundamentally change as a class after Mao died; instead, it advanced its long-term and ongoing interests as a ruling class and provided economic and political rewards to both Maoists and reformers.

Of course, although this book insists on economic and political continuity, it recognizes important economic and political differences between the two periods. The main economic difference was that although Mao and Deng both promoted capitalist development, Mao *failed* to achieve any real economic growth during the first period, whereas Deng and his successors *succeeded* in promoting economic growth during the second period. Mao failed, in part, because he tried to promote development with little external aid. By contrast, Deng successfully mobilized foreign investors to assist the development of capitalism in China. In political terms, Mao initiated faction fighting that divided the ruling class in the first period. In the later period, Deng and his successors united the fractious ruling class and enhanced its power. In my view, the important conflicts within the regime were not struggles between *different* classes—a characterization that depends, again, on a Maoist interpretation of events—but rather between factions of the *same* class. This may seem a trivial distinction, but as we will see, it is a critical difference that has significant consequences.

In general, this book's emphasis on continuity has two important consequences. First, it means that the early, Maoist period must be analyzed to appreciate developments in subsequent years. Second, taking a long view of events means that all of the major developments in China since 1949 need to be reassessed: land reform and collectivization, the Great Leap Forward and famine, the Cultural Revolution, economic reforms, Tiananmen Square, and the rapid economic growth that occurred after 1989.

* * *

This book relies on the work of scholars and journalists who study China. Scholars such as Carl Riskin, Mark Selden, Elizabeth J. Perry, Dorothy Solinger, and Maurice Meisner provided the factual bedrock for the arguments made here. Journalists such as Keith Bradsher, David Barbosa, Sheryl WuDunn, Nicholas D. Kristof, Andrew Jacobs, and Edward Wong made careful observations of contemporary conditions in China. Although China scholars and I agreed on the facts, we often drew different conclusions from them, which is a normal occurrence in a field in which people with different political perspectives sharply contest the interpretation of events.

What's more, this book does not rely on the work of China scholars alone. Many of the arguments made here depend on the theories and analyses of non-China scholars. I relied on Adam Smith to analyze Chinese mercantilism; Karl Marx to criticize Mao's treatment of class; John Maynard Keynes to understand the hoarding behavior of landlords, peasants, workers, consumers, and the state; Richard Nelson to appreciate the problems associated with economic development and population growth, which contributed to a "low-level equilibrium trap"; Maria Mies, Torry Dickinson, and Diane Wolf to understand households, women, and the paid and unpaid work of women and girls; Amartya Sen to put the one-child policy in perspective; Paul Krugman to analyze economic crises in the 1990s; and Immanuel Wallerstein to understand the Cultural "Revolution" and the fractious behavior of the ruling class.

This book also grew out of my previous work on China. I study global problems, China among them, and have written about China in books on partition, democratization, globalization, and gender.[3] I also found that my early work on mercantilism and class analysis helped make sense of the regime's economic policies and political struggles.[4]

Finally, this work is indebted to my colleagues: Torry Dickinson, whose work on gender informed my analysis of women; Wayne Nafziger, who introduced me to Richard Nelson's work; Laszlo Kulcsar, who assisted my analysis of demographic issues in China; Anne Garrett, who provide editorial assistance; and Jeff Dickinson, who prepared the charts.

* * *

The chapters that follow are organized in chronological fashion. The first two examine developments in the 1950s: land reform, collectivization, the Great Leap Forward, and famine. Chapter 3 examines the Cultural Revolution in the 1960s. Chapter 4 describes the battle for succession that followed Mao's death in 1976. Deng Xiaoping and the "reforms" are analyzed in chapter 5. These reforms contributed to economic problems and political turmoil that culminated in events at Tiananmen Square in 1989. This is the subject of chapter 6. During the 1990s economic crises in other countries persuaded foreign firms to invest heavily in China, a development that contributed to rapid economic growth in China. Chapter 7 explores the origin of crises in South East Asia and Latin America and their impact on China. Chapter 8 explains why US officials and private businesses have supported the regime and contributed to Chinese economic development during the 1990s and 2000s. Chapter 9 shows how the ruling class consolidated political and economic power during the 1990s and then used its authority to divide and suppress rural and urban workers in China. Finally, the conclusion examines the problems and prospects for the regime in coming years.

Chapter One

Agrarian Reform and the Consolidation of Power

> "On the basis of your actual conditions, adopt all effective measures, squeeze out all of the labor force that can be squeezed out."
>
> *Mao Zedong*[1]

The development of capitalism in China did not begin with the "reforms" introduced by Deng Xiaoping in 1978; rather, it began with the policies introduced by Mao Zedong in 1949. Although "capitalism" existed before 1949, "China" did not. Between 1911 and 1949 warlords, Japanese invasion, and civil war effectively divided China. The development of "capitalism," in a coherent political entity called "China," began only after Mao took power in 1949. Mao successfully extracted a surplus that the country could use to finance industrialization and promote economic growth in the mainland. But he then squandered the wealth that the regime obtained, at enormous cost, from its citizens. During the first thirty years, the dictatorship under Mao failed to use the surplus it extracted to generate any real economic growth. Like Mao, Deng also promoted capital accumulation, but unlike Mao, Deng successfully used the capital extracted from workers to promote rapid economic growth during the thirty years since 1978.

Why did Mao fail and Deng succeed?

The answer to that question is the subject of this book.

The book is divided into two parts. The first part examines the period from 1949 to 1978, when Mao promoted capitalist development *without* growth. The second part looks at the period from 1978 to 2008, when Deng and his successors successfully promoted both capitalist development *and* rapid growth.

Many scholars have argued that there is a sharp discontinuity between the two periods. They maintain that Mao practiced "socialist" economic policies, initiated a "Cultural Revolution" in politics, and that he promoted a "transition to socialism." Deng, by contrast, is said to have "abandoned" socialism and embarked on a "capitalist road" to economic development. The argument here is that, although Mao failed to promote economic growth, he did create social structures that made it possible for Deng to achieve economic growth in the latter period. In this regard Mao contributed to the development of *capitalism*, not socialism, in China.

The problem for both Mao and Deng was how to create an economic surplus, accumulate capital, and use it to promote economic development. In China, as in most poor countries around the world, people in rural and urban settings typically consumed, hoarded, or saved the wealth they created and were unable or unwilling to invest it effectively. As the British economist John Maynard Keynes argued, "there has been a chronic tendency throughout human history for the propensity to save to be stronger than the inducement to invest. The weakness of the inducement to invest has been at all times the key to the economic problem." The propensity to save, which he described as "the primary evil," was one of the chief obstacles to economic development, not only in poor countries but also in rich ones. "The desire of the individual to augment his personal wealth by abstaining from consumption has usually been stronger than the inducement to the entrepreneur to augment the national wealth by employing labor on the construction of durable assets," Keynes observed.[2] To address this problem, Keynes urged government officials to use public resources to invest in the economy. He argued that this investment, what is called a "stimulus package" today, would persuade private citizens to overcome their inclination to save and instead use their wealth to invest and consume, which would contribute to economic growth.

In China the regime decided that the state would have to use public resources to invest in economic development, both because social classes were unwilling or unable to do so on their own and because Mao and other leaders, like Deng, believed that they knew how best to promote economic development. The problem for them was how to generate the capital they needed to invest. Mao's solution was to wage a series of class struggles that essentially forced people in different classes to produce a surplus, as Mao put it, to "squeeze out all of the labor force that can be squeezed out," and then use the surplus to finance industrialization, promote economic growth, and provide collective and individual wealth for the members of the ruling class.

After taking power in 1949, the regime waged four campaigns to create the conditions for capital accumulation and development. Each of them involved seizing the assets and reorganizing the labor of different social classes. During the first campaign, from 1949 to 1955, the dictatorship seized the assets of rural landlords and the urban bourgeoisie to gain control of their wealth and eliminate them as a political and economic force in China. When this campaign ended, the regime in 1955 seized the assets of rural proprietors and reorganized rural and urban workers so as to increase agricultural production and promote rural industrialization as part of the regime's efforts to spur rapid economic growth during the Great Leap Forward. This second campaign came to a close in 1960 when industry and agriculture collapsed, a development that triggered widespread famine. After a brief hiatus, Mao in 1966 launched a "Cultural Revolution" to struggle against other members of the ruling class. Mao used the Cultural Revolution to purge his opponents, reward his supporters, and make the bureaucracy a more effective instrument of his authority, which had been in decline. This third campaign lasted from 1966 to about 1970. After Mao died in 1975, factions of the ruling class fought to identify his successor. This fourth campaign ended in 1978, when Deng Xiaoping returned to power.

These four campaigns contributed both to the proletarianization of workers in China and to the accumulation of capital. But they also created problems that undermined economic growth. This chapter examines the first campaign, which the regime directed against landlords and the urban bourgeoisie. The regime's campaign against rural proprietors as well as rural and urban workers is the subject of chapter 2. The internecine struggles within the ruling class during the Cultural Revolution are examined in chapter 3, and the battle of succession in chapter 4.

Agrarian Reform and the Destruction of the Ruling Classes

Before 1949 China was ruled by Chiang Kai-shek and the nationalist party, the Guomindong (GMD). The nationalist party represented a diverse coalition of ruling classes: a military-political elite funded by state revenues; a foreign bourgeoisie that controlled much of the large-scale industry in China; a domestic bourgeoisie that owned small-scale firms; and a large rural gentry that owned much of China's arable land. Although these classes were all capitalist, Mao and the Chinese Communist Party (CCP) described them as backward, feudal, semifeudal, or colonial classes because they were either unwilling or unable to use the wealth they extracted from Chinese workers to invest in industry or agriculture and thereby promote economic development. Many scholars have agreed with this assessment, arguing that "the structure of the agrarian economy and rural society combined with the absence of effective political leadership to dissipate potential output surpluses or to prevent their mobilization for investment in future economic growth.... [It was a] social system which guaranteed economic stagnation."[3] By characterizing China's ruling classes as "feudal," Mao was essentially arguing that they were insufficiently *capitalist* and that they should be eliminated and replaced by the communist party, which he believed would be a more effective agent of capital accumulation and economic development.

There is some evidence that China's ruling classes consumed or squandered the capital they accumulated and were unwilling to invest it in economic development, though this is a characteristic feature of many ruling classes in many colonial and postcolonial settings. Chiang Kai-shek and the GMD had successfully used state power to defeat rival warlords and centralize political power in the regions of China that neither the Japanese (before and during World War II) nor the communist party controlled.[4] However, the military-political elite was notoriously corrupt and squandered the economic and military aid the United States provided it. The regime proved incapable of mounting an effective defense against invading Japanese forces or campaign effectively against the communist party's revolutionary armies during the civil war that erupted after World War II. As communist forces advanced, Chiang Kai-shek and members of the regime fled to Taiwan, Hong Kong, and the United States as well as Burma and overseas Chinese communities across Southeast Asia.[5] The foreign bourgeoisie, also fleeing the communist advance, joined them.

Foreign Bourgeoisie. In prerevolutionary China, the foreign bourgeoisie in China controlled "about 42 percent of [China's] industrial assets" and owned most of the country's large-scale industry." But most of their investments were designed to serve "the needs of foreign inhabitants" living in China, not Chinese consumers in domestic markets, and they typically repatriated their profits overseas. They did little to finance the expansion of industry in China, a practice that was typical of foreign firms in postcolonial settings around the world. As a result, "imperialism siphoned off resources that *could* have been devoted to capital formation and economic growth." When communist forces entered the cities, most of the foreign bourgeoisie and their agents abandoned their investments and left the country. When the Korean War broke out in 1950, the United States embargoed trade with China. The embargo "crippled the activities of foreign enterprises [that remained] in China, and they began closing."[6] They would not return until the late 1970s.

Domestic Bourgeoisie. The domestic bourgeoisie owned small-scale industries and businesses in China. They could not compete effectively with the foreign bourgeoisie and could not generate the kind of capital needed to finance large-scale industrial development on their own, a problem common to domestic capitalists in many countries. Indigenous capitalists have sometimes provided the nucleus for industrial development if the state provided them with substantial resources, as regimes did in South Korea and Taiwan. Where foreign capitalists were strong, however, as they were in China until the revolution, foreign interests usually persuaded state officials not to assist the domestic bourgeoisie if state aid would have enabled them to compete effectively with foreign business. Foreign investors in colonial and postcolonial settings successfully argued that state aid violated free-market principles. Although industry in China had grown by 44 percent between 1918 and 1933, the Great Depression, Japanese invasion and occupation, World War II, and the civil war had seriously disrupted industrial development and discouraged investment so that "industrial production in 1949 was only 56 percent of its pre-war peak level."[7] Under these conditions, that the industrial bourgeoisie were unwilling or unable to invest heavily in China's economic development was not surprising.

Rural Gentry. The rural "gentry," the landlords who made up only 4 percent of the rural population but owned between 30 and 44 percent of the agricultural land, was the largest and most significant capitalist class in China.[8] The landlords earned money by renting out their land to tenant farmers. These farmers or sharecroppers paid their landlords about 50 percent of the annual crop as rent. Rents varied considerably by region, from as low as 24 percent in North and East China to as high as 70 and even 90 percent in the Pearl River Delta, but most scholars agree that 50 percent of the crop was the average rent.[9] The landlords frequently demanded that tenants pay some rent in advance and required them to perform some unpaid labor as a condition of their tenancy. The gentry also hired rural workers to till their land and toil as domestic servants in their households. Furthermore, they were not only landlords but also moneylenders. They loaned money, often at usurious rates—"interest rates, while concentrated in the 20–40 percent range, not uncommonly reached over 100 percent per annum"—to rural proprietors, tenants, and landless wage workers.[10]

Villagers used the money they borrowed from landlords to purchase agricultural inputs and land, buy grain to survive in the event of natural disaster or famine, and pay for weddings and funerals. Although some scholars describe the later as "non-productive" uses, the money that peasants spent to marry into a more prosperous family could improve their economic circumstances, an investment they might regard as a "productive" use of their resources.[11]

These income-generating activities defined the landlords as a capitalist class, not a feudal one. As Theda Skocpol argued, "Chinese agriculture was in no sense 'feudal.'"[12] But whereas the landlords were not a feudal class, they typically consumed, saved, hoarded, or loaned the wealth they extracted from their tenants and rural neighbors and did not invest heavily in agriculture. As one scholar has noted, "If . . . the landlord uses his above-average income for above-average (luxury) consumption rather than investment . . . the income inequality associated with property ownership would make no contribution to development." Without investment, food production increased slowly and barely kept pace with rural China's growing population in the years before the revolution.

One study of rural China found that "net investment in agriculture was close to zero in traditional China and numerous case observations confirm the non-investing behavior of the typical landlord."[13] Many scholars have agreed with Mao's characterization of the gentry as a backward, selfish class. Maurice Meisner, for example, argued that "the gentry traditionally had been a basically parasitic class, deriving wealth through rents from their landholdings but contributing little or nothing to production.... They were a class dispensable on economic grounds as well as socially and politically undesirable."[14]

Although Mao and scholars have blamed landlords for their "failure" to invest in agriculture, whether the landlords were entirely at fault is not clear. Between 1918 and 1933 agricultural production actually increased by 22 percent, which suggests that landlords had either invested in agriculture *or* loaned money to rural workers who invested in agriculture.[15] Agricultural production then stagnated after 1933, which suggests that investment faltered, but the timing is key. Agricultural stagnation between 1933 and 1949 was likely due to the Great Depression and world war, which disrupted agricultural production and made investment in agriculture a risky proposition for landlord lenders and rural borrowers. This stagnation may not have been due to the behavior of a "miserly" landlord class. As John Maynard Keynes pointed out, the propensity to save has been a characteristic behavior not only of the gentry but also of virtually *every* social class in contemporary society, particularly when investment is risky, as it is during economic downturns and war.[16]

When Mao came to power, he regarded the residual ruling classes in China—the domestic bourgeoisie and the gentry—not only as a threat to his newly won political power but, more importantly, as backward classes who were unwilling to invest their wealth in industry or agriculture. Because Mao viewed the bourgeoisie and the gentry as a political threat and as obstacles to economic development, he moved quickly to eliminate them as social classes, though he took a very different approach to each: liquidating the gentry but co-opting the domestic bourgeoisie.

Agrarian Reform

In 1950 the regime introduced the Agrarian Reform Law. The first article of the new law explained why the regime thought that the gentry should be destroyed: "The landownership system of feudal exploitation by the landlord class shall be abolished and the system of peasant ownership shall be introduced in order to set free the rural productive forces, develop agricultural productivity, and thus pave the way for China's new industrialization." The measure authorized state officials to "seize the land, draught animals, farm implements and surplus grain of the landlords, and their surplus houses."[17] However, as the law targeted the landlord class for elimination, the regime promised that rich peasants—the 6 percent of the rural population who, like landlords, hired workers, rented land, and accounted for "almost half of total agricultural production"—and "middle peasants" would be "protected from infringement."[18]

To implement the law, the regime instructed its "cadre," or members of the communist party, to set up tribunals and mobilize rural workers and proprietors to attack landlords, "punish, according to law, the hated despotic elements who have committed heinous crimes," seize their property, and redistribute their assets.[19]

Most of cadre who organized tribunals had no legal training, though it hardly mattered because their role was to "prepare evidence and plant witnesses ... make strong speeches and incite the masses against the accused. From the judicial point of view, the defendants were 'judged' before they were brought to the [mass meeting]." The accused landlords were then punished for their "crimes." In this context the tribunals assumed that landlords were criminals and treated anyone who tried to disperse their property, shield their assets from confiscation, or slaughter their animals as "lawless landlords" who would be subjected to severe penalties, including death.[20] While cadre-organized tribunals, which closely resembled the vigilante lynch mobs that local government officials and Klansmen assembled on courthouse steps in the Jim Crow South during the same period, the leaders of the regime in China exhorted cadre to rid their deliberations of a "mentality of peaceful land reform" and encourage the masses to "vent their anger on someone." The difference between lynch mobs in the United States and in China is that mobs in the United States were organized by local and state government officials, not by *federal* authorities, whereas in China they were organized by central government authorities at the highest level. Officials in the central government admitted that this might produce "some overheated activity," but told cadre that "cold water should not be poured on a little ultra-left activity so long as it is the masses' own anti-feudal action." Government officials sought to create a "great burning movement ... to destroy the landlord's political control" and said that they would count land reform as a success when "the peasant raises his head and grinds the landlord into the earth."[21]

During the next three years the regime's local tribunals murdered several million landlords, imprisoned millions more, drove many to suicide, and reduced millions of survivors to poverty on small, residual estates.[22] It is difficult to say how many landlords died during land reform. In Kwangtung province, "local authorities reported 28,000 executions in the 10-month period from October 1950 to August 1951." Zhou Enlai later said in a 1957 speech that, of the "counterrevolutionary cases" handled by the government between 1950 and 1952, "16.8 percent were sentences to death, 42.3 to 'reform through labor [prison],' 32 percent placed under 'surveillance,' and 8.9 percent subject only to 'reeducation.' Using the government's figure of 800,000 counterrevolutionary trials during the first half of 1951, there were 135,000 official executions during that period alone." Other observers have estimated that the regime executed two million people and imprisoned another two million in forced labor camps between 1950 and 1953, most of them landlords.[23]

Of course, because the tribunals did not adopt uniform practices or follow common procedures, they often killed or imprisoned people who had an ambiguous economic status. Take, for example, a widow in Quangdong who owned some land and fishponds and worked the land with the help of her son and a hired laborer. "Although she had never oppressed anyone and was not a hated figure in the village, she fitted the criteria of a landlord and was . . . ordered to deliver a large amount of grain to the peasants' association. . . . She did not have enough money to buy that much grain herself, and her [deceased] husband's relatives . . . refused to lend her [the money]. In despair . . . she committed suicide."[24]

Although millions of landlords were killed, jailed, or driven to suicide, the vast majority of the twenty million landlords and their families survived the pogrom. They were "provided with small plots of land and reduced to the unaccustomed role of cultivators of the soil."[25] Although the regime had changed the gentry's economic and social circumstances, it continued to register them as "landlords," a pejorative—even "criminal"—class category that was also assigned to the other members of their household and to their heirs "so that children acquired the stigmatized status of their parents."[26]

In economic terms the regime seized and redistributed 44 percent of China's arable land to some 300 million peasants.[27] Land reform doubled the average size of poor peasant's farms from one to two acres. Middle peasants owned, on average, 50 percent more land than poor peasants; "rich" peasants owned twice as much.[28] Rural farmers now owned the land they cultivated, no longer paid rent to landlords, and used the savings to eat better and invest in agricultural improvements on their land. Independent, small-scale rural proprietors responded to these developments by working harder and more efficiently. As a result, rural proprietors increased food production dramatically, agricultural output increased 15 percent annually, and in 1952 peasant proprietors produced more food than they had in 1936, which had been "the best of the prewar years."[29]

The Domestic Bourgeoisie

The regime took a very different approach to eliminating the domestic bourgeoisie as a class. Unlike foreign capitalists, the domestic bourgeoisie owned relatively small factories and businesses: half of the factories owned by the domestic bourgeoisie employed less than five hundred workers, and the other half employed less than fifty.[30] Generally speaking, the regime did not mobilize workers and exhort them to murder the owners of industrial factories, banks, and mercantile houses, though "mass campaigns of great *mental* cruelty were used in an attack upon the owners of industrial and commercial enterprises between 1951 and 1955."[31] Instead of killing the urban bourgeoisie, the regime seized their assets, *compensated* them for their losses, and frequently asked them to stay on to help cadre manage the business, though as salaried employees not owners.

The regime's approach to the bourgeoisie contrasted sharply with its campaign against rural landlords. In the cities, communist party cadre went to factories owned by the bourgeoisie and conducted an inventory of the firms' assets. They typically assessed the value of the firms at about one-fifth of their real value.[32] They then issued shares based on this assessment to the previous owners, and the government paid shareholders an annual 5 percent fixed dividend for the shares they owned for a period of seven years (this was later extended to ten years), regardless of whether the firm turned a profit.[33] The owners of the banks in China, however, were less fortunate. To battle inflation, the regime seized their deposits without compensation, which forced most of their owners into bankruptcy. Only a few large banks were taken over by the regime.[34]

Because the regime lacked the expertise to run the factories they seized, they usually asked the owners to stay on as managers, though they assigned cadre to oversee their work. Of course, this provided cadre with opportunity to profit from "corruption, such as the 'five evils' (bribery of government workers, tax evasion, theft of state property, cheating on government contracts, and stealing economic information from the state)."[35]

By seizing their assets and reducing the urban bourgeoisie to wage workers, the regime destroyed their economic base and effectively proletarianized them. Still, by paying them dividends on undervalued shares, the regime cushioned their fall. The state paid compensation to about 760,000 "private industrialists and businessmen" and another 380,000 small shareholders. In 1950 the bourgeoisie in Shanghai had earned 830 million yuan, but by 1956 their collective income had fallen to 123 million yuan.[36] Although their economic circumstances had been reduced, they survived the destruction of their class without significant loss of life, though the party continued to label the survivors and their children as members of "bad classes."

This prompts the question: Why did the regime treat the urban bourgeoisie with restraint? After all, the domestic bourgeoisie had supported the nationalist party and exploited their workers.

The party treated the bourgeoisie with kid gloves because it viewed the bourgeoisie as a "productive" class that promoted industrial development, a goal the party shared, and because it needed the bourgeoisie's managerial skills to run the firms the regime seized. Mao said that the party should "protect the industry and commerce of the bourgeoisie" and argued that "[in] view of China's economic backwardness ... it will still be necessary to permit the existence for a long time of a petty bourgeoisie and middle bourgeoisie [domestic bourgeoisie].... This capitalist sector will still be an indispensable part of the whole national economy."[37]

Nevertheless, if the regime could compensate, not kill, the members of the bourgeoisie, why did it refuse to take the same approach to the landlord class? The regime could have eliminated the gentry as a class, just as it did the bourgeoisie, without using violence. That is exactly what Chiang Kai-shek and the nationalists did after they took power in Taiwan. There, the GMD confiscated landlord property in excess of three hectares, compensated landlords with shares of stock and government bonds, which paid 4 percent interest, and distributed landlords' land to poor rural proprietors.[38] According to Mark Selden, "Land reform [in Taiwan] virtually eliminated the big landlords and consolidated the position of the small-owner cultivator as the bulwark of Taiwan agriculture."[39]

There are several reasons why the communist regime in China chose violence, not confiscation and compensation, to destroy the landlords as a class. First, the bourgeoisie was a small social class, with fewer than one million members. The gentry, by contrast, was much larger, with about twenty million members. It would have been much more expensive for the regime to compensate the gentry, even at undervalued prices. Money spent to compensate landlords would have reduced the amount of money the regime could invest in industrialization, which was a high priority. This cruel calculus suggests that the regime killed landlords to save money.

Second, by murdering a large number of landlords, the regime effectively terrorized the survivors, persuaded them to comply with land reform policies, and discouraged them from hiding assets or slaughtering farm animals before they were seized, which was a serious concern. For example, "The total stock of pigs declined from 102 million in 1954 to 88 million in 1955."[40] The regime blamed this decline on the landlords, though the peasantry's increased consumption also contributed to the slaughter of farm animals. The regime practiced violence to prevent this.

Third, the regime used terror to "empower" the peasantry and get them to overcome their deference to the gentry. According to one scholar who defended the regime's approach, "the violence of 'mass struggle' activity was not only a structural necessity (that is, directed to securing a redistribution of political power in the village), but also a *psychic necessity*."[41] The author here was referring to the sort of psychic necessity advocated in *The Wretched of the Earth*, in which Frantz Fanon famously argued that violence was necessary to overcome the "colonial mentality" that gripped the oppressed masses in colonial settings. Fanon argued that

> Violence alone, violence committed by the people, violence organized and educated by its leaders, makes it possible for the masses to understand social truths and gives the key to them. Without that struggle, without that knowledge of the practice of action, there's nothing but a fancy-dress parade and the blare of trumpets. There's

> nothing save a minimum of re-adaption, a few reforms at the top, a flag waving: and down there at the bottom of an undivided mass, still living in the middle ages, endlessly marking time. From birth it is clear to [the colonized native] that this narrow world ... can only be called into question by absolute violence.[42]

China scholars have routinely rationalized the regime's violence as an economic or psychic "necessity," largely because the victims of violence were members of an "unproductive" or "parasitic" class. Of course, if they had defended the Hutu violence against Tutsis in Rwanda or Nazi violence against Jews in Germany as a "psychic necessity," the flaws in this analysis would be obvious.

Fourth, the regime's violence served to terrorize *other* classes and potential enemies. As one scholar who observed the land reform process wrote, "A great anxiety and tenseness pervaded the village, for now every family was assigned a status fraught with social, economic and political consequences. Those families listed as landlords waited for the axe to fall. Those listed as rich peasants were extremely uneasy, for they knew their fate was undecided, in spite of the temporary policy of 'preservation of the rich peasant's economy' ... the middle peasants experienced considerable suspense ... they were uncertain how long their land and property could be preserved."[43]

In this context, it is understandable that *other* social classes would have been made anxious and "extremely uneasy"—terrorized really—by the murder or suicide of their landlord neighbors. As we will see, they had every reason to be "uneasy" when the regime turned its attention from the landlords to other rural classes. When it came their turn for "the axe to fall," rich and middle peasants submitted *quietly*, which is not surprising given the fact that they had already witnessed the regime's enormous capacity for violence.

The irony, of course, was that the regime's violence was unnecessary. The regime could have eliminated the landlords as a social class, redistributed their property, and increased the production of food without violence. The regime demonstrated that it did not have to kill people—the bourgeoisie—to accomplish their political and economic goals. They could easily have practiced the kind of land reform that the nationalists practiced in Taiwan during the same period, but the leaders of the regime did not. They chose violence instead.

Chapter Two

The Collectivization of Agriculture and the Great Leap Forward

> "We have twenty million people at our beck and call. What political party other than the ruling Communist Party could have done it?"
>
> *Mao Zedong*

At its Eighth Congress in 1956, communist party leaders announced that the "class struggle" in China was "basically resolved."[1] The regime's first class struggle had resulted in the exodus of the military-political elite and the foreign bourgeoisie, the liquidation of the gentry, and the co-optation of the domestic bourgeoisie. The survivors of these classes lived in reduced economic circumstances. Although the struggle between the new regime and the old ruling class had ended, a new one was about to begin. The regime's decision to wage a second "class struggle," this time against the rural and urban working classes in China, came in response to a problem that emerged as a result of the first.

In economic terms, the regime's campaign against the gentry and the bourgeoisie had been a success. By redistributing land to peasants, rural producers became *proprietors.* The ownership of land gave the peasants a powerful incentive to increase their efforts and grow more food—and they did just that. Food grain production increased nearly 50 percent, from 108 million metric tons in 1949, before land reform, to 154.4 million metric tons in 1952.[2]

Peasants grew more food, real incomes increased dramatically, "the poorest 20 percent of the peasantry doubled its income share" as a result of land reform, and rural standards of living improved for the first time in a generation.[3] Between

1953 and 1957 "rural grain consumption for each person rose, in some cases considerably."[4] One observer reported, "At New Years, [the peasants] butchered the fat [pigs] to have feasts, invited guests, had a little extra food, and so gained a little self-respect."[5]

However, although increased food production was good for the peasants, who were eating high off the hog for the first time in a long time, it was bad for the dictatorship's developmentalist agenda. As food production and rural incomes rose, peasants *consumed more* and *marketed less* of the food they produced.[6] The landlord class had marketed as much as half of the food produced by their tenants. But the new peasant proprietors essentially *ate* their newfound wealth, which meant that *less* food was available for the regime, which counted on the sale of grain to feed the urban population and finance its investment in industry.[7] The leadership was "always acutely aware of the need for agricultural surpluses as a condition for rapid industrialization,"[8] but rural proprietors' increasing consumption threatened to reduce those surpluses. As Mao explained in a 1955 speech, if the regime did not "resolve the contradiction between [the regime's] need for commodity grain and industrial raw materials [cotton, oil seeds] and the present generally low output of staple crops ... we shall run into difficulties in our socialist industrialization and be unable to complete it."[9]

The regime had earlier attacked the landlords because they consumed rather than invested the agricultural surplus they took from the peasantry, but after land reform was completed, the peasants, now independent proprietors, behaved the same way: they consumed the surplus. Whereas the regime had earlier regarded the gentry as an obstacle to development, Mao and other leaders quickly came to view rural proprietors as an obstacle that must be removed. As a result, Mao decided to attack the peasantry just as he had attacked the gentry and force rural proprietors to relinquish the surplus they produced. The regime's subsequent campaign to "collectivize" agriculture and industrialize the economy during the Great Leap Forward forced rural peasants to relinquish a surplus that the regime then used to finance industrialization.

The Collectivization of Agriculture

Land reform had eliminated the gentry and created a vast class of small-scale rural proprietors or independent commodity producers. Landownership allowed them to reap the benefits of their labor, and they took advantage of this historic opportunity to increase food production so they could eat better and improve their lives. However, by eating more, they reduced the amount of food available for sale to the state. For the leaders of the regime, rural proprietors had become an obstacle to development. But how could they force rural proprietors to relinquish the surplus they now produced so the regime could use it to finance industrialization? In 1955 Mao decided that the collectivization of agriculture would provide the answer to this question.[10]

Mao opened his attack on rural proprietors by abandoning the promises made in earlier land-reform legislation, which had "guaranteed" that the lands of "rich" and "middle peasants" would be "protected from infringement" and announced that these groups were now a threat. "As it is clear to anyone," Mao argued in the fall of 1955, "the spontaneous forces of capitalism have been steadily growing in the countryside in recent years, with new rich peasants springing up everywhere and many well-to-do middle peasants striving to become rich peasants. If this tendency goes unchecked, it is inevitable that polarization in the countryside will get worse day by day."[11] Mao then demanded that rich and middle peasants be "checked."

Mao's attack was not only a betrayal; it was based on a falsehood. The "rich" and "middle peasants" were not a "class" like the gentry but were instead statistical categories that reflected small economic differences between people in the *same* class. Some "rich" rural proprietors occasionally hired workers to help them farm; some "poor" proprietors hired themselves out to work on other people's farms. Nevertheless, the difference between "rich" and "poor" was incredibly small—miniscule really. On average, "rich" peasant proprietors owned four acres of land, compared to "poor" peasant proprietors who owned, on average, two acres of land. Two acres of land were not sufficient reason to describe them as members of separate classes. As Selden has noted, although there were economic differences between "rich" and "poor" peasants, "they were among the *smallest* in the world." Mao knew that, but he invented three classes—"rich" peasants, "middle" peasants, and "poor" peasants—when in fact they were all members of a *single* class. Moreover, Mao described the "rich" and "middle peasants" as "capitalist" classes, like the gentry, which was also a fabrication. Describing small-scale farmers who essentially grow food to feed themselves, with a little bit of surplus left over, as "capitalists" like the gentry (the 4 percent of the population who owned 40 percent of the arable land) is not meaningful. Mao described these microfarmers as "capitalists" to provide the regime with a pretext for seizing the assets of "rich" and "middle peasants" and, for good measure, to seize the assets of *poor* peasants as well. In 1955 and 1956 "88 percent of China's rural households were swept into large . . . collectives organized on a village or even a multi-village scale."[12]

As part of the collectivization process, the regime seized all of the land and assets—farm implements, draft animals, fruit trees, fish ponds, and irrigation works—owned by rural proprietors and turned them over to the collectives.[13] Some collectives even confiscated "personal property like cooking pots, bedding and furniture."[14] Collectivization reduced rural proprietors to wage laborers, whose "income depended on each individual's accumulation of labor-days or work points (a standard labor-day generally was equal to ten work-points)." Work points were calculated in different ways—based on an individual's strength and skill or on the difficulty or importance of a given task—but its value was determined "only when the harvest was in . . . by dividing the total net income of the collective by the total number of work points awarded."[15]

Although this system was designed to promote "equality," it seriously disadvantaged rural women in a variety of ways. Collectives awarded work points only for "productive" labor in the fields, not for the "unproductive" work—such as raising children, caring for elders, preparing meals, raising garden vegetables and domestic animals, fetching water, grinding grain, gathering fuel, sewing clothes, pickling vegetables—that women were *required* to perform for husbands, relatives, and cadre.[16] Because women were expected to perform various kinds of "reproductive" or "subsistence" labor, they could not devote as many hours to work in "productive" agriculture or earn as much, in general, as men, who could devote themselves full time to work that was rewarded with work points.[17]

Moreover, women were paid less than men were for "productive" work because the collectives compensated work requiring strength and skill—attributes associated with agricultural tasks assigned to men—at higher rates. Elisabeth Croll has noted that "Work points were designed to reward skill and physically hard work and, on both these counts, women or the jobs assigned to women normally received a low estimation. Whereas men were often assigned ten work points for a day's work, women almost automatically received less, whether they were laboring at the *same* or different tasks."[18] In practice, "'women's work was almost universally undervalued relative to that of men, and women automatically received lower work-point norm ratings."[19] In the early days of collectivization, "the remuneration due women was normally paid to the male head of household," which also undermined women's prestige and ability to decide how their income might be spent.[20]

In a study of wage grades in one commune, of the people earning the highest grade, 95.7 percent were men and only 4.3 percent were women; of the people earning the lowest grade, only 22.2 percent were men but 77.8 percent were women.[21]

The gender-based discrimination practiced in the collectives not only affected *women,* it also adversely affected worker households with *dependents,* young or old, male or female. In the collectives, a household consisting of only two adults—perhaps a young, recently married couple—fared best because both partners could devote themselves, more or less, full time to work that would be rewarded by the work-point system. But a household consisting of adult partners with dependents—young children or elderly relatives—fared poorly because the adult female would have to spend a lot of time caring for dependents and could not spend much time earning work points in the field. As a result, "the households with the lowest collective incomes had the largest number of mouths to feed per labor power."[22] For a brief time, the regime instructed collectives to provide communal dining and child care facilities so that adult women with dependents could spend more time in the field, but it quickly abandoned this experiment because the regime thought it was too costly: the communes had to compensate people employed in these facilities with work points, whereas they did not have to provide work points to women or elders if they provided these "unproductive" tasks in their homes.[23]

Rural women were also adversely affected by other steps the regime took as part of the collectivization process. The regime closed rural markets and banned the production and sale of petty commodities. The regime "increasingly squeezed out of existence" rural handicrafts, "like other 'sidelines.'"[24] It did this to prevent agricultural goods from leaking out of the communes and being consumed, rather than sold to the government, and also to deprive rural workers of outside sources of income. This forced them to devote their full attention to producing agricultural goods for the state. Furthermore, this enabled the state to take over rural markets and profit from the sale of goods previously offered by petty commodity producers.[25]

In rural China, as elsewhere around the world, poor rural people, particularly women, wove cloth, made handicrafts, grew garden vegetables, raised animals, and prepared foods that they sold at local markets.[26] They also sometimes loaned small sums of money earned from the sale of their goods or obtained from the "remittances" sent by relatives living in the cities or in overseas diaspora communities. To prevent women from earning interest from money lending, the regime banned the practice and seized most of the remittances relatives sent to residents in rural China.[27] The abolition of rural women's money lending and rent collecting after the revolution "deprived elderly women and widows of the right to receive rent for an income or to use their monetary savings and social knowledge accumulated through kinships and local networks to risk making loans for a living. In a rural society without pensions, money lending and rent collecting may have kept some of the elderly from neglect and destitution when they became too old for manual labor."[28]

The production and sale of petty commodities as well as income from remittances and money lending had provided an important source of nonwage income to women in rural households and furnished goods and credit to rural villagers who were engaged in nonfarm activities: teachers, grocers, innkeepers, masons, butchers, blacksmiths, and even "witches."[29] As Mark Selden observed, "the loss of these supplemental income-earning activities was felt by *all* rural strata and communities," though women felt this loss most sharply.[30]

The regime has long claimed that it improved the rights and status of women and created conditions for the "thorough emancipation of women."[31] Scholars point to the Marriage Law of 1950 as evidence of this. This law allowed women to inherit property, own land, and, if divorced, lay claim to goods acquired during marriage. It also outlawed the "extreme forms of abuse [against women] and legally reduced the power of the males of the family to control the movement of women in marriage and divorce."[32] However, what the state gave women with one hand, it took away with the other. The regime gave women the right to "move" in terms of marriage and divorce, but then limited their ability to "migrate" economically by restricting their movement through the hukou system (see below).[33] The regime undermined women's legal gains by collectivizing land, which prevented both men and women from owning or inheriting land. Moreover, "since the main form of property after collectivization was housing and household goods, and since women married out, in practice inheritances generally went to sons [despite the new law]. In short, women had little control over property."[34] Women may have gained some formal, *social* "rights" under the new regime, but they simultaneously lost important *economic* rights, and a discriminatory, gender-biased approach to collectivization disadvantaged them, thus creating new kinds of inequality in rural communities.

The regime used collectivization to seize land and property, stop workers from engaging in income-generating activities, and make rural workers entirely dependent for their survival on the wages collectives provided, a process of "proletarianization." The regime also required workers in collectives to pay agricultural taxes (as much as 10 to 15 percent of their total income), compelled them to sell their produce to the state "at prices far below those that prevailed in private markets," purchase inputs (farm machinery, fuel, and chemical fertilizer) at prices that the state set artificially high, plant food grains and industrial crops (cotton, oil seeds, and tobacco) that the state required, and work on public works projects (water conservation projects, road and railway building and repairing) without pay.[35] "One hundred million peasants were said to be engaged in water conservancy works during the winter of 1957–58," and evidently many of them received no compensation for what Mao admitted was essentially *corvée* labor, the kind of unpaid labor services that lords and state officials had demanded from peasants under feudalism.[36]

The regime expected workers to produce more food and consume less of it, without providing the collectives with credit to purchase technology or inputs that might help them improve productivity and without the state contributing any substantial investment. As Selden noted, "only 15 percent of state investment was directed to agriculture, where more than 80 percent of the Chinese people labored." The regime canceled festivals, weddings, and holidays so that workers could work longer, and they did.[37] The average number of days worked per labor unit increased from 96 days in 1955 to 175 days in 1957.[38]

These developments enabled the regime to appropriate "a substantial share of that portion of the rural surplus formerly appropriated by the *landlords,*" and by 1957 the "state extracted 80 to 90 percent of the rural surplus above subsistence consumption."[39] Collectivization enabled the regime to increase the rate of capital accumulation from 22.9 percent in 1955 to 43.8 percent in 1959, a very high rate of accumulation for a developing country.[40] Mao then used the capital squeezed from rural workers in agriculture to finance a massive campaign to industrialize the country during the Great Leap Forward, which began in 1958.

The Great Leap Forward

With the capital that collectivization generated in hand, Mao decided in 1958 to use it to finance the rapid industrialization of the country, which would enable China to make what he called a "Great Leap Forward."[41] Still, the regime first had to solve a difficult problem: how to industrialize the country *without* triggering a massive migration into the cities.

As the collectivization of agriculture advanced and living conditions for rural workers deteriorated, millions of workers abandoned farming and moved to the cities in search of employment. Between 1957 and 1960 "the urban population increased from 99 million to 130 million; a year later it had climbed to 149 million."[42]

Rural-to-urban migration created a series of problems for the regime. The migrants needed food, housing, and employment, and the cities needed an infrastructure—water, sewage, transportation, energy, and security—to accommodate them.[43] Rapid urbanization would have been an extremely expensive undertaking for the regime, which would have required it to build cities for roughly twenty million people—cities the size of New York City and Chicago combined—in a three-year period. To accomplish this, the regime would have had to spend much of the capital it had accumulated from collectivization, which would have substantially reduced the amount of money it could invest in industrialization.

Mao's decision to industrialize threatened to make matters worse. If the regime invested heavily in industry, which was, for the most part, located in urban areas, it would need a lot of workers, but there were not enough industrial workers living in urban areas to meet the regime's projected demand. Hence, rural workers seeking employment in expanding urban industries would flock to the cities, and this would exacerbate the problems and the costs associated with urbanization. Basically, whatever gains the regime expected to make by industrializing would be undermined by the costs associated with rapid urbanization.

Although this problem was not unique to China—it has been a problem encountered by virtually every industrializing country—Mao took a unique, three-pronged approach to solve it. First, he introduced a system designed to control internal migration and used it to *stop* rural workers from migrating to the cities. Second, he promoted industrial development in *rural* areas, taking the factories to rural workers rather than bringing the workers to urban factories. Third, to meet the demand for industrial workers, who were in short supply, Mao conscripted male workers from the cities and male workers from rural communities to work in rural industries, and he then drafted rural women to replace the men who had left the fields and entered rural factories.

This complex movement prevented urbanization from becoming a problem, but it also created other, more difficult problems that Mao did not anticipate. To appreciate these developments, detailing their separate steps is necessary.

The regime opposed voluntary rural-to-urban migration—what it called "blind migration"—in the early 1950s. Initially, it tried to persuade rural workers in the cities to return home. When that failed to stem the tide, the regime began to "return" or deport rural migrants from the cities to rural areas. In 1955 the regime forcibly rounded up "over half a million immigrant 'peasants' in Shanghai and deported them to rural areas where they were required to 'join agricultural production.'" But whereas the regime's rustication campaigns in 1955, 1956, and 1957 sent urban youths (many of them were "sent down" because they belonged to "bourgeois" classes) down to the farm, the regime could not persuade the deportees to stay there. These youths returned to the cities as fast as they could because they viewed rustication as a form of "punishment," which in many ways it was.[44] One group of workers from Shanghai, for example, who were rusticated in 1957, returned to the city and petitioned officials to let them stay. Ten of them threatened to commit suicide if they were forced to return to the countryside, which provides some insight into conditions in the countryside.[45]

In 1958, as migration became a more pressing problem, the regime decided to take a tougher approach. Government officials instructed the Public Security Bureau to establish a household registration system (called the *hukou*) that would control internal migration.[46] As the scholar Tyrene White explained, "The regulations established a system to monitor peasant movement and ration access to food grain and other basic supplies. Under this system, peasants who could not produce an authorized work or study permit were ineligible for urban ration coupons that were required for local purchases. Deprived of food and other necessities, they had no choice but to return to, and remain in, the village."[47]

The registration system required individuals to live and "work in the village of their birth or, in the case of women, the residence of their husband." As Selden noted, "To state the matter starkly, the majority of Chinese people since the mid-fifties have been legally bound by the state for life to residence and collective labor within tiny production units . . . typically comprising thirty to forty households."[48] The hukou system thus enabled the regime to stem the migration of rural peasants to the cities, though it took several years for it to establish firm control of population movements.

While the regime clamped down on rural-to-urban migration, it also launched its campaign to industrialize China at a breakneck pace. It decided to finance the development of steel and other basic industries in rural areas to prevent industrialization from drawing rural workers into the cities and to take advantage of the labor supplies located in the countryside.

The regime quickly established "backyard" iron and steel mills in rural areas across the country, with "7.5 million factories and workshops ... set up in the first nine months of 1958." By the end of 1958 "there were several hundred thousand small blast furnaces dotting the countryside, and some 60 million people were at one time engaged in smelting iron and mining and transporting ore."[49] This frenetic activity increased steel production from 5.35 million tons in 1957 to 18 million tons in 1960.[50]

The regime's industrialization program required huge numbers of workers. When the regime took power in 1949, there were only 3.3 million workers employed in industry, which was located in China's cities, and only 6 million in 1955.[51] On the eve of the Great Leap in 1957, the regime could muster only 8 or 9 million industrial workers—only a small fraction of the 60 million that the industrialization effort required.[52] The problem for the regime was that there were *too few* industrial workers, and they lived in the *wrong place.*

To meet the projected demand for industrial workers in rural settings, the regime reorganized labor and redeployed male and female workers on a vast scale. As part of its labor recruitment efforts, the regime first eliminated the "petty bourgeoisie" as a class, drafted its members into the industrial proletariat, and sent many of them off to work in rural factories. Although the proletarianization of small shopkeepers, vendors, pushcart and pole peddlers, itinerant merchants, traveling salesmen, barbers, butchers, craftsmen, and cooks had begun in the mid-1950s, it accelerated in 1958.[53] During the Great Leap the regime banned independent proprietors (the petty bourgeoisie) in the cities from producing or selling goods and services in order to force them to find work in industry, a development that made it difficult for urban residents "to get clothing made, have their hair cut or styled, eat out in restaurants, buy non-staple foods, buy furniture, or get repairs done."[54] However, because the number of independent producers was relatively small—less than one million remained in 1958—they did not make a substantial contribution to the labor supply during the Great Leap, which meant that the regime needed to find another source of labor.

The regime needed a huge number of workers for newly established rural industries, so it drafted male agricultural workers and sent them to work in the factories that had sprung up across the countryside. The number of workers employed in industry tripled in the first year of the Great Leap, growing from 7.9 million in 1957 to 23.7 million in 1958.[55] It then increased to between 50 and 70 million (estimates vary) by 1960. Riskin concluded that "40 million peasants were recruited into the non-agricultural economy" during the Great Leap.[56]

Of course, the departure of forty million male workers from employment in agriculture created a labor shortage on collective farms. Using the slogan, "release men and substitute women," the regime demanded that women take the place of the men who left farms and entered factories.[57] As a result, the percentage of women who worked as wage laborers in agriculture increased from 60 or 70 percent of all women in 1957 to 90 percent of all women by 1958.[58]

At this moment, when rural and urban workers, both male and female, had been redeployed to transform agriculture and industry, was when Mao issued his instructions to the party members responsible for overseeing the Great Leap: "On the basis of your actual conditions, squeeze out all of the labor force that can be squeezed out."[59]

Mao thought he had devised a novel way to promote industrialization while preventing urbanization by controlling migration, locating industry in rural areas, and drafting men into the factories and women into the fields. Nevertheless, his strategy created two new problems that crippled industrialization, undermined food production, and triggered misery and famine for the workers employed in both industry and agriculture.

First, Mao's decision to scatter heavy industries like steel mills across the country created unmanageable logistical problems. Steel mills had to be fed with huge supplies of coal and iron ore, which either ship or rail must deliver. Steel mills in the United States, Great Britain, Germany, and Japan were built alongside rivers, ports, or railway networks so that the raw materials they needed could be delivered promptly, at low cost, and so that finished products could be shipped to industrial markets. However, the Chinese railway system had only 22,000 kilometers of track in 1950—less than Mexico—though its railways served a country the size of the United States. By comparison, the United States in 1950 had seventeen times as much track, 360,150 kilometers in all.[60] Given the weakness of the rail network in China, which was described as "the most heavily used system of any major nation," it was difficult just to deliver raw materials to industry in central urban locations.[61] Mao's demand that the railways deliver ore, at low cost and in a timely fashion, to factories scattered all over China proved impossible to meet.

What's more, the fact that the manufacture of steel required workers with some technical skills, and they were in short supply, complicated the logistical problem of the railways. Scattering steel mills forced the regime to disperse engineers with the requisite technical skills, and many factories lacked adequate supervision. The rural workers who were drafted into factories also lacked the necessary training and skill. Moreover, steel mills are expensive to build, and building them as large as possible would take advantage of economies of scale. However, because the regime built a lot of small mills, it could not achieve economies of scale, and it thus spent a lot of money to produce only a little steel. As a consequence, the regime invested huge sums of money producing low-quality steel, much of which had to be resmelted in "big foreign furnaces" to be usable. Furthermore, the railway system proved incapable of delivering raw materials to producers or finished products to consumers.[62] The result was economic chaos.

The industrialization effort collapsed, and steel production, which had grown from 5.35 million tons in 1957 to 18 million tons in 1959, fell back to only 7 million tons in 1960.[63] As one observer noted, "With planning in disarray, much output was of too low quality to be used, or, as in the case of crude steel, was not produced in the varieties needed by users. Such output, symbolized by steel ingots rusting beside railroad tracks or farm implements breaking at first use, represents a waste of resources."[64]

Consequently, Mao's decision to locate industry in rural areas led to the collapse of the industrialization effort. At the same time, his decision to shift male workers from field to factory combined with other agricultural policies and regional natural disasters to undermine food production and create the conditions for widespread famine.

When the regime collectivized agriculture, it began telling farmers what to grow. Although the production of food grain remained a priority, the regime told farmers to *reduce* the acreage sown with wheat and rice and *increase* the production of industrial crops such as cotton, tobacco, and oil seeds. In 1958, at the beginning of the Great Leap, the regime introduced a new, "plant less, produce more, and harvest the most" policy. As a result of the regime's growing demand for industrial crops, "the acreage sown to grain declined by six million hectares in 1958 and a further 11.6 million hectares in 1959, a total reduction of 13 percent over the two years."[65] The total acreage dedicated to rice and wheat fell from 134 million hectares in 1957 to only 116 million hectares in 1959.[66] In some provinces the acreage devoted to food grain plummeted by as much as one-third.[67]

While the dictatorship shifted agricultural production from food to industrial crops, it also shifted male labor from farms to factories. As a result, "the farm labor force dropped from 192 million in 1957 to 151 million in 1958, a decline of 41 million," virtually all of them men.[68] The women on collective farms replaced them, and the regime told these women to shoulder the burden of producing food for the entire country in addition to performing necessary but unpaid reproductive work and subsistence production.

This shift in the gender of agricultural labor created several problems. First, the departure of men created labor shortages and increased the workload for the men and women who remained on the farm. Because the agricultural labor force was "reduced by over 20 percent in 1958 . . . a peasant who had to look after 8.8 mou in 1957 now had to cultivate 11 mou; and since the number of draft animals had dropped sharply, the work was even harder."[69]

Second, the women who moved into agriculture might not have been as skilled or productive as the men they replaced. Penny Kane has said of the women that "Many—perhaps even the majority—were totally inexperienced in farm work."[70] In truth, were women less productive? This is a difficult question to answer because scholars have not studied the impact of gender on production during the Great Leap and because one does not want to assume that women would be less productive simply because they were women. Still, there are some reasons to think that women might have been somewhat less skilled or productive in *some* agricultural tasks given the prevailing gender-based division of labor and the kind of technologies employed in Chinese agriculture during this period.

First, some adult women may have been less productive than the men they replaced because their parents had bound their feet when they were girls. Foot binding generally ended as a practice in the 1920s. "Girls born from 1910 to 1914, who reached the foot-binding age from 1915 to 1920, were the first cohort in which the majority were allowed to grow up with their feet unbound," one feminist scholar has noted. However, during the Great Leap, there would still be many adult women in their forties, fifties, and sixties whose feet had been bound when they were girls and who would still suffer from the effects of foot binding. For these women to carry heavy loads or to stand for long periods, as they would be required to do to perform many agricultural tasks, would have been difficult because of the pain they would have experienced. On collective farms, "women with bound feet were not exempt from work, but were required to do 'light labor.'"[71]

Second, agricultural tasks require diverse skills that both men and women can acquire. The question is not whether women *could* master agricultural skills. In time, no doubt, they could. The question is this: did women *already* possess these skills when they replaced men in 1958, or did they have to *acquire* them?

There is some evidence that women did *not* possess them. As one woman, the leader of a cooperative, admitted, "Some of the younger women said they also lacked the skill [to farm]."[72] A gender-based division of labor, as elsewhere, long defined agricultural tasks in China. Men performed some tasks, women were assigned to others, and both men and women worked together on some jobs. Nevertheless, it is unlikely that in 1958 women possessed the skill set associated with jobs long performed by men, jobs they were suddenly asked to undertake.

Scholars have conducted careful studies showing that men and women in China regularly performed different tasks, which varied depending on the kind of crop. Not surprisingly, they found that men did "heavy work, such as plowing, carrying heavy loads, digging ditches, and making dikes" and that women performed "lighter tasks."[73] Of course, this did not mean that women did not have the strength or skill to do these jobs as efficiently as men did. Laurel Bossen, a feminist scholar who conducted fieldwork in China, tested the assumption that women could not operate heavy plows and "was once given a chance to try my hand at plowing with an ox [in a village in Yunnan]." She reported that she "found the challenge was not so much one of strength (the animal supplied that) as of skill in keeping the furrow to an even depth and getting the animal to perform properly—the same difficulty an experienced rider has in controlling a horse. Both skills seem a matter of practice."[74]

Bossen's observation that a woman can do a man's work but that obtaining the required skill is a "matter of practice" states the problem well. Whatever women's laboring *capacity* or ability, in 1958 they likely lacked many male agricultural skills that could be developed only from *practice.* They lacked the practice because the regime's gender-based division of labor would not have permitted them to obtain male skills in the years before the Great Leap. It is doubtful that women were encouraged to take a turn at the plow so they could get the experience they needed if they were suddenly asked to replace men in the fields. As a result, women likely did *not* already possess the requisite skills. The lack of practice meant they were probably less productive than the men they replaced. Even if the differences were small, a marginal decline in agricultural productivity, when multiplied 150 million times, could have a dramatic effect on agricultural yields and food production. Some studies have shown that productivity in agriculture did in fact fall during the Great Leap. A study of one village found that output per person fell from 652 kilograms of rice per person in 1958 to 442 kilograms per person in 1959, a substantial decline.[75] How much of this was due to women's lack of experience in performing male jobs, which was a product of a gendered division of labor, is difficult to say, but it likely played an important role.

Furthermore, natural disasters—flood, typhoon, hail, and drought—in different regions accompanied cutbacks in the acreage devoted to food crops and declining yields for food crops, thereby also reducing the overall harvest. Natural disasters were regular and recurrent problems in China, but the acreage affected by disaster—defined as areas where crop production was reduced by 30 percent compared with normal years—rose from 7.8 million hectares in 1958 to 13.7 million hectares in 1959, 25 million in 1960, and 28.8 million in 1961.[76]

The regime's determination to reduce the amount of land devoted to food grains, to shift men from farm to factory, and to replace them with women who had not been prepared with the skills necessary to undertake men's tasks, and natural disaster all combined to reduce food production. Grain production fell from 200 million tons in 1958 to 170 million tons in 1959, to 143.5 million tons in 1960, and 147 million tons in 1961.[77] As a result, rural people began to experience hunger and then famine.

Although food production was falling and rural hunger was rising, the regime continued to demand that farmers pay agricultural taxes and meet the food delivery quotas that the state imposed.[78] In fact, "government procurement demands reached extraordinary heights" during the Great Leap.[79] In 1958 the regime had demanded that farmers deliver 24.6 percent of all the grain that farmers grew, but then it upped the state's take to 29.4 in 1959 and 39.7 percent in 1960.[80]

The regime also exported more food during this period and used the money earned from the sale of grain to finance industrialization. According to Kane, grain exports (mostly of rice) increased from 1.3 million metric tons in 1958 to 1.9 million metric tons in 1959.[81] This is what the British had done during the Irish Potato Famine, but unlike starving Irish peasants, who fled the island during the famine, the regime's migration-control system (hukou) prevented Chinese peasants from migrating in search of food, a system that was "rigorously enforced" in 1960, just as famine struck.[82]

Why did the regime demand more food from farmers at a time when they were producing less?

First, Mao believed what he wanted to believe. Mao thought that collectivization would increase food production. His optimism was based on the fact that food production *had* dramatically increased in the period between land reform and collectivization, when independent proprietors grew more food. He expected that these kinds of gains would continue, but they did not. During the Great Leap, "the state remained convinced that there was plenty of grain if it could only be procured."[83]

When food did not materialize, the regime blamed the farmers and insisted that they must be concealing and hoarding the grain. According to Kane, "Mao estimated that concealed grain amounted to 15 percent of the output, and claimed that the peasants had even buried their output deep and posted sentries to guard it."[84] Of course, this was the kind of charge that Mao had made earlier against the landlords—that they hoarded and consumed rather than marketed and invested. To combat hoarding, the regime announced an "anti-concealment drive," mobilized its cadre, and sent them out to search for the "missing" grain.[85] They searched in vain. This is also what British officials in India had done during the Great Bengal Famine of 1942, according to Nobel Prize economist Amartya Sen. British officials assumed that the harvest had been good, so if the peasants were starving, someone must be hoarding the supply. After explaining why British officials were mistaken, Sen described their search for concealed food as "a search in a dark room for a black cat which wasn't there."[86] In China the regime searched without success for the missing grain. In the meantime, rural workers began to starve.

The annual, per capita consumption of grain fell by one-quarter, from 200 kilograms in rural areas (about 2,100 calories daily) in 1958 to 183 kilograms (1,820 calories) in 1959, and then to 156 kilograms (1,534 calories) in 1960, but averages tell only part of the story.[87] Because rural workers' ability to claim food depended on the work points they earned doing "productive" or "social" labor in the collective, households with a large number of dependents earned *less* and consumed *more* than households with few or no dependents. As a result, many households with young children and elderly parents found it difficult to claim the food they needed to survive. In these households, Kane argues, "The worse off were housewives." According to the economist Chen Yun, "there were about 50 million members of grain-deficient households (due to low income, a large number of dependents, and so on)" during the 1950s, *before* the collapse of food production during the Great Leap. They were the ones who were most vulnerable when famine struck.[88]

Of course, hunger contributed in turn to declining food production, which produced more hunger. People stopped feeding draft animals and instead ate them, which meant they had less animal traction available to plow and transport food, which resulted in less food being produced.[89]

Determining exactly how many people died of famine during and after the Great Leap is difficult. After examining the available demographic data in detail, Kane argues that between fourteen and twenty-six million people died of hunger.[90] MacFarquhar estimates that "anywhere from 16.4 to 29.5 million people died during the Leap, because of the Leap."[91] Furthermore, women, girls, and female infants died in disproportionate numbers. Kane argues that girls "under the age of five but past the age of weaning, would have been particularly vulnerable to discriminatory feeding practices during a famine," and she quotes a report that in some areas, "the peasants have reverted to old times . . . as for girl babies, I think that infanticide has come back."[92]

In comparative terms, this epic social disaster is without parallel. The Irish Potato Famine killed one million people and forced another million to flee. The Great Bengal Famine, from 1942 to 1944, resulted in the deaths of three million people. The African slave trade, which forcibly transported some 12.4 million people across the Atlantic, killed "roughly five million men, women, and children" during the first year of capture and crossing. The Germans murdered six million Jews, another six million other Europeans, and 3.3 million Soviet prisoners of war during the Holocaust. The famine that the Great Leap induced in China likely killed *more* people than *all* of these terrible disasters *combined,* and it did so more *quickly.*[93]

The Aftermath

Mao called a halt to the Great Leap Forward in 1960. Although Mao admitted that "it was impossible not to commit errors," he insisted that "our policy's general line is correct, and actual work has been carried out well"—a startling conclusion to reach in the face of the regime's monumental policy failures.[94] Mao not only failed to appreciate what had occurred, but he also drew two lessons from the experience that made things *worse.*

The first lesson Mao drew from the Great Leap was that there were too many people still living in the cities, so he decided to rusticate them en masse. During the next two years the regime forced twenty million industrial workers to leave the cities and move into the countryside, where they were exposed to penury and famine.[95] Riskin says that "most of [the people who were rusticated] had probably arrived in the cities only recently during the expansionary phase of the Leap," whereas Selden maintains that "industrial workers were laid off and sent to the countryside in virtually the only breach in the lifetime job guarantee enjoyed by state-sector workers in the People's Republic."[96] However, the regime also practiced this policy on subsequent occasions, as we shall see, and "in the years 1960–1976 the Chinese state presided over an historically unprecedented urban-to-rural net migration of forty-eight million people."[97]

After the regime cleared the cities of twenty million workers, Mao boasted to a colleague that "We have twenty million people at our beck and call. What political party other than the ruling Chinese Communist Party could have done it?"[98]

Mao drew a second lesson from the Great Leap. Although he thought that there were too *many* people living in the cities, he also believed that there were too *few* people living in the country as a whole. Mao thought that the Great Leap had failed because of the labor *shortages* in industry and agriculture. Moreover, he believed that the loss of life during the famine would exacerbate these shortages. To remedy these labor "shortages," Mao demanded that the regime abandon the modest population-control policies it had adopted in the 1950s and encourage women to have *more* children.

Mao had long denied that "overpopulation" was a problem. In 1949 he argued, "It is a very good thing that China has a big population. . . . The absurd argument of Western bourgeois economists like Malthus that increases in food cannot keep pace with increases in population was not only thoroughly refuted in theory by Marxists long ago but has also been completely exploded by the realities in the Soviet Union and in the liberated areas of China. . . . Revolution plus production can solve the problem of population."[99]

Although Mao dismissed population growth as a problem, his colleagues were more concerned. Zhou Enlai, Deng Xiaoping, and his wife, Deng Yingchao, worried that food production might *not* keep pace with China's growing population. They persuaded other party leaders to make contraceptives, abortion, and sterilization available and to promote birth control planning, especially among women in urban areas where there were, in Mao's view, "too many people."[100] Zhou argued that "having a lot of people is a good thing but, as the world's most populous country . . . we already have plenty of them."[101]

Mao backed away from his pronatalist views during the 1950s, going so far as to say that "it would be great [if we] could lower the birth [rate] a bit."[102] However, he returned to his pronatalist position after the Great Leap because he viewed labor shortages as a problem and because he thought that a large population would help secure China's national defense in the event of nuclear war. In a 1957 meeting with the Soviets, Mao had asserted that a large population would be an advantage in a nuclear war: "Let us imagine, how many people will die if a [nuclear] war should break out? . . . If the worst came to the worst, and half of all mankind died, the other half would remain while imperialism would be razed to the ground and the whole world would become socialist; in a number of years there would be 2.7 [billion] people again."[103]

After the Great Leap Mao began to attack other party leaders on the issue of population growth, arguing that "the more people there are, the more, faster, better, and thriftier we can build socialism."[104] In 1960 his attacks on the proponents of population control forced the party to abandon its population-control efforts and "made all discussion of population planning unacceptable for more than ten years."[105] By the time the issue was revived in the early 1970s, "there were two hundred million more Chinese."[106]

Mao's decision to abandon population-control efforts had serious consequences for economic development in China. It ensnared China in what the economist Richard Nelson called a "low-level equilibrium trap."[107] [See chart, Appendix I, p. 189] In the 1950s development economists argued that if poor countries successfully used investment to promote economic growth, their efforts to raise per capita incomes would fail if the population continued to grow. This argument emerged during this time because the problem of population growth was a new development. Postwar improvements in public health had reduced infant mortality and death rates, though birth rates remained high. Recognizing this, economists then warned that rapid population growth would consume the benefits of economic development. As Simon Kuznets pointed out, rapid population growth in less developed countries "is a recent phenomenon, which has emerged only since the early 1940s. Before the 20th century, and back to the late 18th century, population in developed countries had grown more rapidly than in the less developed."[108]

In China's case, the regime, at tremendous social cost, promoted economic growth during the 1950s. Economic growth collapsed during the Great Leap and then resumed at a much lower rate in the mid-1960s. (Think of economic growth as the upper jaw of a steel bear trap. In the 1950s the top jaw opened wide, but then, during the Great Leap, began to close.)

In the 1950s China's population grew, though by how much is difficult to say because the regime did not have the means to assess its true size. The famine brought population growth to a halt in the early 1960s, but the population soon started growing again—and at a fairly rapid rate—both because people worked hard to replace their losses (a common practice after war or famine) and because the regime, which had abandoned population-control efforts, encouraged them to do so. (Think of population growth as the lower jaw of the steel trap. Anemic economic growth closed the upper jaw and robust population growth raised the lower jaw. The two jaws snapped together, catching China in a low-level equilibrium trap.)

Of course, the economy made some gains during the 1960s and 1970s. The regime built industries and infrastructure and developed nuclear weapons, detonating its first atomic bomb in 1964, but this was an extremely costly development. Lewis and Xue estimated that the Chinese nuclear weapons program cost at about "U.S. $4.1 billion in 1957 prices." The regime devoted "37 percent of the budget for the year 1957" to developing nuclear weapons, and "the burden of these allocations undoubtedly fell disproportionately on budgets in the 1960s, the years of economic distress." Cost, however, did not deter the regime from procuring nuclear weapons. Yen Yu, the minister of foreign affairs, said that the program would continue at any cost, "even if the Chinese had to pawn their trousers for this purpose."[109]

During this same period agricultural output "increased by only 2.3 percent per annum, barely keeping pace with an average yearly population increase of 2 percent."[110] As a result, "the gains were, quite literally swallowed up by the extra mouths."[111] This is what economists described as a low-level equilibrium trap. The only reason that food production stayed ahead of population growth, and then only just barely, was because the regime poured huge amounts of chemical fertilizer into agriculture, nine times as much in 1965 as it had in 1957.[112]

For the vast majority of rural and urban workers, the meager economic growth associated with industrialization in this period did not yield any appreciable benefits. The diets of rural workers failed to improve between 1958 and 1975. In 1958 the average rural worker ate 201 kg of food grain. They then ate *less* grain per year over the next seventeen years (until 1975).[113] Although food consumption did increase in the late 1970s, still, in 1980 "it was reported that 100 million peasants each year have a grain ration of less than 150 kg [which was equal to the average per capita consumption of food during the famine years, 1960 and 1961]."[114] As Selden has noted, "at the most basic level of food consumption, twenty-five years of collective agriculture brought no gain."[115]

Urban workers fared better in terms of food consumption. The regime provided industrial workers with a higher-calorie diet than rural workers—between 10 and 25 percent more grain per capita.[116] However, the average urban wage *fell* in real terms between 1957 and 1977, even though worker productivity had increased.[117] Urban workers also lived in more crowded conditions: "The average per capita housing space in urban areas declined by 20 percent from ... 4.3 square meters per person in 1952 to 3.6 square meters in 1977."[118]

To summarize, during the 1950s Mao directed a series of "struggles" against different classes in China. The regime first attacked the gentry, killing millions of landlords and reducing the survivors to penury. It then stripped the urban bourgeoisie of their assets, barred the petty bourgeois from practicing their trades, forced them both into the urban proletariat, and sent large numbers of them to rural areas, which further impoverished them. The regime then stripped the "rich" and "middle peasants" of their meager landholdings and assets and drove them into the lower echelons of the rural working class, where they were collectively immiserated and exposed to hunger and famine, which killed them by the tens of millions.

The developments associated with agrarian reform, collectivization, and the Great Leap took people from different social classes, stripped them of their assets, impoverished them, and made them all members of the same class: the proletariat. Scholars have made much of the distinction between rural and urban workers in China and have clung to the idea that the "peasantry" is somehow different from the urban, industrial "proletariat," but this is not a useful analytical or class distinction; rather, it is simply a description of *where* people in China lived. During the 1950s the regime turned different classes into a vast, single class of people who worked for wages. The fact that the regime offered different compensation to rural and urban wage workers—and generally favored the latter—did not mean that they were different classes; it meant only that wage-workers in China, as in every other country, were divided by income, geography, and gender and age, as we have seen.

In China the process of "proletarianization"—stripping people of their assets, reducing their circumstances, requiring them all to rely on state-given wages for their survival—reduced members of different classes to the same economic status, that of wage workers. However, the regime did not stop there. It then prevented workers from engaging in activities that provided them with nonwage sources of income—producing and selling goods and services on their own account. It also seized income-generating property: land, livestock, farm implements, carts, and tools. As a result, wage workers in China became entirely dependent on the income earned from wages for their survival.

Moreover, the regime did not permit wage workers to sell their labor freely. The regime assigned them to work for the duration of their lives in agricultural collectives and urban workshops. Workers could not move from these jobs unless, of course, the regime decided to deport them from the city or draft them into rural factories. Without a license from the regime, wage workers could not change their residence to marry or care for elderly parents in a nearby village, much less search for jobs that paid better wages or offered better conditions.

During the 1950s proletarianization in China resulted in the creation of a coerced, less-than-free, wage-labor force in both urban and rural settings. Historically, proletarianization has often led to the creation of free-wage labor, as it did when capitalism emerged in Holland, England, and parts of the United States in the early modern period. However, it did not always do so. Immanuel Wallerstein has argued that the development of capitalism, and the proletarianization associated with it, also resulted in the creation of less-than-free forms of labor: *encomienda* in Spanish America, the "second serfdom" in Poland, sharecropping in Italy, and, of course, slavery in the Americas.[119]

In comparative terms, the kind of coerced wage labor that emerged in China during the 1950s most closely resembled the kinds of labor employed under the *encomienda* system in Spanish America or the second serfdom in Poland, largely because both of these systems were designed to create a low-wage labor force *and fix it in place,* where it could be used to create agricultural commodities that landlords and the state could then sell on external markets. In Poland and Spanish America, workers were fixed to the land because there was a *shortage* of labor to work agricultural estates. In China, by contrast, workers were tied to the land because there was a *surplus* of workers who, if left to themselves, would have migrated in large numbers from rural areas to the cities. The proletarianization of workers in China, as well as in Spanish America and Poland, differed from the proletarianization that resulted from the "enclosures" the English landlords and state practiced. These enclosures drove workers *off* the land and turned many workers into "free wage laborers," though in the seventeenth century this meant the "freedom" to find work or starve. It also differed from slavery, which of course did not provide wages of any kind.[120]

The regime proletarianized workers so that they could generate a surplus that the state could use to invest in industry and promote economic development. Although the exploitation of Chinese workers in the 1950s created the conditions for capital accumulation and economic development, it did not immediately lead to economic growth because the regime's economic policies squandered the capital that had been so painfully extracted from landlords, the domestic bourgeoisie, and urban and rural workers. Therefore, the regime's policy failures foreclosed the possibility of economic development for a generation. However, whereas proletarianization in the 1950s lead to capitalist development *without* growth in the 1960s and 1970s, it contributed to capitalist development *and* rapid economic growth after 1978. Essentially, proletarianization in the 1950s created a coerced, low-wage labor force that the regime would *later* use to promote economic growth in the 1980s.

Worse than Landlords?

The regime's first "class struggle" took aim at landlords in China, who were widely despised, but given the regime's behavior toward rural workers in the 1950s, one might reasonably ask, Was the regime under Mao worse for workers than the landlord class that it replaced?

Of course, asking this question casts into doubt the regime's long-standing claims that it was "good" for the peasantry. Still, the evidence suggests that during the Maoist period the communist regime was worse for rural workers than it was for the much-despised landlord class.

Property. In prerevolutionary China rural people owned 60 percent of the agricultural land, and the gentry owned 40 percent. When the regime introduced agrarian reform, it seized the gentry's land and turned it over to rural workers, making proprietors of most rural people. Nevertheless, the regime subsequently seized all of the land rural proprietors' held when it collectivized agriculture. Although the collectives nominally "owned" the land, the state in fact owned and controlled it, told farmers what to plant, and took a portion of the crop as payment—a form of sharecropping. Thus, agrarian reform made proprietors of most rural farmers, but collectivization in the late 1950s sharply reduced individual ownership from 100 percent to 0 percent. In terms of land ownership, peasants owned more land under the gentry (60 percent) than they did under the Party (0 percent).

Rent. The regime under Mao demanded that rural workers deliver a percentage of their crop to the state. Farmers delivered 34.6 percent of the harvest to the state in 1958, 29.4 percent in 1959, and 39.7 percent in 1960.[121] In addition, the regime levied agricultural taxes, which were "twice the pre-1945 rate," that amounted to another 10 percent of all grain production.[122] The regime took somewhat *less* of the harvest from rural workers in rent and taxes than the gentry—49.7 percent in 1960—and it was less than this in the years before and after 1960.

However, although the regime took a slightly smaller cut, it took this percentage from *more* people. Recall that the landlords took 50 percent of the crop, on average, from the vast majority of the rural people who were tenant farmers. Farmers who owned their own land paid nothing to the landlords. After collectivization swept rural proprietors (the so-called "rich" and "middle" peasants) into collectives, the number of people owing rent and taxes *increased.* Thus, whereas the regime took a smaller percentage of the total crop than the gentry had done, it took its cut from more people. As a result, the regime likely took a larger percentage of the total harvest than the gentry had done.

Of course, the 50 percent of the crop landlords took and the 40 to 50 percent of the crop the regime took are not strictly comparable. The landlords took their share and sold it, whereas the regime "procured" or "paid" for the share they took. One might argue that the regime gave rural workers a better deal. However, the regime's payments for food were set artificially low (so it could sell the food at a higher price to urban workers and use the profit to finance investment), and payments were distributed to workers through the work-point system in the collectives, which discriminated against women and households with dependents, as we have seen. Furthermore, the income that workers earned from the sale of food could not be used to *purchase* food, which was rationed, so the money farmers received for their produce during the Great Leap did not enable them to buy the food they needed to keep from starving.

Wage and Nonwage Income. Landlords frequently hired peasants to farm on the gentry's estates or to labor as their domestic servants. Although the landlords paid their servants low wages, these wages were an important source of income for poor peasants and particularly for landless peasants. The gentry also allowed tenants and rural proprietors to produce goods for sale on local markets, which provided an important source of nonwage income for the peasantry, particularly for women.

After the regime collectivized agriculture, it prevented workers from selling their labor outside the collectives, which deprived workers of wage income, and it curbed the production and sale of commodities in local markets, which in turn deprived households, particularly the women who produced and sold these goods, of nonwage income. The regime also confiscated remittances that relatives sent to rural households. Thus, the regime deprived rural workers of both wage and nonwage income, which meant that the regime was worse for workers than the gentry.

Migration. Landlords tried to restrict worker mobility and used debt to bind tenants to disadvantageous contractual arrangements and keep them on the land. Nonetheless, many farmers migrated. Mobility increased workers' bargaining power with landlords and employers and helped restrain landlord behavior.

Of course, the regime, like the gentry, wanted to restrict worker mobility. To do so, the regime introduced the household registration system to restrict migration and make it more difficult for workers to search for jobs, beg for food during the famine, or use migration to improve their bargaining power. Therefore, the regime's migration-control policy was more disadvantageous to workers than the kind of debt-peonage that the gentry practiced.

Credit. Money-lending landlords extorted high interest rates from borrowers and used debt as leverage to coerce peasants and reduce their bargaining power in contractual relations. Still, some peasant borrowers used loans from landlords to purchase land, invest in agricultural improvements, build homes, and pay for weddings and funerals. When the regime eliminated the gentry, it also prohibited money lending, but the regime did not replace individual moneylenders with financial institutions that provided credit to rural borrowers.[123] The regime refused to extend credit to rural borrowers because it wanted to *prevent* people from spending money on religious festivals, funeral services, and weddings, which it regarded as frivolous expenditures and a misuse of scarce resources. Restricting credit was part of the regime's campaign against civil society and nonparty institutions, which gave people the opportunity to build social networks (social capital) and kinship-based family alliances *outside* the party. Workers had previously spent money on weddings and funerals to create and cement family alliances, viewing social networks as important because they assisted them in times of economic distress. Although the credit the gentry provided had been advantageous for some peasants and disadvantageous for most, the regime's complete elimination of rural credit made conditions worse for rural workers.

Investment. The gentry and the regime were alike in one respect: neither of them used the money they extracted from rural workers to *invest* in agriculture. The gentry generally consumed or hoarded the surplus, though they often loaned some of it out with interest. Nevertheless, they did little to invest in ways that might have increased food production. Conversely, the regime used the money extracted from rural workers to invest in industry, not agriculture, and did so ineffectively.[124] Except for the brief period in the early 1950s, when independent proprietors made agricultural investments that increased food production substantially, neither the gentry nor the regime made the kind of agricultural investments needed to increase food supplies or food consumption for workers in China.

Famine. Famine in China was common in the years before the revolution, but when it occurred, it was generally the product of natural disaster not public policy, was generally restricted to particular regions, and was mitigated by the fact that some hungry peasants could borrow money from landlords to purchase the food they needed to survive (though at the cost of future indebtedness) or move out of the region struck by famine and beg for food. As a result, the famines that occurred under the gentry were fairly small and localized. By contrast, the regime adopted policies that contributed directly to famine, failed to take decisive steps to ameliorate the famine, and prevented rural workers from migrating in search of food or even to beg for food. This resulted in a harrowing famine that killed tens of millions of people, an unprecedented catastrophe in Chinese history.

Taken together, that the regime eliminated landownership, extracted a large share of the harvest from the entire rural population, eliminated wage and nonwage sources of income, curbed credit, restricted migration, and refused to invest in agriculture is clear. For rural workers, the regime was arguably worse than the gentry.

Chapter Three

The Cultural Revolution

> "Whenever a Chinese artist painted a picture of me with Stalin, I was always shown shorter than Stalin."
>
> *Mao Zedong*

The Great Leap Forward and the accompanying famine undermined Mao's authority, which was already weak, and made it weaker still. To strengthen his position, in 1966 Mao initiated a new class struggle called "The Great Proletarian Cultural Revolution." He described the Cultural Revolution as a struggle that pitted the proletariat against a new, bureaucratic, capitalist class, but this characterization of the Cultural Revolution depended on Mao's idiosyncratic definition of "class" and "class struggle." The Cultural Revolution should more accurately be described as a struggle *within* the same class—a large, socially diverse ruling class that refused to heed Mao—and as a struggle that was designed not to *curb* the bureaucracy but to make it *more responsive* to Mao's edicts.

To appreciate these events, we must first identify the developments that had combined to weaken Mao's authority: the growing reluctance of a large, diverse ruling class to follow his instructions; the policy failures of the Great Leap and famine; and China's growing political and economic isolation. Then we will show how Mao's idiosyncratic treatment of class allowed him to create fictitious classes and to depict the conflict between them in a way that helped him define and win the struggle that ensued. Finally, we need to explain how Mao used the Cultural Revolution to purge his opponents, reward his allies, and make the bureaucracy more responsive to his demands.

Mao's Weakness

Some scholars have portrayed Mao "as the supreme leader with unchallengeable authority."[1] But Mao was weaker and had less real power than Joseph Stalin or the leaders of many other developmentalist dictatorships in the postwar period. As Lynne White has argued, "Even Mao Zedong often had to cooperate with leaders [within the party] who had different social preferences, in a complex process of 'conflict and consensus building.'"[2] Other scholars have argued that in the early 1960s "Chairman Mao's influence ... was at a low ebb," that he "was subject to much criticism during the crisis years," and that "Mao's power was weak, and within the small world of the elite he was subject to attack by followers of one of his rivals, Peng Zhen."[3]

Some scholars have argued that Mao's declining authority within the party could be observed as early as 1955 when "the leadership consensus began to unravel" or in 1956 when Chairman Mao was forced to share power with four vice-chairmen, who included Liu Shaoqi and Deng Xiaoping, a new General Secretary.[4]

It was evident by the 1960s, if not earlier, that Mao was weaker and had less real authority than Stalin. Unlike Stalin, Mao had to share power with other leaders—Liu Shaoqi, Peng Zhen, Deng Xiaoping, Lin Biao, Zhou Enlai—who had interests and constituencies of their own. Of course, Mao regularly fought with his rivals and usually defeated them, but the fact that Mao fought with successive rivals demonstrates that he was not a "supreme leader with unchallengeable authority." Moreover, when Mao fought with his rivals, his behavior was constrained. Stalin had his rivals arrested, "tried," and then shot in the back of the head. Some, like Trotsky, escaped arrest, so Stalin had him assassinated in Mexico. In China Mao stripped rival leaders of their power but did not or could not murder them at will. When Mao forced Peng to resign, Peng "turned in his Marshal's uniforms, his fox-fur coat and the carpets and paintings that adorned his room ... retained only his bodyguard" and took up gardening.[5] Like Peng, Deng Xiaoping was removed from office, but he was not killed and so later returned to power. There is little doubt that Mao was as ruthless as Stalin, but his ability to order the murder of rivals within the regime was more limited than Stalin's.[6]

Mao greatly admired Stalin and regarded him as a role model. He objected when Soviet leaders denounced Stalin after his death, and Mao defended his legacy: "To beat Stalin to death with a single stick was something however with which we don't agree. [The Soviet leaders] don't hang his portrait, we hang it." Still, Mao himself complained that in China he lacked the unchallenged authority or political stature of Stalin: "Whenever a Chinese artist painted a picture of me with Stalin, I was always shown shorter than Stalin." Stalin was in fact the shorter man.[7]

Mao was "shorter" and weaker politically than Stalin because a series of developments had combined to weaken him. During the 1950s and early 1960s the emergence of a large, socially diverse ruling class, Mao's own capricious behavior, the failure of his domestic policies, and the regime's growing political and economic isolation combined to weaken Mao's authority.

After the revolution, the regime had exiled or eliminated the classes that belonged to the old ruling class: the military-political elite, landlords, and the international and domestic bourgeoisie. The destruction of the old ruling class made it possible for a new ruling class, which was built around a communist party nucleus, to emerge. When Mao took power in 1949, the communist party counted 4.5 million members, many of whom had recently joined the party. In contrast with communist parties in the Soviet Union and Eastern Europe, where the party recruited heavily from the urban working class and intellectuals, the Chinese communist party had a socially diverse membership: 69 percent were drawn from rural classes, 14 percent from the urban working class, and the rest from bourgeois and petty bourgeois backgrounds.[8]

Still, though the party was quite large, it did not have enough members to run government agencies, the military, and the businesses it seized from the bourgeoisie.[9] Consequently, the party recruited bureaucratic personnel and industrial managers from other classes—chiefly the domestic bourgeoisie and the petty bourgeoisie, who had held government positions or run businesses under the old regime.[10] The party did not, however, allow landlords or intellectuals to become members.[11]

Nonetheless, during the 1950s the regime needed additional cadre to direct new industries, agricultural collectives, and government bureaucracies, which administered its economic plans and controlled population movements. So it recruited additional members from the urban and rural working class. As a result, membership in the communist party rose from 4.5 million members in 1949 "to 6.5 million in 1954, and to 12.7 million in 1957."[12] It would double in size, to 22 million members, by 1966.[13] Keep in mind, however, that the party provided the nucleus of a larger ruling class that coalesced around it.

The new ruling class that emerged in China was considerably larger and more socially diverse than most of the developmentalist dictatorships in the postwar world. Small, socially homogeneous classes ran most of the developmentalist dictatorships in the West. In some countries, heads of families—Somoza in Nicaragua, Salazar in Portugal, Marcos in the Philippines, Stroessner in Paraguay, Mobutu in Zaire, or Diem in South Vietnam—organized the dictatorship, a development that created regimes with likewise small, socially homogeneous, narrowly based political structures. In these settings, ruling *elites* rather than *classes* ran regimes, and these were smaller than class-based dictatorships. In other Western countries—Greece, Argentina, Brazil—military officers ran regimes on behalf of ruling classes: the landed gentry, leaders of the Catholic or Greek Orthodox churches, and the domestic bourgeoisie and foreign investors.

Regimes in a few Western countries invited other, larger social classes to participate. Francisco Franco, Pinochet Ugarte, and Saddam Hussein drew middle-class supporters into the regime, as did the Institutional Revolutionary Party in Mexico. The apartheid government in South Africa invited white South Africans from different economic strata into the ruling class, while, of course excluding blacks and "coloreds" from participating.

In the East, developmentalist regimes in the Soviet Union and Eastern Europe created fairly large ruling classes based on communist parties, which recruited heavily from the urban working classes, while families organized communist dictatorships in North Korea and Albania. Most communist regimes were fairly homogeneous in social terms, drawing their members primarily from the urban working class and the petty bourgeoisie. The communist party in Yugoslavia was perhaps the exception to this general rule. It drew members both from different social classes *and* a diverse set of ethnic groups. In this context, the ruling class in China was larger and more socially diverse than the ruling classes in most developmentalist regimes, with the possible exception of South Africa.

Of course, the regime in China described itself not as a "ruling class" but rather as a "dictatorship of the proletariat" that represented the interests of urban and rural workers. However, this claim was not credible for three reasons. First, the regime might credibly claim that it represented the "interests" of working people *before* the revolution. But by incorporating members of the domestic and petty bourgeoisie into the government and industry, the regime created a socially diverse ruling class that no longer represented *only* workers. Second, in the 1950s the regime adopted policies—the collectivization of agriculture and rapid industrialization during the Great Leap—that proletarianized and immiserated urban and rural workers, eliminated their ability to generate nonwage sources of income, deprived them of credit, seized their property, and restricted their freedom to migrate. No genuine "representative" of the "proletariat" would have done to working people what the regime did to rural and urban workers in China during that time, and no working class would have willingly visited these collective miseries on itself. Karl Marx argued that classes act in their own self-interest. To sustain the assertion that the regime "represented" it, then, one would have to imagine that the working class in China was an exception to this rule, that it would consistently and repeatedly act *against* its own self-interest.

Third, the new regime in China acted *like* a ruling class. As Selden says, "The dominant class or classes are, by definition, those who control the disposition of the surplus."[14] In China, once the regime took power it organized the acquisition and disposition of surplus wealth in China. As we have seen, the regime adopted policies designed to seize and accumulate capital for landlords and the bourgeoisie as well as from rural and urban workers. Like other developmentalist regimes, it used the surplus collected or extracted from other social classes to finance rapid industrial growth. And like other developmentalist regimes, it used some of this surplus to provide collective and individual wealth to its members, which is a characteristic of ruling classes the world over. Historically, ruling classes provide both collective and individual wealth to its members, though some ruling classes emphasize the former and some prefer the latter.

Collective Wealth. The recent global financial crisis has underscored the proliferation of collective wealth—corporate jets, lavish expense accounts and housing allowances, private security details, corporate retreats, club memberships, executive dining rooms, and personal physicians, chefs, trainers, and lawyers—that corporations or government agencies pay for and provide, free of charge, to the executives and government officials that belong to the ruling class. Members of ruling classes often prefer that much of their compensation take the form of collective wealth because it allows them to leverage or use resources that individuals could *not* otherwise afford (such as a corporate jet), because it is not taxed by the government, and, importantly, because it is less *visible* to the employees, shareholders, taxpayers, and voters who foot the bill. Even if this wealth does not end up in an individual's personal bank account, it is an important form of wealth for members of the ruling class.

Although developmentalist regimes and ruling classes in democratic states provided both collective and individual wealth to their members, the ruling classes in the "capitalist" West preferred to distribute wealth to *individuals.* (They sometimes regarded the distribution of collective or "public" wealth as "corrupt" or immoral.) By contrast, in the "communist" East, ruling classes preferred to provide its members with wealth in its collective form. (They sometimes viewed the distribution of individual wealth to their members as "corrupt" and immoral.)

Before taking power in 1949, the Chinese communist party provided free food, housing, clothing, living allowances, education, and other necessities to soldiers and cadre under the "free supply system" (*gongjizhi),* which was designed to provide collective wealth to its members. Of course, the quality and quantity of free supplies varied by rank, so, for example, the party provided a "Big Kitchen" for commanding officers and a "Small Kitchen" for rank-and-file soldiers. After 1949 the regime stopped providing free supplies to many of its cadre, paid them salaries, and reserved the provision of *collective* wealth to high-ranking members of the ruling class, who were provided with apartments, furniture and houses, lavish banquets, free food and other necessities, private security details (see Peng, above) and bodyguards, cars and chauffeurs, air transport, private trains, personal physicians, commissary privileges, and schools reserved for their children's use. The managers of army units, businesses, and collective farms could also appropriate collective assets or "minor public family holdings" for their collective use, though the regime later discouraged this practice and demanded that the assets held by small public households be delivered to the central government, which then made this wealth available to high-ranking members of the ruling class.[15]

The wartime system of free supply helped the regime rationalize the provision of collective wealth to its members. As one senior cadre explained, "I am part of the supply system. Even I as a person belong to the public family. It does not really matter if I use some of the stuff belonging to the public family." Another cadre, who spent two years in prison for embezzlement (taking unauthorized *individual* wealth) explained how he had come to appreciate the value of legal, *collective* wealth: "Now I have realized that only fools embezzle. They have to do it illicitly at the risk of breaching the law. Smart ones do it openly. Now I am living a luxurious life but do not have to *pay* for it [collective wealth]. It's all covered by the entertainment expenses. It is not embezzlement."[16]

Although the regime provided substantial collective wealth to its high-ranking members—for instance, the real value of a free apartment or house in the Forbidden City—their claim on collective wealth often ended when they were retired (or purged). Thus, officials who neared retirement age—sixty—often tried to engage in "corrupt" activities that would enable them to convert their access to collective wealth into individual wealth that they could draw on after they lost power, a practice the regime described as the "59 [year-old] phenomena."[17]

This is one reason why members of the ruling class viewed admission to China's elite schools or military academies as an important prerogative.[18] If they could place their children in elite schools or military service, which would enable them to secure elite jobs in the "Big Kitchen," ruling class *households* could retain their access to the collective wealth made available to high-ranking members, even after they retired.[19] Because of this, competition over admission to elite schools and military service would become an extremely important issue for factions of the ruling class during the Cultural Revolution.

Of course, leaders of the ruling class portrayed themselves as living frugal lives. Liu Shaoqi "ate simply, often leftovers," made his children wear hand-me-down clothes, and had "his own suits and shoes mended when they wore out."[20] Zhou Enlai "was renowned for the same qualities."[21] However, this threadbare, sack-cloth-and-ashes frugality was designed for public consumption. Liu Shaoqi himself admitted in 1956 that an "aristocratic strata" had emerged that threatened to alienate the masses, though he neglected to count himself as one of its members and beneficiaries.[22]

Individual Wealth. In China "state employees with power and access to resources [collective wealth] have many opportunities to divert for their own comfort or benefit [individual wealth]."[23] Although the regime in China has long viewed the private appropriation of collective wealth as a form of "corruption" (*tanwu,* which means "greed and dirt"), in 1997 the ruling class "was rated as one of the world's most corrupt countries . . . ranking twelfth overall." Much of this corruption was a product of the reforms the regime adopted in the late 1970s, which will be discussed in a subsequent chapter. Nevertheless, it is clear that member of the ruling class began early on to acquire individual wealth. Soon after taking power in 1952, Mao launched the first of many campaigns against corruption, which meant that it was already a common practice. In Shanghai, auditors in 1952 found that 81 percent of the city's businesses, which were run by members of the party, had evaded taxes, and "38 percent of cadres in government agencies and state enterprises . . . were found to have committed graft/embezzlement."[24]

The private acquisition of individual wealth took many forms. Members of the ruling class embezzled money; demanded bribes and kickbacks; misappropriated collective resources; used public money to pay for lavish feasts, prostitutes, and mistresses; secured favors for relatives and friends; engaged in profiteering; and evaded taxes.[25] They also used their police powers to coerce, assault, rape, arrest, and detain people to extort money and services from the rural and urban workers under their authority and to silence opponents and intimidate people who objected to their official behavior. Liu Shaoqi's widow, Wang Guangnei, recalled "the widespread physical assaults by local officials that she and her husband witnessed when they visited Hunan: 'every agency and cadre could detain or beat up someone at will, not bound by any rules.'"[26]

Although the regime under Mao preferred to provide members of the ruling class with collective wealth, clearly the acquisition of individual or private wealth was a common practice that the regime did not effectively curb or sanction, and the regime did not introduce a comprehensive criminal code for corruption until 1979.[27] In the 1970s the ruling class embraced the idea that its members should be allowed to acquire individual wealth, and Deng advanced the slogan, "to get rich is glorious." Still, this idea was rooted in practices that had existed for a long time.

The emergence of a large, new, capitalist ruling class with diverse social origins, access to collective and individual wealth, and a determination to defend its interests and prerogatives presented increasing challenges for Mao to wield power unilaterally. It also constrained his behavior, thereby making purging or disciplining other members of the ruling class, as Stalin had done, difficult. Mao was "weak," in part, because the new ruling class was "strong," but Mao was weak for another reason: his capricious behavior made the bureaucracy increasingly reluctant to follow his edicts.

Bureaucratic Resistance. In many countries, China among them, postwar dictatorships created large state bureaucracies to direct economic development. However, as Joel Migdal observed in *Strong Societies and Weak States,* bureaucrats in these organizations typically used their offices to consolidate power, gain access to collective wealth, line their pockets, and pursue their own economic and political agendas. To curb this kind of behavior, dictators shuffled the managers of state agencies to prevent them from establishing an independent power base, appointed inexperienced cronies and loyalists to manage state bureaucracies, purged managers who might challenge the leadership, and charged some with corruption, a behavior that was tolerated so long as its practitioners did not present a political threat to the regime. Nevertheless, efforts to control the bureaucracy impaired their efficiency and made low-level, front-line bureaucrats wary of taking action that might invite sanctions from above. The result was the creation of large but ineffective bureaucracies that did little to implement the policies or advance the political agendas dictators adopted. As Egyptian dictator Gamel Abdel Nasser once complained, "You imagine that we are simply giving orders and the country is run accordingly. You are greatly mistaken."[28]

In China the regime's incessant "class struggles" and administrative campaigns, which placed huge demands on its members, and Mao's capricious behavior and policy flip-flops, which increased the risk to bureaucrats who *followed* the Chairman's line, exacerbated this problem of bureaucratic inefficiency and bureaucrats' reluctance to implement government policy. As an administrator, according to Ezra Vogel, Mao insisted on "careful planning and groundwork at all levels" followed by "a sudden burst of mobilization" and "waves of assault."[29] These incessant campaigns placed heavy demands on cadre assigned to implement them, particularly because they were graded by results and classified into three categories: the good, the not-so-good, and the bad—or "red flag," "green flag," or "white flag." Cadre designated as "white flag" were exposed to disciplinary measures by their superiors. As one cadre recalled after his superior told him that his group had failed to meet the objectives of a campaign in 1958, "At that time, everyone was scared of being a 'rightist,' [because] several hundred people in government agencies [nearly] ... lost their jobs or were sent to labor camps after being labeled as 'rightists.'"[30]

For members of the bureaucracy, the risk associated with failure was substantial. At the outset of the Great Leap in 1958, for example, "half a million party members received disciplinary action [for lack of 'revolutionary enthusiasm']; the number of people expelled from the party equaled 80 percent of the total number of expulsions from 1951 to 1957."[31]

Not surprisingly, these disciplinary measures were counterproductive. As Xiaobo Li observed, "the methods employed to reduce what the leadership perceived as bureaucratism ... induced non-professionalism and produced highly politicized administrative staffs who were not only timid politically but also inefficient and incapable professionally." Under these circumstances, as the risks to cadre increased, they became more cautious. As one cadre explained, "Nobody wanted or dared to tell lies because the Communists were supposed to be truthful; yet without telling lies, the pressure was on and everyone could feel it."[32] One actor echoed this sentiment. During the Hundred Flowers Movement, when the party invited intellectuals to criticize the government, he cautioned, "Only lies are safe."[33]

Mao urged the party to create "an atmosphere of speaking out and correct shortcomings," and he argued, "People are entitled to their own opinions."[34] However, by punishing bureaucrats and intellectuals who did speak out, Mao increased the risk of doing so and effectively silenced those who dared, which made the bureaucracy a less effective policy tool.

Mao's capricious behavior and policy flip-flops also increased the risk to bureaucrats who followed his line. Mao never advanced a policy or principle that he was not prepared to abandon if the "conditions changed." This approach was informed, in part, by his experience with guerilla warfare, which put a premium on adopting to rapidly changing conditions on the battlefield, and also in part by his ruthless pragmatism and utter lack of any principle save one: his determination to hold on to power.

As we have seen, Mao constantly changed his positions. As Frederick Tiewes observed, "The Chairman changed [the] rules virtually at will."[35] He first defended the rich and middle peasants and then denounced and betrayed them; he ridiculed population control, then supported it, and then condemned it; and he turned against almost every one of his cohorts in the communist party, with the possible exception of Zhou Enlai. In 1971 Mao said that the Party had been tested by ten great crises in his lifetime. This list did *not* include the Japanese invasion, civil war with the GMD, the Korean War, the Sino-Soviet split, the Great Leap Forward, the famine, or the Cultural Revolution. Instead, they all involved disputes with other leaders and the threats these disputes posed to his personal leadership, and this view of party crises was indicative of his obsession with the personal, not the political.[36] He promoted disastrous economic policies—collectivization and the Great Leap—and blamed their failure on others, and during the Cultural Revolution he used the Red Guard to pursue his goals and then had the army suppress them once he had achieved his objectives.

Mao hedged his bets and positioned himself on both sides of every issue so he could claim, after the results were in, that he had been right all along. He rationalized this unscrupulous behavior by expressing everything in terms of its myriad "contradictions," which he claimed was a product of the dialectical method employed by Marx. However, his dialectical method was a crude caricature of Marx's method.

Take, for example, Mao's speech about leadership: "Take the problem of whom to follow. Whom should one follow first of all? First of all, we should learn from the people and follow them. The people have so much energy, [they are] more, faster, better.... That is why we follow the people first, and afterwards the people follow us."[37] Mao was asked to clarify these instructions, so he amended them: "This statement needs modification. One should follow and yet not follow. An individual is sometimes right and sometimes wrong. Follow him when he is right and do not follow him when he is wrong. We follow whoever has truth in his hands. Even if he should be a manure carrier or a street sweeper, as long as he has the truth he should be followed."[38]

Got that? How exactly should Mao's followers follow his instructions? How would they know *whom* to follow, and yet *not* follow? How would they know whether a person was "right" and had "truth in his hands?" Mao's discussion begs all these questions. Imagine the difficulty, for cadre, of correctly interpreting, applying, and "following" these instructions, particularly if they knew that failure to "follow" them could expose them to serious penalties.

Making sense of Mao's directive about development in a socialist society is equally difficult: "Balance is relative, imbalance absolute. This is a universal law which I am convinced applies to socialist society. Contradiction and struggle are absolutes; unity, unanimity, and solidarity are transitional, hence, relative. The various balances attended in planning are temporary, transition, and conditional, hence relative."[39] At one point, Mao insisted that "all empty words are useless," which is a non sequitor, but it seems a good description of this passage.[40]

The problem for Mao was that his continual flip-flopping and contradictory blather made it difficult for the members of the bureaucracy to follow the party line, which was extremely difficult to divine, changed all the time, and made them liable for the "mistakes" or "errors" that emerged if they incorrectly interpreted or applied Mao's policies.

Bureaucrats in China were responsible for following and implementing the regime's policies, but they were subject to punishment if the policy changed or failed, as it did frequently. Because of the risk associated with following Mao's edicts, members of the ruling class became increasingly reluctant to follow Mao's dictates and implement his will. Bureaucratic resistance, which grew in response to Mao's capricious behavior as a dictator, further undermined his authority and weakened his real political stature. By the early 1960s Mao's efforts to make the bureaucracy an effective instrument of his will had become increasingly *in*effective.

Events in the 1950s further weakened Mao's authority. During the Great Leap, food production collapsed. The resulting famine led to the deaths of tens of millions of people and brought Mao's ambitious industrial development plans to a halt. The scholar Hong Yung Lee concluded, "The disastrous failure of the Great Leap Forward shattered the confidence of the Chinese people in Mao's thought and his personal power."[41] The regime's growing political and economic isolation further compromised Mao's ability to exert his authority.

Political and Economic Isolation. After the outbreak of the Korean War, in 1950 the United States and its allies imposed a political and economic embargo on China, barred it from membership in the United Nations, and banned trade with and investment in China. Because of this, during the 1950s China relied on loans from the Soviet Union, trade with the Soviet Union and its allies, and technical assistance from Soviet scientists to assist its economic development. However, in 1960 Soviet Premier Nikita Khrushchev broke with Mao, withdrew Soviet scientists and advisers, and banned further investment and trade with China. Carl Riskin said of the Soviet withdrawal, "It would have been impossible for Khrushchev to have chosen a moment when China was more vulnerable: a major famine in progress, the economy in organizational disarray, Chinese technical and administrative leadership scattered and demoralized, and the moves to resurrect planning and central control just beginning."[42]

In political terms, the Sino-Soviet split deprived Mao of international allies. During the 1960s only a few socialist countries recognized Mao's regime, so Mao was reduced to counting poor and politically insignificant countries like Albania, Tanzania, and Zambia as his only allies. Although he had portrayed himself as one of the leaders of the world's revolutionary, anticolonial movements, none of the revolutionary movements in Africa (Guinea-Bissau, Angola, Algeria, Mozambique, Rhodesia, and South Africa), Latin America (Cuba, Bolivia, Argentina, Brazil, Chile), Asia (Malaysia, North and South Vietnam, Indonesia, Cambodia, Burma), or the Middle East (Iran, Afghanistan, Syria, Egypt) looked to Mao for leadership, guidance, or military assistance. This is because political isolation undermined Mao's claim that he led a "revolutionary" party that was an important "anti-imperialist" force in the world. It would not be until Mao launched the Cultural Revolution that some marginal, anti-imperialist student movements and ultra-left terrorist movements in the United States and Western Europe (Students for a Democratic Society, Progressive Labor, Weatherman, Baader-Meinhof, and the Red Brigades) would adopt Maoist rhetoric and look to Mao for political inspiration.

Economic isolation meant that Mao could not adopt many of the strategies other developmentalist regimes used to foster economic growth. China could not rely on the sale of raw materials or export commodities to earn money that could finance development, as Taiwan and South Korea had done. It could not borrow money from the International Monetary Fund or the World Bank, which made loans available to members of the United Nations (they are agencies of the United Nations), as both capitalist and communist regimes around the world had done.[43] It could not use the money earned from foreign troops based in the country or military assistance provided by a superpower ally to promote economic development or defray the cost of defense, as Taiwan, South Korea, the Philippines, South Vietnam, Thailand, or countries in Eastern Europe had done.[44] It could not use foreign direct investment to finance development, as regimes across the US sphere, particularly in Latin America, had done. Just about the only strategy China could adopt was import-substitutionist industrialization (ISI)—building domestic industries that could supply goods that had previously been imported, which regimes in Latin America had also adopted.[45] However, in China this strategy was a product of necessity, not of choice, as it was elsewhere.

Of course, many of the regimes that adopted these different economic strategies failed to promote development, but some regimes, like those in South Korea and Taiwan, used them successfully to promote rapid economic growth. However, political isolation deprived Mao of strategies that *might* have provided economic benefits in the 1950s, 1960s, and 1970s. With these alternatives off the table, Mao was forced to practice a punitive, primitive strategy of economic development that relied heavily on exploiting rural and urban workers to generate a surplus that could then be used to invest in rudimentary industries and provide collective and individual wealth for members of a large and growing ruling class.

Mao's Idiosyncratic Class Analysis

Mao described the Cultural Revolution as a struggle between two classes: the proletariat and a bureaucratic class that "is sharply opposed to the working class and the poor and lower-middle peasants." He argued that "these people have become or are in the process of becoming bourgeois elements sucking the blood of the workers."[46]

This rhetoric is important to note because "in China," Hong Yung Lee has argued, "differences in the definition of class are not merely empty, ideological polemics. They had direct and concrete consequences for various groups during the Cultural Revolution, because they defined who would be the major targets and who the participants in the mass movement."[47]

However, Mao's interpretation of events during the Cultural Revolution relied on an extremely idiosyncratic definition of "class" and "class struggle." Before and during the Cultural Revolution Mao used arbitrary, racial, and spiritualist criteria to define class. His non-Marxist approach to class enabled him to create fictitious classes—a proletariat and a bureaucratic class—and depict the conflict between them as a struggle between two separate classes when in fact they were factions of the same class: the ruling class. This ruse allowed him to frame and win the struggle that ensued. To understand how Mao framed the debate during the Cultural Revolution, scrutinizing his theoretical and practical approach to class is necessary.

As a practical matter, Mao directed the party to assign individual heads of households to different classes—worker, rich, middle, lower, and poor peasants, capitalist, landlord, petty bourgeois, and vagabond—that were largely defined by their *source of income.* These class identities, as well as some nonclass categories such as "revolutionary cadre," "revolutionary solider," or dependent of a "revolutionary martyr," or "student," or "intellectual," were then entered in the household registration books that the police, employers, and work units kept, together with information about their "name, address, sex, birth date, nationality, marital status, years of schooling, the place of the family's ancestral origin, and class status."[48]

The regime used "family origin" to describe an individual's class and source of income in the years *prior to* the revolution, but it also generally used this category to identify a person's class in the years *after* the revolution. This meant that people kept their prerevolution class identities even if their actual economic status had changed. Moreover, the rest of the household were generally assigned to the same class status as the head, and if a "person moved into a new family (for example by marriage), her (practically never his) origin remained unchanged."[49] As a result, children generally inherited their father's assigned, prerevolutionary class identity, irrespective of their actual material circumstances. The regime used the dossier containing all this important social information in the late 1950s to record the place of residence as part of the regime's household registration system (hukou) to keep rural workers from migrating to the city.

This class-registration system had important consequences for people both before and during the Cultural Revolution. In the 1950s and 1960s people with "good" class labels (worker, peasant, revolutionary cadre) received economic and social advantages, whereas the regime penalized and sometimes singled out and attacked people assigned to "bad" classes (bourgeois, landlord, intellectual) during its campaigns against landlords, the bourgeoisie, the petty bourgeoisie, rich, upper-middle peasants, and intellectuals—sometimes with lethal results. (As we will see, this would change during the Cultural Revolution.) For example, during one "anti-rightist" campaign in 1957, the regime ordered work units and universities in Shanghai to identify 5 to 7 percent of their employees as "rightists," a task that cadre accomplished by examining the household registration books of their employees and identifying employees with "bad" class status, which was based on their prerevolutionary class identity, to make their quota.[50]

Consequently, in the early 1950s Mao and the regime defined and assigned class labels to virtually everyone in China, but it is clear from its practice that Mao used arbitrary, racial, and spiritual criteria to define the classes to which people were assigned.

Arbitrary Criteria. Mao used the attributes associated with specific *kinds* of work to define classes in economic terms, and he used the source and level of income that people received to determine their class. Thus, people who received wages were classified as workers, and people who received a share of the crop were peasants, who were then subdivided into several classes depending on their level of income. People who received salaries were petty bourgeois, people who received rent or interest were landlords, and people who received profits from the sale of goods that workers produced were capitalists. Mao also used other specific job attributes to define class. The regime defined intellectuals, in part, by the fact that they performed "mental" as opposed to "manual" labor, a characteristic that landlords, capitalists, and the petty bourgeoisie also shared. It also defined intellectuals by the fact that they engaged in "unproductive" labor (labor that did not produce economic value), a characteristic of landlords but *not,* according to Mao, of capitalists and the petty bourgeoisie, whom he saw as contributing to economic development.[51] Mao viewed some classes as combining the attributes of different classes. For instance, upper middle peasants worked their own land, which made them like other peasants, but they also hired workers to assist them, which made them like landlords. In the 1950s the regime used upper middle peasants' latter characteristic (that they were like landlords) as its rationale for eliminating them as a class, their peasantlike characteristics notwithstanding.

Curiously, sociologists in the United States and Western Europe have widely adopted Mao's idiosyncratic approach to class analysis. Scholars like C. Wright Mills, John and Barbara Ehrenreich, James O'Connor, Nicos Poulantzas, and Erik Olin Wright have used specific attributes associated with different kinds of work to assign people to membership in different classes.[52] In the 1950s and 1960s American sociologists like Mills distinguished between a "white-collar" and a "blue-collar" class based on a set of job attributes. For Mills white collar was shorthand for skilled, college-educated, salaried workers who performed mental labor in the service sector; blue collar described less-skilled, high school–educated wageworkers who performed manual labor in factory settings.

During the 1970s sociologists influenced by Mao and the Cultural Revolution used distinctions between mental and manual, productive and unproductive as a way to identify the emergence of what they described as a new, "professional-managerial," "petty bourgeois," or "new middle class."[53] Some scholars, like Erik Olin Wright, argued that this new class took characteristics from both capitalist and workers and thereby occupied a "contradictory class location" within the class structure, much like Mao's upper-middle peasants.

However, the use of job-related attributes based on income (wage, salary, rent); education, skill, apparel (white or blue collar); kind of work activity (manual or mental); and the end use of goods workers make (whether they are productive or unproductive of value) is problematic for several reasons. First, capitalist development has continually changed the specific character of work in any given job. Capitalists have introduced new technology, reorganized the division of labor in field, factory, and office, eliminated old jobs, combined others, and created new ones with new sets of tasks that require different sets of skills. Capitalists have also used different systems of payment—piece rates, wages, tips, salaries, bonuses, stock options, pension plans, health care benefits—to persuade workers to maximize their efforts. The specific attributes associated with work and income change all the time. As a result, these changes have undermined the meaning of classes that a particular set of job-related attributes defined. What happened to "white-collar" and "blue-collar" classes that figured so prominently in the sociological literature of the 1960s and early 1970s? Factories closed and laid-off workers took jobs in the retail service sector—McDonald's, Home Depot—where managers dressed them in new uniforms: polo shirts and khaki pants. However, even though "blue-collar" jobs have been eliminated and new jobs have been created for people wearing polo shirts, did that mean that a new class, a new "polo-tariat" has emerged? No. It does not mean that wage work or the working class has disappeared; it simply means capitalists have substantially reorganized work and workers.

Second, if specific set of job-related attributes defined class, people who changed jobs or had their work reorganized would change class. Sociologists using this method would define a person employed by a temporary agency—a janitorial or cleaning service such as Manpower or a firm providing temporary office workers such as Kelly Services—as the member of a "manual, productive" class one day, and the member of another, "mental-*un*productive" class the next, depending on where they worked. Given the fact that many workers now have diverse career paths, they might change their class identity many times in a lifetime. Thus, this kind of "pop" sociology is arbitrary and capricious. It is arbitrary because scholars can use any particular attribute or set of characteristics—income, skill, type of work, end use—as a criteria to define class. It is capricious because scholars who define class in this way imagine that people change their class identity as easily as their change their shirts.

If arbitrary criteria can be used to define class, there is no reason why other job-related criteria cannot also be used to define class. We know, for example, that gender, race, age, and ability are closely associated with different kinds of work and that people are frequently assigned to jobs based on these social attributes. Why not then use these social attributes to define separate classes? After all, they are no less important than economic attributes. The problem, of course, is that this would lead to an endless profusion of "classes," which would be divided, each from the other, in complex ways. Unfortunately, many social scientists in the United States and Western Europe have in fact taken this direction, using a growing number of social and economic criteria to identify smaller and narrower social/economic "classes." In a recent book, for example, Andrew Ross, an American sociologist, identified a new "service" class, a "knowledge" class, a "gray-collar" class, a "permatemps" class, a "digitariat," and a "cognitariat," which he suggested might join together in a cross-class alliance he called the "precariat."[54] This is useless nonsense.

The bureaucratic class that Mao invented on the eve of the Cultural Revolution has all of these socioeconomic attributes. Mao used an arbitrary set of job-related attributes to identify the emergence of a new bureaucratic class. According to Mao, the bureaucracy consisted of workers who engaged in unproductive, mental labor and derived their salaries from the surplus created by the proletariat, wageworkers who were engaged in manual labor.

The approach taken by Mao and pop sociologists in the West owes more to Max Weber's discussion of "status groups" than to Marx's analysis of "class." As Lynn White has argued, "It is worth noting that most of the Marxist innovators since Marx and Engels (Bernstein, Kautsky, Lukacs, Gramsci, Althusser, Polantzas and others) have spent much of their intellectual effort trying to capture the practical virtues of making economically generated classes almost synonymous with Weberian status groups. The labeled classes [Mao] used were closer to status groups, despite their [Marxist] names."[55]

Marx, however, took a different approach. He defined class *not* on the basis of *specific* or what he called "concrete" characteristics of work. Instead, he defined classes in terms of people's "abstract" or general relation to the "means of production." For Marx, the landlords who owned land and the capitalists who owned land, labor, and capital (technology, machinery, raw materials, and the money needed to purchase all of these things) *both* belonged to the capitalist class because they *owned* the means of production, which was an important, general kind of social relation. By contrast, people who owned neither land nor capital, who therefore had a different relation to the means of production and relied on the sale of their labor to survive, were, in Marx's view, members of the proletariat.

Marx might have added that although people in most households have to sell their labor to make a living, household members also engage in nonwage work—reproductive and subsistence activities, sharing, and petty commodity production—to help them survive. They do so both because wages are usually insufficient to survive as a group and because these activities—cooking, cleaning, childrearing, and elder care—are necessary if they are to survive from one generation to the next.[56]

Marx argued that most people belong to one of these two great classes (the bourgeoisie or the proletariat), though he said that small groups of people belonged to classes—the petty bourgeoisie, beggars, criminals, and vagabonds (what he called the "lumpen proletariat")—that he thought would soon disappear. (In fact, they have proved more durable than Marx expected.) Marx used abstract criteria to define class in very general terms. This enabled him to argue that the great majority of workers could and should act together politically, based on their shared mutual economic interest. Marx also viewed class as a durable social structure, one that persisted despite the fact that capitalists constantly "reorganized" the means of production and, by doing so, transformed the character of work and the workers associated with it. This enabled him to take a long-term view of social change. Whatever the merits or demerits of Marx's approach, it contrasts sharply with the one Mao and pop sociologists in the West advocated. Not only did Mao adopt an arbitrary approach to the definition of class, he also viewed class in racial terms.

Racial Criteria. Mao and the regime assigned people to classes that they defined in arbitrary, non-Marxist terms, and they registered these assignments with the police and employers. But Mao also insisted that their children be assigned and inherit these given identities, for generations to come, even if their economic circumstances had changed. Mao did this because he thought that people inherited class traits, and he advanced a "theory of blood heritage," or "blood pedigree theory," that informed his view that "a hero's child is a brave man, and a reactionary child is a bastard."[57]

People who were given good class labels could pass the privileges and often their own job assignments on to their children, and "the practice of job inheritance [was] 'in force everywhere.'"[58] By contrast, people who were arbitrarily assigned to bad classes not only experienced the sting of discrimination and the stigma associated with it, but they also watched this stigma attach itself to their children. The American sociologist Erving Goffman would describe Maoist practices as creating both "blemishes of individual character" and "tribal" stigma.[59] By making class an *inherited* social attribute, Mao and the regime effectively *racialized* the meaning of class in China. It was racial because he imagined, like race theorists, that socially constructed attributes (physical characteristics, national origins, or, in Mao's case, economic class identities) were automatically passed down from one generation to the next and could not be changed.

This development in China was very similar to what the Belgians did in Rwanda during the 1930s. During the 1933 census, the Belgian administrators of their colony in Rwanda divided the population into two different groups—Tutsi and Hutu—and registered these designations on their identity cards.[60] The Belgians treated these groups as separate races and insisted that these racial identities be passed on to their children. The irony, of course, was that Tutsi and Hutu were not different races or even different tribes. They both belonged to the same ethnic Bantu people, spoke the same language, and, after the Belgians introduced Christianity, practiced the same religion, Catholicism. They were, however, different in one respect. They belonged to different *economic* groups: the Tutsi were pastoralists who herded cattle; Hutu were farmers who cultivated the land.[61] The Belgians took these economic differences and, by making them permanent and inherited, *racialized* them. Of course, even though these "racial" assignments were a fiction the Belgians invented, they had real social consequences for the people assigned to them, contributing later to conflict, war, and genocide.

Like the Belgian colonists, Mao and the regime took economic differences, which, as we have seen, were often small or based on arbitrary criteria, and turned them into racial categories. Despite the fact that Mao invented these social categories, they had real and enduring consequences for the people assigned to them. As Thomas and Thomas have argued, "If men define situations as real, they are real in their consequences."[62]

Marx, of course, did not think that class membership was inherited. After all, during the French Revolution, the bourgeoisie had fought *against* inherited wealth and privilege, arguing that political, economic, military, and social advancement should be based on "merit" not "birth." Marx believed that classes were durable social structures but nonetheless thought that their membership changed as a result of social and economic developments. As a class, the bourgeois was open to successful leaders of the military, industry, politics, and, in our own era, to entertainers and sports figures. Likewise, the proletariat was open to people who fell from other classes and became proletarianized. In this regard, Marx believed both in upward and downward mobility. But he thought that class structures remained intact even if their particular membership changed.

Of course, although the members of ruling classes champion "merit," they try hard to create structures of opportunity (private schools, entrance to elite universities, low tax rates on inherited wealth) for their children, and this of course makes "birth" a more salient feature of membership than "merit." Still, despite their best efforts, whereas members of the ruling class try to emphasize birth, their fortunes are divided or squandered, and children marry "beneath" them, waste the opportunities provided by their parents, and fall, headlong, into the proletariat. Likewise, some members of the working class use public structures of opportunity (public schools, scholarships to private schools, scrimping and saving) to ascend into the ruling class. Those who succeed infuse the ruling class with new money, energy, and ideas.

In China the new ruling class used racialized class categories as a mechanism for ensuring that that they could transfer wealth and power to their children and make membership in the ruling class a matter of *birth,* not *merit.*

Spiritualist Criteria. Mao was a spiritualist. He believed that people in one class could possess the consciousness of another class that *no longer existed.* In his 1957 pamphlet, "On the Correct Handling of Contradictions among the People," Mao argued that the bourgeois political superstructure survived the loss of its economic power and that bourgeois ideology was transmitted to a new generation of people who belonged to other classes.[63] This was a remarkable position to take because the regime had earlier eliminated the bourgeoisie as a class. It had killed, exiled, imprisoned, incorporated, or proletarianized its members; seized its assets; and destroyed its social networks and political institutions. The party in 1956 had even announced that its struggle with the bourgeoisie and the landlords had ended.

Nonetheless, Mao argued that although the bourgeoisie's *economic* base had been destroyed, its ideas and consciousness lived on. Mao insisted that class-consciousness could survive the destruction of its material base. "Although socialism eliminates class," Mao warned, "in its process of development, some problems of groups with vested interests still persist."[64] Some of his colleagues disagreed; Liu Shaoqi argued that economic or material circumstances defined class.[65]

In 1966, when Mao announced the Cultural Revolution, he admitted that the bourgeoisie no longer existed as an economic class but insisted that its ideas lived on and had taken possession of another class: "Although the bourgeoisie has been overthrown, it is still trying to use the old ideas, culture, customs, and habits of the exploiting classes to corrupt the masses, capture their minds, and stage a comeback."[66]

However, if the bourgeoisie was dead, how could "it" still be trying to "capture the minds" of people in *other* classes and use them as a vessel to "stage a comeback"? This is the language of J. K. Rowlings, the strategy of Lord Voldemort, who was killed but nevertheless plotted his "return to power."

As a guide or medium of the spirit world, Mao argued that the consciousness of the bourgeois had taken possession of another class—the bureaucratic class—and persuaded it to travel down the "capitalist" road. "Adopting the reactionary stand of the bourgeoisie," Mao warned darkly in 1966, "[the new bureaucratic class has] enforced a bourgeois dictatorship and struck down the surging movement of the great cultural revolution of the proletariat."[67]

Voldemort had returned!

Taking this spiritualist nonsense seriously would be difficult except that it had important consequences for millions of people in China. As Lee has noted, "In China, differences in the definition of class were not mere empty, ideological polemics. They had direct and concrete consequences for various social groups in the Cultural Revolution because they defined who would be the major targets and who would be the participants in the mass movement."[68]

The problem with Mao's spiritualist approach to class consciousness is that it owed more to "idealist" philosophers like Friedrich Hegel than to "materialist" thinkers like Marx. Like Hegel, Mao imagined that class-consciousness could be divorced from the material world and economic reality and could persist even in the absence of material conditions. Marx, of course, viewed this kind of thinking with disdain and criticized the German idealists in his early works, including *The German Ideology.* Marx considered himself a materialist and argued that people's consciousness grew out of and was tied to their material economic conditions. In this context, Mao's spiritualist view of class was profoundly anti-Marxist.

Consequently, after the revolution Mao and the regime developed and practiced an arbitrary, racial, spiritual, non-Marxist approach to class in China. I have argued that this was both problematic and consequential, but why would Mao and the regime depart from a Marxist approach to class? After all, Mao and his cohorts professed to follow Marx, so why would Mao and the other leaders treat class and class struggle in this idiosyncratic fashion? I maintain that they did so because it provided several political advantages to the regime, and to Mao in particular.

First, doing so allowed Mao to use arbitrary criteria to define as a "class" enemy any person or clique who challenged his authority, even if this group had no material, economic base as a class, much less a "consciousness" of itself as a class. The "rich" and "middle" peasants were targeted as a "class" even though they were simply income groups, a statistical category without any awareness of themselves as a class. They became aware of themselves as a class only when the regime defined them as an enemy of the state and targeted them for destruction.

Second, it allowed Mao and the regime to create fictitious classes and engage in fictitious class struggles. During the Cultural Revolution Mao invented a fictional bureaucratic class, which, he said, was imbued with the spirit of the dead bourgeoisie, and he then mobilized people to struggle against it. However, even though many of the class struggles that Mao waged were fictions, they nonetheless had real and serious consequences. As William Hinton, a close observer of developments in China, has written, "Cadre who treated all contradictions as class conflicts raised them artificially to absurd levels of antagonism, created 'class enemies' where none existed, and ended up fighting battles that never should have been fought."[69]

Third, this practice allowed Mao to identify "problems" and frame the debate about how to "solve" them. As the American sociologist William Gamson has argued, the ability to "name" and "frame" a debate is the key to winning the struggle that follows.[70] By using his command of class language, Mao was able to define the terms of debate within the party. He generally persuaded his colleagues to accept his definition of class and engage in class struggle on his terms, and this ability to set the terms of the engagement gave him a tactical advantage in the struggle that followed. This was particularly true during the Cultural Revolution. Mao named the classes and framed the struggle between them as a conflict between two distinct classes: the proletariat and the bureaucracy. This was a triple fiction: the people who fought were not members of the "proletariat" but of the ruling class; the "bureaucratic" class was not the representative of the dead bourgeoisie but a faction of the new ruling class; the struggle that ensued was not a conflict between *two* different classes but a struggle within the same class.

Fourth, this approach debased the political language and deprived Mao's opponents of using a class vocabulary to express their grievances, defend themselves in a debate, or persuade others to support them. By debasing the language of class, Mao effectively silenced his opponents. The demonstrators who gathered in Tiananmen Square in 1976 and 1989 groped with difficulty for words to describe the regime, articulate political demands, and mobilize like-minded people. In 1978 they denounced the "feudal fascist dictatorship" of Mao Zedong, which was an awkward, inaccurate characterization. Its only advantage was that it was an epithet; it used words that were anathema to the regime. What else could the demonstrators say? What kind of class language could they use? All the good words in the class vocabulary—words that might have had meaning and power—had been debased by Mao or perverted by the regime's incessant use. The students could not use the language of *class* to express their own "class-consciousness" or engage in "class struggle."

Actually, this is a common problem. Ruling classes in the United States and Western Europe work hard to create a political language that makes articulate expression difficult for their opponents. In the United States, for example, Richard Nixon used the term, "the silent *majority,*" to describe his supporters. He thereby created a political vocabulary that framed the debate and made it difficult for his opponents to "speak up" and articulate dissent because to do so marked them as the "vocal *minority.*"

In China dissidents have faced difficulty waging a class struggle against a ruling class that has altered and debased the language of class, a regime that has defined itself as the "proletariat," and a regime that has argued that anyone who struggled against it must be an "enemy" of the working class. Furthermore, many scholars and observers have uncritically used the debased class vocabulary Mao articulated. This has made it difficult for them to explain what the Cultural Revolution was *really* about.

The Revolt of the "Disadvantaged"

In 1966 Mao launched the Great Proletarian Cultural Revolution to strengthen his authority within the ruling class and make the bureaucracy more responsive to his rule. As we have seen, the emergence of a large, socially diverse ruling class, his own disastrous policies (the collectivization of agriculture, Great Leap Forward, and famine), and events (political and economic isolation) weakened Mao's authority. His incessant campaigns and political flip-flopping had exposed the bureaucrats in government, industry, and agriculture to risk, which made them wary and increasingly reluctant to implement his policies. Although Mao wanted to purge his opponents, increase his authority, and bend the bureaucracy to his will, he was not strong enough to accomplish this on his own; he needed allies to assist him. "Lacking the organized intra-Party power base of Stalin," Andrew Nathan has argued, "Mao prepared to mobilize student power to drive his rivals out of office."[71] So Mao enlisted the slightly *dis*advantaged members of the ruling class—the students and cadre who had been given or inherited "bad" class labels—and asked them to attack the more *advantaged* members of the ruling class—cadre who had obtained or inherited "good" class labels. With help from the slightly disadvantaged, Mao was able to drive his rivals in the ruling class from power.

Initially, Mao called on "good" label cadre to assist him, but he soon turned to "bad" label cadre because their resentment made them more enthusiastic allies, so they became Mao's foot soldiers during the Cultural Revolution. By the fall of 1966 "the radical rebel factions, with the support of the radical Maoist leaders at the top, managed to seize the leadership of the student movement from the children of high-ranking cadres, and shifted the target of the movement to the top level party and government leaders."[72] Scholars who interviewed members of Mao's Red Guard in Guangzhou found that "three quarters of the radical Red Flags came from families with 'middle and bad' labels.[73] As Lynn White has persuasively argued, during the Cultural Revolution, "people who disliked the [class] labels or their bosses rose up to change them."[74]

Why did the slightly disadvantaged cadre join Mao and rise up against their betters? Cadre with "bad," "bourgeois" class labels responded to Mao's invitation to revolt because they resented their inferior status. They resented the fact that they were stigmatized by bad class labels, complained that they were treated as "born criminals," and, as a result, "were discriminated against in job opportunities, in admission to the People's Liberation Army, in some important positions, and in some institutions of higher learning"; in short, they were denied the structures of opportunity provided to some members of the ruling class.[75] They viewed admission to college as an important issue because it was a structure of opportunity that allowed them to *stay* in the ruling class. They worried that colleges increasingly gave preference to cadre with good labels, who had spots reserved for them, even if they were unqualified, and that the colleges discriminated against bad-label cadre, even if these cadre had a better academic record. The preferential treatment given to good-labeled cadre threatened to shut the bad-labeled cadre out of the ruling class.[76] The bad-labeled cadre had good reason to fear this development. Between 1951 and 1963 the percentage of bad-label students enrolled in college had declined by more than half, from 81 percent of admissions to 33 percent—a troubling prospect for bad-label cadre.[77]

The disadvantaged cadre made common cause with Mao not only because they regarded the discrimination associated with their arbitrary and racialized class identities (which, ironically, Mao had given them), but also because "those from bourgeois and other 'bad' families saw an opportunity . . . to enhance their political position," to displace their "betters," and move up, as a group, within the ruling class.[78]

During the Cultural Revolution Mao and the disadvantaged rejected the old (Maoist) argument that class identity was inherited and insisted instead that it be based on performance and "merit." Recall that Mao had earlier said "if the father's a hero, the son's a good chap; if the father's a reactionary, the son's a bastard." Nevertheless, during the Cultural Revolution he changed his position, as he often did, and argued, "A person's class *origin* should be distinguished from his *performance,* which is more important than his class origin. It is wrong to assume that class status is everything." Mao and his followers now criticized the earlier view of class inheritance and "claimed that the original couplet represented a 'feudalistic hereditary blood theory' or a 'theory of natural redness.'"[79] Mao's wife, Jiang Qing, even penned a new slogan: "If the father is a hero, the son is in the successor generation; if the father is a reactionary, the son betrays him," which, of course, tried to have it both ways.[80] She defended those from bad family backgrounds because "an individual cannot choose his background, but can choose his performance."[81]

Of course, Mao and his wife defined "performance" or merit as being "red," or loyal to Mao. This forced cadre with good labels to defend their "privilege," which was based on their inherited claims to membership in good, prerevolutionary classes. This new definition put them in a difficult political position. Mao and his allies could claim that they supported advancement based on "merit"—which, incidentally, was the position bourgeois revolutionaries during the French Revolution took—and denounce their opponents as defenders of inherited "privilege," which then forced said opponents to become representatives of a class "aristocracy." One cadre with a "good label" ruefully described the topsy-turvy feeling of vertigo that this switch caused among his peers: "In the past, we had privileged thought and suppressed out classmates from 'bad' family backgrounds. We admit that. But now it is reversed. These sons of bitches want to discriminate in reverse and suppress *us*."[82]

Mao had mobilized the disadvantaged against the advantaged on previous occasions. During the agrarian reform, he and the party had successfully mobilized the upper, middle, and lower peasants against the landlords and incited them to violence. During collectivization, he mobilized the lower peasants against middle and rich peasants. Because Mao promised disadvantaged groups that they would benefit from an attack on advantaged groups and because he rewarded them with the land and assets seized from their superiors, he gave them an incentive to participate in the process and join the "class struggle." During the Cultural Revolution Mao again used the prospect of upward mobility within the ruling class as an incentive—as the bait—to persuade the resentful members of disadvantaged groups to attack their betters. Naturally, they responded with enthusiasm, and the Cultural Revolution took on a violent and undisciplined character. The political conflict during the Cultural Revolution, like the conflict during agrarian reform, resulted in considerable violence, which Mao encouraged. "The more ferocious, the better, don't you think?" Mao told his supporters. "The more people you kill, the more revolutionary you are."[83]

Mao's allies in the Red Guard attacked, humiliated, beat, tortured, and killed their opponents. They "subjected the 'class enemy' to physical abuse and torture in their private jails and torture rooms.... The 'red terror' against the ... intellectuals reached its peak ... when Red Guards maliciously broke the fingers of Yeh Chien-ying's son-in-law, a famous pianist."[84] During August and September 1966 "1,772 people were murdered in Beijing," and in Shanghai in September there were 704 suicides and 534 deaths."[85] Public humiliation and the use of coercion and torture to force confessions of personal "error" persuaded many victims to commit suicide. "Many people have committed suicide or been killed," Lin Biao acknowledged, and Public Security minister Xie Fuzhi said that many people killed themselves "out of fear of punishment for their crimes."[86]

Determining how many people died during the Cultural Revolution is difficult. Lynn White and others have argued persuasively that about one million people died, which was about half as many people who died during the campaign against the landlords during the agrarian reform.[87] Whatever the actual numbers of deaths, scholars agree that millions of people were sent down from the cities to the countryside and proletarianized. Carl Riskin and Thomas Bernstein have separately argued that twelve million people were rusticated between 1968 and 1975, whereas Tyrene White put the figure at fifteen million.[88]

The rustication of Mao's political opponents had several important social and political consequences. First, it allowed Mao and his allies to purge his opponents and expel their families and children from the ruling class. When Liu Shaoqi, the head of state and number-two ranking person in the Politburo after Mao, was purged, more than "20,000 of Liu's family, friends, and supporters were purged, and imprisoned," and many of them rusticated to remote rural areas.[89] Although some would later be "rehabilitated" and allowed to return to the cities, their lives were shattered by long-term proletarianization, which destroyed the career prospects of victims and their children.

Second, the rustications associated with the Cultural Revolution, like the smaller-scale rustications practiced in the late 1950s and early 1960s (see above), reduced the urban population. During the Cultural Revolution Mao killed two birds with one stone: he purged his opponents *and* reduced the demand for urban jobs, which were in chronically short supply.[90]

Third, by purging his opponents and removing them, along with their families, Mao made it possible for his allies to take their jobs, their positions in the bureaucracy, and their places in the university and then settle into their apartments and move up within the ranks of the ruling class. Thus, Mao rewarded his allies for acting on his behalf. In return, this group, which owed its advancement to Mao, pledged him their loyalty.

By purging his opponents and promoting his allies, Mao simultaneously rid the bureaucracy of people who had been unresponsive to his edicts and replaced them with cadre who were more responsive to his demands. As Lin Biao's son observed in 1971, "the Chairman commands such high prestige that he need only utter one sentence to remove anybody he chooses."[91]

Mao and many scholars have argued that the Cultural Revolution was a revolt "against" the bureaucracy.[92] As Hong Yung Lee has argued, "Mao wanted to reverse the trend toward restratification caused by the bureaucratization of the Party."[93] However, if Mao was against bureaucracy, why did it grow so dramatically during the Cultural Revolution?

Between 1969 and 1973 Mao *increased* the number of people in the Party, which staffed and directed state bureaucracies, by *six million* members, from twenty-two to twenty-eight million.[94] Mao's attacks on the bureaucracy, like that of Republican presidents in the United States, were rhetorical, not substantive. Antibureaucracy leaders in both countries regularly attacked "bureaucracy" but then took steps to increase its size.

The fact that Mao increased the number of Party members and admitted his allies as a way to reward their loyalty belied his claims that he was opposed to bureaucracy. Mao was only against a bureaucracy that was insufficiently "red," which paid him no heed. He supported a loyal bureaucracy that heeded his demands.

In some respects, then, the Cultural Revolution resembled the French Revolution. Scholars have often cast the French Revolution as a conflict between two great classes: the rising bourgeoisie and the declining aristocracy. But Immanuel Wallerstein has long argued that the French Revolution was *not* a conflict between rival classes. "Far from this being a class struggle ... it was a mere power struggle, 'a matter of rivalry between competing teams" who were then in the process of merging. The bourgeoisie bought titles; the aristocracy married into bourgeois, merchant houses.[95] An aristocracy-bourgeoisie led by King Louis XVI went into the revolution, and a bourgeoisie-aristocracy led by Bonapart Napoleon came out of it. Wallerstein asked whether it even deserved to be called a "revolution." Ruling classes can and do struggle against themselves. Wallerstein argued that this was quite common.[96] As a result, he argued that the French Revolution was not a struggle between different classes, nor even much of a revolution.

In China the "Great Proletarian Cultural Revolution" might be seen in the same light. First, it was not a "Great" conflict, but a miserable, violent, and tawdry affair that killed a lot of people and ruined millions of lives. Second, it was not a struggle between two classes—the "proletariat" and the "bureaucracy." These classes were fictions Mao created. He and his allies were not members of the "proletariat" but rather members, slightly disadvantaged ones, of the ruling class. The bureaucracy was not the representative of the old "bourgeoisie," which had been eliminated, but instead part of the new ruling class that Mao led. The conflict within the new ruling class emerged because Mao wanted to purge his opponents, replace them with loyalists, enhance his authority, and make the bureaucracy more responsive to his will. Consequently, the Cultural Revolution was not an attack on bureaucracy but rather a campaign designed to *strengthen* it.

Finally, we should ask whether it was in fact a "Revolution." If it was a revolution, what did it *change*? Many scholars have gotten so caught up in the turmoil, the thick fog of battle, the violent clash of arms that they fail to observe what did *not change.* As Mao admitted, it was difficult even for him to figure out what was going on. "In the past we could easily fight the war ... because our enemy was clear. Compared to that kind of war, the GPCR was much more complicated ...

the main reason was that [the line between friend and foe] was unclear, because of the confused mix of ideological mistakes with antagonistic contradictions."[97] Thus, even the "Great Helmsman," as Mao was sometimes called, found it difficult to navigate the deep waters of the Cultural Revolution.

Let us recap. A new ruling class led by a politically weakened, short-in-stature Mao entered a period of conflict, from about 1966 to 1970. This conflict resulted in downward mobility (purge) for many members of the ruling class, who had previously had "good" class labels, and upward mobility (promotion) for other members of the ruling class, who had previously been assigned "bad" class labels. When it was over, a ruling class with a slightly different social composition (more members with "bad" class labels and fewer members with "good" class labels) and led by a slightly stronger, taller Mao emerged to rule the country, much as it had done before.

The regime's economic and political policies remained unchanged. The economy was still stuck in a low-level equilibrium trap of Mao's making. The regime remained politically and economically isolated. (This would change in 1971, but US recognition and China's subsequent reentry into the world economy was *not* a product of the Cultural Revolution or of any initiative Mao took.) The great mass of urban and rural workers in China remained in the same, miserable condition—slightly worse in fact because the Cultural Revolution disrupted grain production and reduced per capita food consumption for several years.[98]

Some scholars and the leaders of the Communist Party that succeeded Mao have argued that the Cultural Revolution lasted for *ten* years, from 1966 to 1976, when Mao's widow, Jiang Qing and the "Gang of Four" fell from power.[99] This official periodization "is criticized by some Western scholars ... as a distortion of historical reality."[100] If one takes this longer view, many of cadre that had been purged and rusticated eventually purged their opponents and tormentors (Jiang Qing and the Gang of Four) and were rehabilitated and returned to power, Deng Xiaoping chief among them.[101] Although I think this longer periodization is inaccurate and self-serving, it does, however, make the case for "continuity," not "revolution," stronger still.

Of course, to say that the Cultural Revolution was not a "revolution" does not mean that it was inconsequential. Many people were abused, tortured, and killed, and millions of people were rusticated and proletarianized, which was a real misfortune in the Chinese context. Although some of these people were eventually rehabilitated and allowed to return to the cities, a whole generation of cadre was "lost," forced to labor alongside the rural workers that they, or their parents, had helped immiserate. Victimized by the purge, families lost their children, and children lost their future. That was a terrible price to pay for so *little* change. It makes the whole episode even more of a needless tragedy.

Chapter Four

A Crisis of Succession

> "Sex is engaging in the first rounds. What sustains interest in the long run is political power."
>
> *Jiang Qing, wife of Mao Zedong*

During the 1970s economic and political crises created serious problems for the regime. For twenty years Mao had promoted the relentless accumulation of capital to finance industrialization, but he had failed to achieve any real economic growth because he had encouraged the population to grow without restraint. The rapidly growing population ate up the country's modest economic gains. According to one scholar, "In 1976 . . . the growth of total production was, at 1.7 percent, *below* the rate of population growth."[1] As a result, China remained caught in a low-level equilibrium trap of its own making. For urban and rural workers this meant that living standards, incomes, and diets were actually lower in 1977 than they had been twenty years earlier in 1957.[2] At the end of the 1970s the regime admitted that the economy had been pushed to "the brink of disaster."[3]

As we have seen, Mao waged a Cultural Revolution that divided and weakened the ruling class. The bureaucracy that emerged was more responsive to Mao but was less effective as an agent of social change or public policy. Then in 1976 the deaths of Zhou Enlai in January and of Mao in September triggered a battle of succession between factions of the ruling class.[4] As such, their deaths reignited the conflict between the "beneficiaries" of the Cultural Revolution who wanted to *retain* their hold on power and the "victims" of the Cultural Revolution, who wanted to *return* to power.[5]

The beneficiaries were composed of the slightly disadvantaged members of the ruling class who had inherited "bad" class labels. During the Cultural Revolution Mao had mobilized them to attack his opponents, the advantaged members of the ruling class who had inherited "good" class labels. Mao enlisted the slightly disadvantaged against the advantaged because the latter disregarded his directives and he wanted to make the bureaucracy more responsive to his will (see chapter 3).

The beneficiaries were divided into two groups. Jiang Qing, Mao's wife, led a radical faction who wanted to renew and extend the Cultural Revolution. They wanted to expel the "victims" who had been rehabilitated and who had rejoined the ruling class in the early 1970s, Deng Xiaoping among them. Hua Guofeng led a more moderate group of beneficiaries who championed the "two whatevers." Hua argued that they would defend "whatever policy decisions Mao made, whatever instructions Mao gave." Naturally, this group was "dubbed the 'whatever' faction."[6] Finally, the victims of the Cultural Revolution—the ruling-class cadre who had been attacked, humiliated, sent down to the countryside, or demoted by Mao's supporters—wanted to return to power and reestablish themselves in the positions of authority they had held before the Cultural Revolution. Deng Xiaoping, the ultimate survivor, led the victims, a leader whom his peers demoted three times but never voted off the island.

Deng was first demoted in 1931, but worked his way up through the ranks and ascended into the leadership in the 1950s. In 1966 Mao again demoted Deng during the Cultural Revolution. Mao subsequently rehabilitated Deng and returned him to office in 1973, along with many of Deng's colleagues and supporters. Deng then worked closely with Zhou Enlai until Zhou's death in 1976.[7]

Deng, a pragmatist, represented a diverse coalition of ruling-class victims. Some of them had been rehabilitated, like Deng, in the early 1970s; some of them had been consigned to political limbo and waited for a chance to return to power; and some of them had remained in power, albeit as junior partners in a regime dominated by radical and moderate Maoists.[8] Deng promised his supporters that he would rule on the basis of a negotiated consensus rather than enforcing Mao's dictates, "whatever" they might be.[9] "While [Deng's] most ardent support [came] from those who had suffered at Mao's hands," one scholar observed, "more fundamental backing [was] derived from the wider elite whose members [recognized] Deng's long association with Mao [and saw Deng] as capable of 'delivering the goods,' which for them meant tackling the economic problems facing the regime."[10]

The battle between the "beneficiaries" and the "victims" began in January 1976 when demonstrators gathered in Tiananmen Square to commemorate the death of Zhou Enlai.[11] Jiang Qing and the radicals blamed Deng for the demonstrations, which they regarded as a revolt by cadre whom the Cultural Revolution had victimized. They argued that Deng was using the demonstrations as surrogates and persuaded Mao to remove Deng from power, for a third time, and forcibly suppress the demonstrators.[12]

The radicals won the first round but lost the second. Although Mao supported his wife Jiang Qing and the radicals in January, he soon soured on them. The previous year Mao expressed his annoyance with his wife's politics, telling her not to "flaunt yourself in public ... you've already got too many complaints against you," and warning her, "Don't function as a gang of four." After the Tiananmen Square incident, as Mao grew ill, he abandoned Jiang Qing and the radicals and appointed the moderate Hua Guofeng as his successor, saying, "With you in charge, I am at ease."[13]

Hua used Mao's endorsement to consolidate power, assume the leadership, and, a month after Mao's death, move against his radical rivals. In October Hua ordered the arrest of Jiang Qing and three associates, who were dubbed the "Gang of Four," to prevent them from challenging his authority, and then he arrested thousands of their supporters. Hua claimed that Jiang and her associates had conspired to organize a coup. When these arrests were made public, many of the victims of the Cultural Revolution celebrated in the streets.[14]

The diverse coalition of cadre who Mao had victimized or who wanted to depart from Mao's disastrous economic policies and the primitive, divisive politics of the Cultural Revolution persuaded Hua to reinstate Deng, for the third time, in 1977. Deng then successfully organized a coalition against Hua's "whatever" faction and in 1978, at the Third Plenum of the Eleventh Central Committee, replaced Hua and became the regime's "primary architect."[15]

At the December 1978 meeting, Deng announced that the "'period of large-scale class struggle' [between factions of the ruling class] had come to a close."[16] In practical terms, this meant that Deng rehabilitated the victims of the Cultural Revolution and restored hundreds of thousands "to positions of power and influence."[17] Like his predecessors, Deng punished the losers by demoting Hua and his associates. Nevertheless, the new leadership did not rusticate the moderates or expel them from the ruling class. Instead, Deng urged the victims, now victors, to "have a large heart and not hold grudges."[18]

Deng took a lenient view toward the moderates because he wanted to end the fighting that had divided the ruling class and because he wanted them to assist the reform effort. In effect, he offered something to both factions as a way to affect reconciliation. For the "victims," Deng restored the old *order*—good cadre on top, bad cadre below—and the privileges associated with it, primarily by "allowing children to inherit the jobs of their retired or deceased parents."[19] This restored privileges based on inheritance, not merit, privileges that Mao had undermined during the Cultural Revolution.

For the "beneficiaries," Deng promised a "new order" based on "merit." As part of the reforms, Deng provided members of the ruling class with the opportunity not only to secure collective wealth but also to secure individual wealth. When Deng announced, "Let some get rich first," and "prosperity to some, to most, then to all," he was inviting the members of the ruling class (both factions) to seek individual wealth.[20] But their success in securing this wealth would be based on "merit," which would encourage the "beneficiaries," cadre whom the system of privilege had in the past disadvantaged, to participate in the reform project and support his leadership. By offering "privilege" to the "victims," and "merit" to the "beneficiaries" of the Cultural Revolution, Deng offered a grand compromise designed to knit together the different factions of the ruling class in a joint enterprise that would provide both with some measure of collective and/or individual wealth and power.

However, while Deng extended an olive branch to the moderate Maoists, he exacted his revenge against the radical Maoists by demonizing Jiang Qing and putting the Gang of Four on trial in 1980. The regime charged Jiang and the others with killing 34,800 people and torturing 726,000 others during the Cultural Revolution as well as conspiring to carry out a coup d'état.[21] The leaders of the regime designed the trial to humiliate Jiang Qing and, indirectly, to attack Mao.

Jiang Qing, an actress and three-time divorcee, had wooed and wed Mao, a much older man, after persuading him to divorce his second wife in the late 1930s.[22] Male party members had long viewed her with suspicion and disdain and allowed Mao to marry her only if "she never exercised any political power." Of course, Jiang ignored this injunction. "Sex is engaging in the first rounds," she once told an interviewer. "What sustains interest in the long run is political power."[23] During the Cultural Revolution, Jiang used her relation with Mao to rise to the top of the party leadership.

The trial was designed as a public pillory, an opportunity for the regime to humiliate publicly the upstart actress. But Jiang refused to accept the role the state assigned to her. She defiantly rejected the charges, mounted a vigorous defense, and insisted that she acted on Mao's behalf, not her own. "I was Chairman Mao's dog," she testified. "Whomever he told me to bite, I bit."[24]

In gender terms, the all-male leadership exacted their revenge by attacking a woman who they called a "white-boned demon." But they lacked the courage to attack Mao himself because to do so would call into question their own responsibility as his collaborators, heirs, and successors. So instead of attacking Mao, they kicked his dog. Of course, Jiang was convicted and sentenced to death, a sentence that was commuted to life in prison. She died, purportedly of suicide, in 1991.[25]

Surviving the Crisis

The death of a dictator can trigger a crisis of succession that can prove fatal to a regime. In Spain the death of Francisco Franco in 1975 caused a succession crisis that led to democratization in 1978. In Yugoslavia, when Marshal Broz Tito died in 1980, the battle for succession that ensued contributed to the collapse of communism and the country's division. The deaths, in rapid succession, of elderly and infirm Soviet leaders—Leonid Brezhnev died in 1982; his successor, Yuri Andropov, died two years later in 1984; his successor, Konstantin Chernenko died in 1985—likewise created a crisis for the regime.[26] The battle for succession did not end with the selection of Mikhail Gorbachev in 1985 but continued until 1991, when competitors forced him from office and assumed power in separate republics, much like what occurred in Yugoslavia.

In China, as elsewhere, the deaths of elderly leaders Zhou and Mao triggered a succession crisis. This political turmoil occurred at a time when the regime was struggling unsuccessfully to escape from the low-level equilibrium trap, which had been decades in the making. The combination of economic crisis and political turmoil might have proved fatal for the regime, as it did for other developmental dictatorships, both capitalist (Spain) and communist (Yugoslavia and the Soviet Union), during this period, but it did not. The question is: why?

There are several incidental reasons why the regime survived. First, there was no alternative. The regime's destruction of social institutions outside the party meant that no other social groups or classes could step in to provide an alternative, as Solidarity and the Catholic Church did in Poland or as the monarchy did in Spain. Second and significantly, the regime had not created a federal system of government that allowed political institutions to emerge in constituent "republics," as occurred in Yugoslavia, Czechoslovakia, and the Soviet Union. When economic and political crises struck, factions of the communist party used political institutions based in the republics to organize constituencies against the central government. This contributed to the decline of central authority, the dissolution of union, and the creation of separate, independent republics that former communists led in Yugoslavia and the former Soviet Union. In China, by contrast—and also in Poland and other nonfederal communist states in Eastern Europe—the regime had not created institutions that factions of the ruling class could have used as a base to organize a challenge to central authority. Whatever their political differences, ruling-class factions in China shared a determination to seek power in the central government, which was the product of the party's long campaign against warlords and separatist forces that had divided and weakened China during the first half of the twentieth century.

Third, during the crisis the regime could draw on some of its political assets. The regime had developed nuclear weapons, at great cost, and these were a source of pride for many Chinese. The regime reminded them that it had defeated wartime opponents: Japan during World War II, the nationalists during the civil war, the United States in Korea, and India and Tibet in border wars. This provided the regime with a residual source of legitimacy.[27] Still, the regime's 1979 attack on Vietnam undermined this residual legitimacy, an attack that was designed to punish Vietnam for invading Cambodia and overthrowing Pol Pot's genocidal regime (China supported Pol Pot) and to burnish the regime's military credentials. As Deng told US President Jimmy Carter, "It's time to smack the bottom of unruly little children [Vietnam]."[28] However, the battle-hardened Vietnamese forces inflicted heavy casualties on the Chinese army and forced them to withdraw after a few weeks—and after making only limited progress. Instead of burnishing Deng's military credentials, the war "tarnished the image of the new Peking government . . . [and demonstrated] that the People's Liberation Army had deteriorated into something less than an effective military force."[29]

Fourth, although Deng was seventy-eight when he took power, he would live long enough to manage an orderly transition from the old guard to a younger generation in 1989.

These developments helped the regime weather the economic and political crises of the 1970s, but they were not actually crucial to its survival. The regime survived for two more important reasons. First, US recognition of China gave Mao's moribund regime an enormous political and economic boost that enabled it to emerge from political isolation, re-enter the world economy, and pursue a successful development strategy under Deng. Second, the regime under Deng initiated a series of domestic reforms that took advantage of China's re-entry into the world economy and allowed it to escape from the low-level equilibrium trap that had gripped the economy during the first thirty years of capitalist development. These two developments made it possible for the regime to consolidate its authority in the years after Mao's death.

US Recognition

In 1971 President Richard M. Nixon invited China to participate in secret talks that might lead to US recognition of the regime. One year later Nixon and Henry Kissinger traveled to China, met with Mao, and established a new set of relations with the regime. When they first met, the star-struck Kissinger described Mao as a political "colossus" who exuded "in almost tangible form the overwhelming drive to prevail."[30]

Nixon initiated the opening to China with two goals in mind. First, he thought that by aligning the United States with China, he could undermine the Soviet Union, which he regarded as the principle threat to US interests. As Kissinger explained, "it is better to align yourself with the weaker [China], not the stronger [the Soviet Union] of two antagonistic powers."[31] Second, by aligning with China, Nixon hoped to turn it against North Vietnam and force Hanoi to negotiate an end to the war in Vietnam. As Nixon explained to Secretary of Defense Melvin Laird, "The offer of U.S. relations with China might persuade the Chinese to offer assistance in other areas. In particular, China might put pressure on the North Vietnamese to come to an agreement with the Americans."[32]

Nixon's opening to China was successful in that it antagonized the Soviet regime and soon persuaded the regime in North Vietnam to agree to a cease-fire and conduct negotiations that allowed Nixon to withdraw US forces from South Vietnam. Kissinger argued that it was successful insofar as the "drama," as he called the US opening to China, "eased for the American people the pain that would inevitably accompany our withdrawal from Vietnam," an act of stage management that would provide a useful public distraction.[33] However, it was unsuccessful insofar as the US-North Vietnamese negotiations resulted in a peace agreement that enabled the North to win the war and reunify the country soon after US forces withdrew.

For Mao, Nixon's uninvited initiative provided his regime with enormous political and economic rewards. In political terms, Nixon helped admit China into the United Nations, which expelled Taiwan, and secured the regime a permanent seat on the UN Security Council. Moreover, Nixon agreed to recognize the regime's claims to Taiwan and Tibet as well as to Hong Kong and Macao, territories held by the United Kingdom and Portugal.[34] In economic terms, Nixon ended the economic embargo on China and facilitated its re-entry into the world economy, which in turn provided the regime with access to foreign loans through the International Monetary Fund and the World Bank (both UN institutions), foreign investment, natural resources, consumer markets, and preferential trade relations.

In return for all this Nixon asked only that China betray North Vietnam. This was easy for Mao to do because it cost China nothing. After all, North Vietnam was a *Soviet* ally, like virtually every other anticolonial regime or movement in the world, with the exception of the genocidal regime in Cambodia. By betraying North Vietnam, Mao could antagonize the Soviet Union, which had been his principle antagonist since the Sino-Soviet split in 1960. As Mao put it, "It is the Americans who need something from us, not the other way around."[35]

Nixon had insisted that there was "one cardinal rule for the conduct of international relations: Don't give anything to your adversaries unless you get something in return."[36] But in negotiations with China, Nixon violated his own rule. Nixon gave Mao *everything*, whereas Mao gave Nixon *nothing* in return that the Chinese valued. This kind of US "give" and Chinese "take" has characterized US-Sino relations ever since.

US recognition gave an enormous boost to the regime, helping it survive the economic malaise of the 1970s and political crisis of succession that followed

Mao's death. In 1978 the regime also took advantage of the economic windfall US recognition provided by introducing a series of domestic reforms that enabled it to both escape the low-level equilibrium trap that had gripped China under Mao and promote capitalist development *with* growth.

Chapter Five

The Reforms

Problems and Solutions

> "They will eventually comply with this new [one-child] policy. . . .The first time will be the most difficult, just like when you put a yoke on an ox's back for the first time. It will resist and struggle. But once the yoke is accepted by the ox, you can tighten it repeatedly, even to the point of choking it to death. Peasants are like oxen. Once they accept something as inevitable, you can continue to tighten the screw."
>
> *Huang Shu-min, Party secretary in Fujian*

After taking power in 1978, Deng worked to free China from the low-level equilibrium trap. Because he lacked a "viable blueprint for systematic institutional reform," Deng was forced to adopt a series of ad hoc policy initiatives and so was compelled to "cross the river by groping for stones."[1] In practice, this meant that the regime took policies from the 1950s and adopted them for use in the 1980s. In many ways, the reforms Deng introduced represented a "return," not just an "advance."[2] Scholars have described the policies the regime adopted as "reforms," which suggest that they involved a "substantial relaxation (*fangsong*) and increased permissiveness."[3] However, to think of the reform policies as introducing greater "freedom" because some of the reforms were accompanied by a reassertion of "control" would be a mistake. As one scholar observed, "For Deng, a new authoritarianism was a prerequisite for rapid economic advance."[4] The regime's draconian, coercive population-control policies, which were a centerpiece of the "reforms," were one expression of this "new authoritarianism." In fact, the regime said that the goal of reform was to create what it called a "birdcage" economy: "The concept was presented . . . by likening the planned economy to a cage in which the market adjustment mechanism, like a bird, could fly freely . . . this concept was commonly called the 'birdcage economy,' in which 'freedom' was contained by 'control.'"[5]

To pry open the jaws of the low-level equilibrium trap, the regime had to find solutions to four problems associated with agriculture, investment, labor, and population. The first and most important problem for the regime was how to increase food production.

The regime decided to transfer collective land to individual rural households and give them incentives to increase food production. But although this solution *increased* food production, it also *reduced* the surplus available to the regime, a surplus that it had long used to finance industrialization. This created a second problem: how to finance industrialization.

The regime decided to take advantage of the economic aid provided and invite foreign capital to "return" to China. The regime used access to foreign loans along with direct investment from the overseas Chinese community and from the United States and Japan to finance industrialization and promote the expansion of export commodity production, which was based in the special export processing zones in the southeast, an area that became known as the Gold Coast. However, this solution immediately created a third problem: how to create a cheap labor force for industries in cities along the coast without triggering a massive migration into China's cities.

The regime decided to allow rural workers to migrate to the cities but also treat them as illegal migrants so that they could be returned, if need be, to rural areas, thereby restricting the migration of workers into the cities. This enabled the regime both to regulate the size of the industrial labor force and keep the wages of illegal migrants and legal urban workers relatively low.

Finally, the regime had to find an answer to the problem of how to curb population growth. A growing population would eat up the economic gains made by the regime's efforts to increase food production, attract foreign investment, create a cheap labor force, and prevent the regime from escaping the jaws of the low-level equilibrium trap. Therefore, the regime decided to introduce a one-child policy, forcing women to reduce birth rates, and use it to pry open the jaws of the low-level equilibrium trap.

To appreciate these developments in detail, we will now turn to examine the agricultural, investment, labor, and population policies the regime adopted in the first decade of reform: 1978–1989.

Agriculture

During the first thirty years the regime squeezed agriculture to produce a surplus that could be used to feed the urban population, finance industrialization, and provide collective and individual wealth for members of the ruling class. As Mark Selden observed, "By keeping prices on agricultural commodities low and those for tractors, fertilizer, electricity, and other modern inputs high, the state effected a major resource transfer at the expense of agriculture and the countryside. This was the primary vehicle for China's rapid accumulation and urban-centered industrialization."[6] However, by forcing rural workers into collectives, where they were systematically deprived of food grains and investment, the regime sapped the energy of rural workers and the productivity of natural resources. After the Great Leap and famine in the early 1960s, agriculture slowly recovered, a development achieved primarily by increasing the hours of rural workers and applying chemical fertilizers to boost productivity.[7] By the mid-1970s grain production had increased a little, though rural workers' consumption of grain had increased not at all. "By 1977, the Chinese diet still did not equal the 1957 level of 2,000–2,100 calories a day, a level of subsistence which itself fell below the food requirement for Chinese estimated by the United Nations Food and Agricultural Organization."[8] In Northwest China, "per capita food consumption and income in the late 1970s not only were significantly below the levels of 1949 but even lower than the levels prevailing prior to the Sino-Japanese War."[9] The regime estimated that 260 million rural workers lived in poverty in 1978, and some scholars have argued that 100 to 200 million rural workers lived under conditions of "semi-starvation."[10]

At the Third Plenary meeting in 1978, the regime admitted that "agriculture, the foundation of the national economy, has been seriously damaged in recent years" and went on to warn that "if agricultural development is not accelerated, industrialization ... cannot be achieved."[11] As Daniel Kelliher has argued, "Years of abusing the peasantry had produced a deepening anxiety the leaders could no longer ignore. Their relationship with the rural population had changed: they were now a little afraid of the peasants."[12]

When Deng came to power in 1978, he was determined to increase food production. He had little choice. Given China's growing population, he had to increase food production to keep up and, if possible, get ahead. The problem for Deng and the regime was *how* to increase food production *and* keep rural workers on the land.

As a first step, Deng in 1978 provided rural workers with incentives to increase food production. The regime raised by 20 percent the prices it paid for the grain rural workers produced, paid an additional premium for grain that exceeded their assigned quotas, and allowed rural workers to sell grain in excess of state quotas on newly opened rural and urban markets for even higher prices.[13] The regime also allowed rural workers to engage in petty commodity production, which had long been prohibited, and organize village enterprises to produce and sell agricultural products. These two developments were particularly beneficial to households with women and dependents, young and old, who could once again engage in "sideline" activities—"cultivating vegetables, tending livestock, and producing handicrafts"—that could provide them with important new sources of income.[14]

Rural workers responded to these changes with enthusiasm. However, they wanted more: they wanted individual households, not the collective, to organize production and profit from it. Rural workers had long asked that households be allowed to farm the land, a demand going back to the 1950s, when land had briefly been given to "the tiller."[15] Of course, the regime had betrayed private farmers and had collectivized land, though it allowed households to keep small private plots (about 5 to 7 percent of the land) for their own use.[16] In 1978 the regime allowed the collectives to expand the size of private plots and said that the decision about how to organize production should be devolved from the collective to small work groups consisting of a few families, though it refused to endorse a return to family farming.[17] Rural workers took advantage of this opportunity and began expanding private plots, effectively redistributing collective land and letting households, not work groups, organize production—what one scholar called a "rush to freedom."[18] As a result, "the small group was merely a way-station on the quick trip back to the household" as the central actor in agriculture.[19] The rapid spread of household farming, which began to decollectivize agriculture, caught the regime by surprise. However, the regime recognized that it proved an effective way to increase production, so its attitude softened. Although the regime had "forbidden" household-based agriculture in 1978, it soon "permitted," then "encouraged," and finally "required" its adoption, and the household-based responsibility system, as it was called, became "nearly universal in the countryside by the end of 1982."[20] As Deng said in 1981, "We should let every family and every household think up its own methods of doing things, and let them find ways to raise production and increase incomes."[21] Whereas some scholars argued that the regime responded very pragmatically to change, others claimed that the regime was forced to respond to changes that a "spontaneous, unorganized" grassroots initiative initiated.[22] Andrew Watson has argued that "the pressures came from below and proceeded to force the pace of change thereafter." David Zweig agreed: "As soon as the opposition acceded to one step on the path to decollectivization, new demands for change arose from the localities, keeping pressure on the policy process in Beijing until collective agriculture was dismantled." Daniel Kelliher argued that the change was initiated from below, which the state reluctantly adopted and then "forced the new policy on all rural communities, whether they were willing or not." As a result, he states, "a vast change overtook rural China, driven by peasants who were neither victims nor revolutionaries."[23]

Nevertheless, these accounts of change, which focus on the roles of rural households and the central government, neglect the role that cadres may have played. There is some evidence that cadres may have supported the rural households *against* the central government, which employed them, because they wanted to distribute collective land and assets and reserve the best for themselves, much like cadre in the Soviet Union and Eastern Europe after the fall of communism, where privatization had provided cadre with the opportunity to secure public assets as a way to provide individual wealth for themselves. As Carl Riskin observed, "The authority to allocate such opportunities meant a considerable retention of local cadre power in the villages."[24] Some scholars have observed that in the privatization process, "cadres seem to have had an advantage" and managed to acquire many of the collectives' best land, fishponds, and orchards, which they used as a source of capital in various rural enterprises.[25] Of course, farm machinery and draft animals were not easily "divided" when collective assets were redistributed, and that cadre claimed them and then demanded that rural workers pay high fees for their use is not surprising. Income from rent quickly became a source of individual wealth for local cadre.[26] Furthermore, the regime subsequently endorsed cadres' seize-the-assets privatization initiatives, saying, "Rural Party members should serve as models for working hard to get rich."[27]

By 1984 the regime had transferred public lands, which it had seized first from landlords and then from rich, middle, and poor peasants in the 1950s, to individual households. Of course, the regime might have simply given land away. That's what the US government had done with Western lands that it had purchased from empires or seized from Native Americans. The US government made a gift of theft and distributed public lands to individual farmers and railroads, virtually free of charge, through the 1860 Homestead Act. But although the regime in China was willing to redistribute land, it did not want to transfer title to the land and decided instead to "lease" it. Why? Because if the regime transferred *title* to the land, many rural households would have sold their land to richer farmers, who would have consolidated and expanded their holdings. Although consolidating land would have created economies of scale and increased productivity and yields, it would have also *displaced* landless rural workers. Recall that the problem for the regime was how to increase agricultural production *and* keep rural workers on the land. To prevent rural workers from migrating in large numbers to the cities, the regime decided to lease public land to households, for periods of fifteen years or longer.[28] Households could sublease land and pass leased land on to their children, but they could not acquire title to the land or sell it.[29] Rural households paid rent on the land they leased by selling a portion of the crop to the state, under a quota system, which was essentially a form of sharecropping.[30] By redistributing and leasing land to individual households and providing them with higher prices and market opportunities, the regime gave rural workers the tools they needed—indeed demanded—to increase food production *and* incentive to stay on the land.

Rural workers took immediate advantage of reform and increased food production dramatically. Between 1978 and 1984 grain production increased by one-third, from 304.8 million metric tons (mmt) to 407.3 mmt.[31] What's more, higher prices and increased production contributed to rising rural incomes, which grew for the first time since the 1950s. Rural workers, particularly women, also earned more from petty commodity production or "sidelines," which tripled in value from 1978 to 1983.[32] As a result, the real income of rural households doubled between 1978 and 1985.[33] Food consumption increased, diets improved, the number of semihungry and very poor people fell, and rural workers, for the first time, closed the gap between urban and rural standards of living.[34] Still, in 1988 "an estimated 100 million out of China's 1.07 billion, or about a tenth of the population [were] still unable to feed or clothe themselves adequately."[35] Overall, however, food production increased even faster than population growth during the first ten years of reform.

By providing higher prices, breaking up the collectives, and redistributing land to individual households, the regime provided rural workers with the incentives and the means to increase food production dramatically. But these reforms created three new problems that the regime did not anticipate or appreciate: first, they encouraged rural workers to consume rather than invest their earnings; second, they contributed to inflation, budget deficits, and urban discontent; and third, they reduced the role that agriculture played in financing industrialization.

Consumption, Not Investment

The regime reluctantly agreed to redistribute land to rural households, but it refused to give them title to the land they cultivated, offering them long-term leases instead. The regime insisted on leasing the land so as to prevent rural workers from selling it, a development that would consolidate land holdings and displace landless workers, who might then migrate to the cities looking for work. By leasing land, the regime solved one problem (preventing displacement) but created another: workers who *leased* land were reluctant to *invest* in improving the land if they could not claim the benefits of improvements. Why spend time and money building an irrigation system or planting trees or applying fertilizer to increase soil fertility if they worked the land as a tenant, not as an owner? Furthermore, not only were rural workers reluctant to invest in the land, they also refused to participate in collective projects—irrigation works, road construction and maintenance—upon which their individual efforts depended. When cadre tried to round up farmers to work on collective land improvement, one man reported, "Nobody would come in for flood control work. The cadres beat the gong until it split."[36] Instead of investing in agriculture, rural workers spent their newfound wealth to improve their diets, purchase consumer goods, and, most importantly, improve their *housing*.

Rural workers used their hard-earned gains to improve their diets. Between 1978 and 1987 grain consumption increased 30 percent, sugar consumption 97 percent, and alcohol a whopping 300 percent.[37] They decided not to invest in farm machinery—tractor sales fell sharply after reforms were introduced—but purchased consumer goods instead. Sales of sewing machines increased from 48,000 in 1978 to 1,087,000 in 1983, largely because the women who used them wanted not only to mend clothes but to make apparel for sale in markets. Furthermore, bicycle sales tripled, from 8.5 to 27.5 million in the same period.[38] But whereas rural households improved their consumption of food and drink and splurged on consumer goods, they spent most of their money to improve their houses, to which they *could* claim title. "In the past," one leader observed, "the peasants' primary want was 'enough food to be full and enough clothes to be warm. Now they demand to 'eat well, be well dressed, and have good housing.'"[39]

Rural workers with money in their pockets were overcome with what one official called "house building fever," working hard to build new homes and improve old ones.[40] The home-improvement boom, which households savings and independent credit (not by government banks) financed, increased the rate of construction from 100 million square meters in 1978 to 980 million square meters a year in 1986, a tenfold increase, which was "the single largest housing boom in world history."[41] Half of all rural families moved into new homes between 1978 and 1986 and per capita living space doubled, from 10 to 19.4 square meters.[42] Many households "treated contracted land as their own and built houses and put graves on it" despite regime efforts to prohibit this practice.[43]

Naturally, this housing boom led to conflict. In one village a man who built a three-story house incurred the wrath of his neighbors, who all lived in two-story houses. They complained that "with your house higher than the others, you are taking away the good fortune of all the other villagers," and they then gathered together and tore down the offending third floor.[44]

By using their savings to improve their housing, rural workers invested in an asset that they could claim, an asset that was both functional (providing living space) and valuable (providing a way to invest savings and as a hedge against inflation) in a context in which other investments were unrewarding (investment in leased land might not provide a return and investment in a government savings bank would provide only minimal returns).[45]

The problem for the regime was that the reforms had encouraged rural workers to engage in the kind of saving, spending, and "hoarding" behavior that John Maynard Keynes had identified as inimical to capital accumulation, behavior that the regime had previously associated with landlords and then with rural workers during the agricultural boom that accompanied land reform in the early 1950s. During the 1980s reform "produced a sharp drop in agricultural investment . . . as households . . . channeled investment into more profitable industries, sidelines, and commerce, or into housing and consumer durables."[46] So whereas "the rate of savings of rural households *rose* in the 1980s . . . these savings were not channeled into productive investment."[47]

By the mid-1980s officials in the regime complained, "The peasants are selling their agricultural products at high prices and accumulating money. If we cannot think of a way to make an exchange to recover it, then the peasants will just end up with more and more paper money in their hands," which would contribute to inflation and take money out of the hands of the regime.[48] The regime, it turned out, realized that agricultural reforms did not promote investment but instead promoted consumption and contributed to rising inflation.

Inflation and Backlash

In 1978 the regime paid rural workers higher prices for the food they produced. This provided rural workers with an incentive to grow more food, and they did. But higher prices contributed to two problems. First, it increased government spending, which meant the regime had less money to spend on other things.[49] Second, it contributed to inflation. Between 1978 and 1984 food prices on urban markets rose by more than one-third, and this fueled rising inflation.[50] Rising food prices also undermined the living standards of urban workers and contributed to urban unrest. "In Tianjin, workers were reported to have a 'bitter reaction' to the price hikes on non-rationed food stuffs," and this contributed to widespread dissatisfaction with agricultural reforms.[51]

To address these issues, in 1985 the regime decided to cut the prices it paid farmers, raise the price of farm inputs (machinery, fertilizer, oil) by about 10 percent (thereby taking money out of the hands of farmers and putting it back into the government's hands, see above), and take steps to control food prices—measures that Kelliher has described as "the backlash reform of 1985."[52]

Rural workers then responded to lower food prices and higher input prices by producing less food. The 1985 harvest "decreased by 25 million tons," and food production stagnated for the next four years.[53] Although the regime's reform in 1978 helped increase food production for a time, its decision to cut prices in 1985 curbed incentives and limited further gains. For rural workers the 1978 reforms increased their incomes, for the first time since the 1950s, and helped them close the income gap between rural and urban workers, whom the state had long privileged, from 1 to 4.6 in 1978 to 1 to 3.1 in 1987.[54] But the 1985 backlash halted rural workers' upward progress, and the gap between rural and urban workers started to widen once again.[55]

INVESTMENT

The reform of 1978 greatly reduced the regime's exploitation of rural workers, though the 1985 backlash demonstrated that the regime decided it had gone too far and needed to increase the exploitation of rural workers slightly. Still, the regime understood in 1978 that if it adopted agricultural reforms, it could not exact as much of a surplus from agriculture as it had in the past. So how was it going to finance industrialization?

As a first step, Deng cut military spending by 25 percent over the next ten years, reduced the army by one million men, reduced the representation of the military in the Politburo, encouraged the military to devote more attention to producing arms for export, and used the savings and earnings to finance industrialization.[56] "The army must be patient," Deng told military leaders.[57] Still, the savings from defense spending cuts and the earnings from arms sales (US$1 billion in 1988) did not generate the kind of money that the regime needed to finance its ambitious industrialization goals. It needed a *large* source of capital. So it turned to foreign capital to provide the loans and investment it needed to finance industrialization and provide individual wealth for the members of the ruling class.

Foreign Investment

As part of the reforms Deng introduced in 1978, the regime turned to foreign capital to provide the funds and technology it needed to promote rapid industrial growth. First, it asked foreign banks and international lending agencies to provide loans that the regime could use to finance industrialization. Second, it encouraged the overseas Chinese business community, which had fled into exile during the revolution, to invest in and travel to China, which would provide the regime with hard-currency income from tourist receipts and remittances. Third, it invited firms based in Japan and the United States to invest in China or contract with domestic cadre to manufacture goods that could be sold on foreign and/or domestic markets.

Foreign Loans. Between 1978 and 1988 the regime took advantage of US recognition, which made it possible to enter global financial markets, and borrowed US$40 billion from foreign creditors, commercial banks, international lending agencies such as the World Bank, and foreign investors who purchased Chinese government bonds. From this, foreign debt grew from US$2.1 billion in 1979 to US$42 billion in 1988.[58]

During the 1970s developmentalist dictators in China, Latin America, Africa, and Eastern Europe borrowed hundreds of billions of dollars to finance industrialization—US$810 billion by 1983. Western banks with access to the Euro-dollar currency market as well as the World Bank provided much of the money. But when the United States raised interest rates to battle inflation in 1979–1983, thereby triggering a recession that in turn lowered commodity prices, many of the regimes that had borrowed money experienced a debt crisis. The problem for them was that high interest rates forced them to spend more money to repay their debts while falling commodity prices reduced their income. This debt crisis contributed to the fall of dictatorships across Latin America and in the Philippines in the early 1980s.[59] Although the regime in China borrowed heavily—more than Poland (US$27 billion) but less than Mexico (US$90 billion) or Argentina (US$100 billion)—these developments did not create a debt crisis in China. So how did the regime avoid getting trapped in the debt crisis?

The regime escaped the debt crisis for three reasons. First, when the regime re-entered the world economy in the late 1970s, it decided to produce manufactured goods for export in special economic zones that were modeled after the maquiladoras in Mexico. In these zones along the southeast coast, the regime allowed businesses to manufacture goods for export. The Chinese used loans and investment to finance the export of *manufactured* goods, not raw materials.[60] That turned out to be a good thing because the price of raw materials fell sharply after 1980s, which then reduced the incomes of regimes that relied heavily on the sale of oil, coffee, sugar, and minerals to earn the money they needed to repay debt.

Second, the regime devalued the yuan. By 1987 the yuan had fallen by about 75 percent against the yen and the Taiwan dollar and by about 50 percent against the US dollar and the South Korean won.[61] Devaluations made Chinese exports cheaper and easier to sell in foreign markets, and they made imported goods more expensive. As a result, the Chinese increased their export earnings from $9.7 billion in 1978 to $52.5 billion in 1989.[62] Because they did not allow imports to grow as fast, they created a growing trade surplus and were able to use the hard currency they earned from trade to repay their debts and avoid the kind of debt crisis that crippled other dictatorships during the same period.

Third, the regime could also use foreign direct investment to repay debt. In other countries, foreign and domestic investors fled at the onset of the debt crisis, a development that left many regimes strapped for cash. But whereas investors *withdrew* their money from many indebted dictatorships during the 1980s, they *invested* their money in China during the same period.

Foreign Direct Investment

The regime also invited foreign capital, which had exited during the revolution, to "return" to China and invest in the four Special Economic Zones that it had set up along the coast.[63] Between 1979 and 1988 foreign firms contracted with the regime to invest US$28 billion, of which US$11.6 billion was actually delivered.[64] However, determining the exact origin of FDI in China is difficult because for many years Chinese investors from Hong Kong made investments on behalf of firms in Taiwan, which prohibited investment and trade with China, and after Taiwan again permitted investment in China in 1986, both groups acted as intermediaries for Japanese firms, "who often relied on the Overseas Chinese to grease their way into China."[65] During the late 1980s "the capitalists of Hong Kong employed an estimated two million industrial workers in the People's Republic of China, about twice the number that they employed in Hong Kong."[66]

There is serious irony here. Many members of the overseas Chinese community had fled from China during the revolution and were bitterly opposed to the communist regime. But several developments persuaded them to return. The regime offered to provide them with low-wage workers who could produce cheap manufactured goods for overseas markets, devalued the yuan so that these goods were cheap in comparison with goods from Hong Kong and Taiwan, allowed the investors to produce goods in tax-free enclaves, and offered them access to China's vast domestic market.[67] Under these conditions, that overseas Chinese investors overcame their economic skepticism and their political scruples and invested in China is not surprising. The regime successfully persuaded overseas Chinese investors to bring their money but leave their politics at the door.

The regime also encouraged members of the Chinese diaspora to return to China as tourists. As a result, the number of tourists traveling to China, 90 percent of them from the overseas Chinese community, increased from 1.8 million in 1978 to 31.8 million in 1988, a fifteenfold increase.[68] In 1988 China earned US$2.2 billion from tourist receipts, providing the regime with an important source of hard-currency income (which could be used to repay debt or purchase imported goods). Many foreign visitors also gave money to their relatives in China, and these remittances provided the regime with another source of hard currency. (When people in China received money from relatives who lived abroad, they had to exchange the foreign currency for yuan before they could spend it. When they changed money, the government obtained "hard" foreign currency that it could use to purchase imported goods—oil, food, and technology.) In this regard, the overseas, anticommunist Chinese tourists who went to China in the 1980s provided a boost to the regime, much as anticommunist refugees from Cuba and Vietnam have done for dictatorships back home.[69]

Foreign Investment, Privatization, and Individual Wealth

The return of foreign investors enabled cadre to forge alliances with foreign firms—mostly overseas Chinese businesses—as partners and subcontractors. These alliances then gave them access to individual wealth. Furthermore, a slow-motion privatization of state enterprises during the 1980s accompanied the alliance between the domestic ruling class and the "old" Chinese bourgeoisie. As part of its reforms, the regime shifted public resources from state-run enterprises to individual-controlled firms, and state-run enterprises, which accounted for nearly 80 percent of all domestic production in the late 1970s, declined to about 50 percent in 1990.[70] Joseph Fewsmith has argued that this development reflected "the state's continual effort to 'buy' [cadre's] political compliance by increasing the incomes of [individual cadre]."[71]

Gordon White agrees, arguing that the "emergence of a 'new, post-communist bourgeoisie' [was] generated by dual trends: on the one hand, a strata of economic influentials is rising in the 'private' sector aided by connections with state officials and foreign (mainly overseas Chinese) business and, on the other hand, state officials are attempting to convert their power into control over economic assets, transforming political into economic power."[72]

During the 1980s, cadre seized the opportunities reform provided (much as rural workers did) to transfer collective assets (political power in the case of cadre, collective land in the case of rural workers) into individual wealth. They did not, in my view, constitute a "new bourgeoisie," as White suggests, but rather an "old" bourgeoisie (the ruling class that emerged in China after 1949) with a "new" source of income, which its alliance with the overseas Chinese bourgeoisie and the regime's privatization of public assets during the reform era provided (see chapter 9).

On Hainan Island, for example, cadre in charge of the regional government used their access to foreign exchange in the special economic zone "to import (tax free) an astonishing 2.86 million color television sets, 252,000 video cassette recorders, 122,000 motorcycles, and 10,000 cars and minibuses, most of which were resold throughout the country at double or triple the original prices." As Riskin noted, "Where personal gain is legitimized [by reform] but administrative fiat [dictatorship] still runs the show, the distinction between private gain and public responsibility is easily blurred."[73]

"Illegal" Migration

After 1978 the regime secured foreign capital to finance the growth of industries in urban areas along the coast. Of course, these export industries needed a large supply of cheap labor. During the Maoist period the regime had rusticated millions of urban workers to keep the urban workforce from getting too large and restricted migration from rural areas to prevent workers from migrating to the cities. As a result, the supply of urban workers in 1978 was relatively small and unable to meet the demand of growing industry. Of course, there was a huge supply of rural workers who might be used to fill jobs in industry: the 150 to 250 million "surplus" workers who lived in rural areas.[74] The problem for the regime was how to provide a supply of cheap workers for emerging industries *without* triggering a migratory flood that would swamp the cities and burden the regime with the cost of providing food, housing, services, and infrastructure that would be needed to accommodate them.[75]

The regime developed an ingenious answer to this concern. Deng decided to allow rural workers to migrate to the cities but keep them "illegal." Deng kept the 1955 hukou system intact and treated migrant workers as "illegal" workers in their own country. Because the regime treated migrants as illegals, it refused to provide them with food, housing, education, or health care.

In the early 1980s the regime began to allow small numbers of rural workers to move to the cities and take jobs. At first, rural workers took low-end, marginal jobs "in factories, restaurants, construction sites, elevators, delivery services, housecleaning, child-rearing, garbage collecting, barbershops and brothels" so that urban workers could move out of these jobs and into the industries financed by foreign capital.[76] However, because the supply of legal urban workers was insufficient to meet the growing demand, many rural workers soon moved into the growing industrial sector as well.

Of course, rural workers who migrated to the city needed food to eat. Because they were "illegal," they could not obtain ration cards from the government, so they had to rely "on food they had brought in themselves."[77] The government's restrictions on food constrained the number of rural workers who could move to the city and work for an extended period of time. But as the demand for rural workers grew, the regime eased its regulations and allowed migrants to store and then buy food from markets in the cities, which then allowed a larger number of workers to come and stay.[78] By treating migrants as illegal and making them pay for their own food rather than providing it to them, as it did for legal workers, the regime avoided the cost of providing food rations to migrant workers.

The regime took a similar approach to housing. Instead of building housing for migrant workers, the regime required businesses to provide housing for workers at or near the factory, where migrants were crowded into substandard dormitories.[79] State and private businesses then charged workers rent for the housing they provided.

The regime also refused to provide migrant workers with access to public education for their children, even though "China's Law on Compulsory Education stipulated that all children must enroll and receive education for nine years." As a result, migrant workers either left their children behind in rural areas or organized their own schools and paid for them out of their own pockets or kept their children out of school altogether. Consequently, "In Beijing, where 100 percent of [legal] children were enrolled in school ... only 40 percent of migrant ones were [enrolled]."[80]

The regime also refused to provide health care for migrants, so workers "were forced to try their luck with untrained traveling 'doctors' who floated among migrant communities."[81] As a result, "pregnant migrant women and their children suffered mortality rates between 1.4 and 3.6 times the national average."[82]

By allowing workers to migrate but keeping them illegal and by refusing to pay for their food, housing, education, and health care, the regime reduced the costs associated with industrialization in the cities. At first, the number of rural workers allowed to migrate was fairly small, only about two million in the early 1980s. However, the number of rural migrants grew rapidly in the mid-1980s, and by the end of the decade "the number of migrant laborers reached 50 million," which was almost as many workers as had been drafted into industry twenty years earlier during the Great Leap Forward.[83] Most of these rural workers, both male and female, migrated to cities along the coast, though a number of male workers also migrated west to Xinjiang and south to Tibet. The regime used male settlers to increase the Han population and secure these regions with large, ethnic "minority" populations.[84]

The growing supply of migrant labor in the cities lowered or suppressed wages. Nearly half of the migrants were women, and businesses paid them less than men—only 55 percent of male wages in 1988 and 42 percent in 1992.[85] The growing supply of female migrants lowered the wages paid to male migrants, and the growing supply of male *and* female migrants—who collectively were paid only 58 percent of legal urban workers—then lowered or suppressed the wages paid to legal urban workers.[86] Some analysts have argued that migrant workers "depressed China's wages by 47 percent to 86 percent" and maintained that low wages in China "created an incredible downward push on wages and production in the rest of the world's economy."[87]

The regime's policies toward migrant workers created a new social category in China: a large population of workers who were treated not as "citizens" but as "denizens" in their own country.[88] As Cindy Fan argued, "By maintaining an institutional and social order in which peasants are inferior to urbanites, and by permitting rural-urban migration without granting urban citizenship to most migrants, the state has engendered a migrant-labor regime conducive to industrial and urban development at low cost with far-reaching social consequences."[89]

The creation of a denizenry is not unique to China. Although most nation-state republics grant "citizenship" to adult males and females, they do not extend the full benefits of citizenship to minors, legal immigrants, or, for that matter, gay men and lesbian women.[90] And they treat prisoners, convicts, and illegal immigrants as "subjects" who have few rights and are subjected to direct state authority.[91] In China the regime essentially *deprived* adult men and women of their rights as "citizens" that they enjoyed in rural areas (among them the right to food, housing, education, and health care), instead treating them as "denizens" in their own country, a development that had important legal, economic, and social consequences.[92] First, the regime deprived migrant workers of their constitutional rights: "Article 90 of China's Constitution that was promulgated in 1954 states that Chinese citizens have the right to change their residence." Of course, "constitutional" rights are problematic in a dictatorship. In 1958 officials of the regime defended restrictions on migration by arguing that "the freedom [to migrate] guaranteed in the Constitution refers to the freedom under leadership rather than freedom without government. It is concerned with the freedom of the entire people rather than the absolute freedom of a minority of people."[93] Thc regime also denied migrants the rights that it made available to *other* citizens in rural and urban areas. Moreover, because the regime viewed migrants as "illegal," it could arrest and deport them from the cities if they became too numerous or complained about wages or working conditions. For instance, in Beijing the government demolished the stalls of migrant vendors in open-air markets and expelled many of the vendors.[94] And in Guangzhou the city government in 1989 "forced many transients out of the city and refused to allow others to get off trains at the train station."[95]

Second, the regime's treatment of migrants allowed employers to pay below-minimum wages and to withhold pay from workers. Migrants who worked on construction projects "were owed $43 billion in unpaid wages and some have remained unpaid for up to ten years," one government official admitted.[96] Employers routinely demand that migrants work long hours—"we have less than ten minutes for meals ... we must take turns to eat because the machines never stop," a garment worker explained—and employers deny workers sick leave or holidays. Most employers require workers "to eat and sleep in the factory dorms" so the employers can charge high rates and deduct these charges from workers' pay.[97]

Employers can cut worker pay and fire workers without notice and regularly replace older workers with younger migrants who they regard as more compliant. "It is difficult for married women to find work," a migrant worker in Guangdong reported. "Employers prefer young, single workers. When women have a family, they need days off and employers don't like that."[98] If workers are injured or killed on the job—about thirty thousand workers die in industrial accidents each year—they receive lower compensation than legal urban workers. Employers paid US$17,000 to the families of legal workers killed in a gas-line explosion, but paid only US$5,000 to migrant workers' families.[99] Employers can engage in these practices and subject workers to poor working conditions and wages because the regime treats migrants as illegal and permits this kind of behavior. As one seamstress in Jiangsu explained, "These bosses always want to find ways to squeeze our pay.... Nobody in the government, either at home or in the city, speaks for us. If governments at both ends ... supported us, then we [could] have a place to turn to when cheated by employers ... we know we are exploited, but we have no choice but to work as hard as possible."[100]

Third, the regime's treatment of migrants contributes to legal workers' discrimination against migrants; they view the "floating population" and "blind drifters" with animosity and disgust.[101] Legal urban workers blame migrants for "urban crowding, crime and health problems," and "women migrants are often ... blamed for engaging in prostitution, conducting extra-marital affairs with local men, and destabilizing marriages." Migrants, particularly women, are frequently targets of rape and sexual assault, in part because they are seen as naïve and easily tricked, and in part because the perpetrators think that the women will be unwilling to complain to authorities or report crimes to the police because they are illegal.[102]

Why do migrant workers participate in this?

The common answer is that they migrate to the cities to earn money that they can send back to their families.[103] As one woman who migrated with her son to work in Beijing explained, "In addition to the money we sent home [to her husband and mother-in-law], we paid back some debts, built three rooms, and bought a cow."[104]

But millions of migrant workers do not earn enough to support themselves in the cities, much less send money back home. "How much did I bring home?" one eighteen-year old migrant woman asked. "I am embarrassed to say. I brought home very little money . . . let's say 300 yuan. Some of my friends cannot even support themselves and need their parents to send *them* money."[105] A woman whose migrant husband worked in mining and construction admitted, "For several years, he didn't bring back a cent."[106] Thus, instead of assisting families back home, family members supported many migrants. Many households supported migrant workers by working harder, and elderly women and young girls often took over the responsibilities of male migrants.[107]

Of course, some migrants can save money on below-subsistence wages if they live frugally and lower their standard of living. But they can do this only for a relatively short period of time, not for a lifetime. As one Sichuan man explained, "This is not a long-term strategy. I have a wife, child, and a house in the home village. I will eventually return to farm."[108] In fact, most migrants eventually return home and few apply for or receive the right to become permanent, legal residents in the cities because they cannot survive in the cities on the wages paid to migrant laborers.[109]

By working on a temporary basis for below-subsistence wages in substandard working conditions, migrants and the rural households that support them have essentially *subsidized* the industrialization of China in the years after 1978. Rural households made it possible "for employers to pay workers wages that are lower than the cost of maintaining worker households" over a lifetime.[110] Rural households often subsidized migrant workers, particularly young women who were paid half as much as male migrants, because it cost them less to support girls who earned *some* money as migrants than to support them back home, where they would earn even less. For many rural households, the migration of young girls was not seen as an investment in their collective future, largely because girls eventually joined another man's household. As one Sichuan woman explained, "Daughters married out are like water spilled out. They don't usually send their remittances to the natal family. Even if they do, it is largely symbolic. Sons are different. They are expected to shoulder the responsibility for the family."[111] Employers that hire migrant workers in China understand that rural households view migrant daughters as a liability, as "water spilled out," not as an investment, and pay them accordingly. As a result, industrialization in China takes advantage not only of migrants generally but also of young female migrants who, for social reasons, rural households see as economic liabilities, not assets.

By encouraging migration but keeping it illegal, the regime created a large supply of low-wage workers. As we will see, governments in other countries would find difficulty creating a labor force that could compete with China's low-wage urban workers, lower-wage migrant workers, and even lower-wage female migrant workers because to do so they would have to deprive large numbers of workers of their rights as citizens, insist that they work for below-subsistence wages, and demand that households support or subsidize this endeavor. Although some dictatorships could organize a cheap-cheaper-and-cheaper-still supply of labor in the early 1980s, the collapse of dictatorships in the 1980s and early 1990s made this virtually impossible for states to do in the years since then.

Population Control: All for One and One for All

When Deng came to power, the regime took steps to increase food production, secure foreign investment, and create a workforce of low-wage migrants to labor in the expanding export industries. But Deng's efforts to promote rapid economic growth would have come to nothing if the population continued to grow at a rapid rate, a development that would keep China in a low-level equilibrium trap.[112]

Deng and his wife had long been proponents of birth control. In the 1950s they had joined with Zhou Enlai to advocate for population control policies.[113] However, Mao had derailed population-control efforts in the late 1950s, arguing that "one billion plus [people] would be no cause for alarm."[114] During the 1960s Mao even denounced birth-control advocates, dismantled birth-control programs, demoted personnel, and sent them to detention centers in the "cowpens."[115] Mao's wife, Jiang Qing, dismissed birth planning as a "feminine triviality."[116] In the early 1970s, however, Mao relented, allowing Zhou to reintroduce some modest birth-control programs that promoted voluntary family planning under the slogan, "Later, Longer, Fewer."[117] But the effort lacked conviction, and "in the late 1970s, population control was only a verbal slogan; there were no policy documents making it official." Determined to change this when he took power, Deng adopted a "muscular approach to population control."[118]

When Deng took over, he announced that "[we] must greatly increase our efforts in [birth] planning" and vowed to use "economic and administrative methods" to reduce fertility rates and population growth.[119] In 1980 he announced the goal of limiting the population to 1.2 billion by the year 2000, a target that the regime said would require the immediate imposition of a "one-child" policy.[120] This meant that "with few exceptions, each childbearing-age couple was to bear only one child, state officials were to decide who had permission to conceive in a given year, and contraception after birth was required and state administered."[121]

The regime argued that drastic measures were required both "to make up for the lack of population control" during the Maoist period and to overcome the "feudal" fertility preferences of rural households, which "could and should be eradicated through ideological persuasion or, if that did not work, veiled force."[122] It denounced peasants who "clung to 'outmoded reproductive beliefs,' remained 'ignorant and superstitious,' and lived in 'primitive economic conditions' that fostered high fertility."[123] By characterizing rural households as "feudal," the regime provided a pretext, an ideological rationale for imposing coercive measures against this new "class enemy," a tactic the regime frequently used to attack its opponents during the Maoist period. As one scholar observed, "There was great irony in the decision to launch a massive one-child campaign at this moment . . . when much of Mao's legacy, including Mao's preference for mobilization campaigns, was being officially repudiated."[124] Whereas previous campaigns against class enemies had been directed at landlords, peasant proprietors, rural and urban workers, and, during the Cultural Revolution, factions of the ruling class, the regime now aimed its campaign to control population growth at rural women and girls.

To accomplish its objective—1.2 billion by 2000—and implement its one-child policy, Deng introduced a number of programs designed to monitor women and households, provide a set of rewards to induce compliance, impose a set of penalties to punish noncompliance, and use invasive procedures—inserting IUDs, abortion, sterilization—to ensure that women and men complied with the policy.

The regime allowed some people to have a second child if, for example, they belonged to a small national "minority," the first child was disabled or dead, one spouse was a deep-sea fisherman or worked for more than five years in an underground mine, or the spouse was the single child of a revolutionary martyr.[125] But the regime granted few exemptions and worked assiduously to enforce the one-child policy for one and all.

Monitoring Women

As a start, the regime required women to attend meetings where cadre exhorted them to comply with the one-child policy.[126] But the regime also instructed cadre to compile detailed records of each woman's reproductive history—"their menstrual periods, births, pregnancies, and contraceptive use, including IUD insertions, sterilizations, and abortions"—and update these records on a regular basis. Cadre enlisted the help of "granny police," or "voluntary enforcers who kept an eagle eye out for anomalous behaviors and tracked down the non-compliant."[127] In some villages cadre "went so far as to post public records of women's menstrual cycles." Cadre efforts to monitor women in the village and in the workforce was supplemented by "shock attacks," which authorities used to check up on cadre who, they worried, might not pursue the policy with sufficient zeal.[128] During a shock attack administrators made surprise inspections to "check one family after another, have talks, examine [cadre] records, and even count how many children's clothes are around" to see if households or cadre had concealed unreported births.[129]

Rewards and Penalties

The regime offered modest monetary incentives to households who complied with the policy. They provided an annual bonus of about 40 yuan and in some cases promised health care subsidies, school tuition relief, extra maternity leave, and extra space allowances for housing and gardens.[130] Although the regime offered some incentives, it relied on penalties to persuade people to comply. As one cadre explained, "We first resort to persuasion and education. If someone still does not mend his ways, we meet out fines. In serious cases, we tear down houses and take away land."[131]

The regime levied fines of up to 20 percent of a household's income if they had an unplanned second pregnancy or violated spacing requirements. Between 1985 and 1993 the regime collected 21.40 billion yuan in fines.[132] If a couple managed to evade surveillance and give birth to a second child, they could be fined from 15 to 20 percent of their income for the next fourteen years.[133] The regime also deprived these households an allowance of grain, land, or housing for children born outside the plan; demoted or forced violators from their jobs; revoked the operating licenses and government contracts from business owners; fined cadre for failing to enforce the regulations or meeting their assigned quotas; and levied fines and sanctions on work units for failing to report violations.[134] If a household lacked the income to pay the assessed fines, cadre reported "confiscating stored grain, taking away pigs, and dismantling the houses of households . . . putting handcuffs on and putting into prison those who have an attitude."[135] As the demographer Thomas Scharping concluded, "Whoever ignored the official one-child limit was driven to financial ruin."[136]

Of course, the power to fine rural workers provided cadre with the opportunity to pocket fines and "use their new powers to maintain their political leverage and to enrich themselves, their families and their village clients."[137] Some cadre even "encouraged unauthorized births in order to fine them."[138] In one case, cadre seized the "television, bed, table, bureau and other furniture" of a man who could not pay his fine, "auctioned off the possessions, and pocketed the proceeds."[139]

Invasive Procedures

To prevent pregnancies outside the plan, the regime required women to use IUDs as the primary method of conception. They did not support the use of oral contraceptives because they regarded IUDs as more effective and they insisted on metal IUDs, not plastic, because they could be detected with X-ray machines, which were used to monitor compliance.[140]

The problem with the stainless steel IUDs was that "they provoked menstrual bleeding and led to expulsion rates of more than 30 percent two years after insertion." The regime regarded the purposeful removal of IUDs as a crime, even though it was difficult to tell whether it had been voluntarily removed or involuntarily expelled. In 1981 "the Ministry of Justice ruled ... that unauthorized IUD removals would be treated as fraud ... [and] two years later, breach of public order and hooliganism were added to the list of crimes liable to prosecution in connection with IUD removals."[141] As a result, women could be prosecuted for the "crime" of IUD removal even if it had been expelled because the technology the regime required was inherently defective.

If cadre discovered a woman had become pregnant without permission, they first tried to persuade her to have an abortion by haranguing her for days at public meetings. If intimidation meetings were insufficient to gain compliance, "more direct forms of coercion could be used. One approach was to seize and hold family members until the couple had complied." Cadre forced women to undergo involuntary abortions, "including women in the eighth or ninth month of pregnancy." One woman "who had locked herself in her home and refused to undergo an abortion found her home surrounded by armed members of the brigade militia. When they threatened to take her by force, and demonstrated their will by firing into the air ... she gave herself up."[142] During one "particularly vicious" campaign in Guangdong, "pregnant women were treated like the enemy." According to one observer, "big-bellied women were put in cowpens, handcuffed and escorted to operating areas by armed personnel."[143]

The number of abortions tripled from 5.39 million in 1978 to 14.37 million in 1983, and by 1988 "almost 17 percent of all married women in China had experienced one induced abortion, and a further 8 percent had already had two or more."[144] To reduce "recidivism," if that is the right term, or rather, to prevent women from repeatedly engaging in criminalized reproductive behavior, the regime in 1982 launched a "one cut of the knife" campaign "with the goal of sterilizing by 1985 all childbearing-age couples with two or more children."[145] Although the regime announced that "one spouse of rural couples ... should be mobilized for sterilization," it "mobilized" women much more often than men.[146] In 1983 at the height of the campaign, the regime sterilized more than sixteen million women, "nearly three times as many as in 1979," and performed more than four million vasectomies.[147] Between 1983 and 1991 "more than 30 *million* women were forcibly sterilized."[148] The authorities were four times more likely to perform invasive surgery on women them than men. Of the four-fifths of a billion operations (male and female sterilizations, abortions, IUD insertions and removals) performed from 1971 to 2001, "95 percent were performed on women," one scholar reported.[149] "It does not matter if problems come up in your work," the regime told birth-control cadre. "Stiffen your back for a couple of years."[150]

Collateral Damage

The programs designed to enforce the regime's one-child policy produced a variety of social problems that adversely affected women and girls. Susan Greenhalgh has argued that they "damaged women's reproductive health and exacerbated discrimination and violence against infant girls."[151]

Women's Health and Safety

The regime's reliance on invasive procedures undermined women's health. Women risked infections and perforations from repeated IUD insertions and abortions. In the early 1990s young women could expect to have 2.3 abortions on average during their lifetime before being sterilized. Poorly trained medical personnel typically performed the invasive medical procedures without anesthesia—women who underwent abortions described the pain as "so unbearable it is like having one's heart cut out"—under unsanitary conditions, and in rudimentary hospitals: "When beds were in short supply, the ground was used instead." Naturally, this took a heavy toll on women's health.[152]

The regime's population control efforts also compromised women's safety. Under the one-child policy, nearly one-half of all households after 1978 raised a girl as their only child. When girls married, her earnings went to support her husband's household, not her own, and she would be expected to care for her in-laws, not her own parents, in their old age. This meant that "50 percent of couples are being asked to face old age without a male heir."[153] Given these social practices, the one-child policy effectively deprived households with female off-spring of the income they might have received from a male child before marriage and the income and care his wife would provide after he married. Over the course of a lifetime, households would pay a substantial economic penalty for having a female child. Under these conditions, that men and their parents would direct their anger about the economic consequences of the one-child policy at women who gave birth to daughters should not be surprising. "Husbands, mothers-in-law and other relatives have been reported to beat, scold, and maltreat infant girls and their mothers, chasing them away from home to live in chicken coops."[154] In-laws blamed women who had female children for terminating their family line and frequently urged men to divorce them.[155] Violence by "son-hungry husbands" and in-laws against women with daughters increased dramatically during the 1980s, as did divorce, with men whose wives give birth to daughters instigating more than 50 percent of divorce actions.[156] This psychological and physical abuse drove many women to suicide, not only women with daughters but also elderly women without grandsons.[157] Greenhalgh reported that "young Chinese women have been committing suicide at an alarming rate, 66 percent higher than that of rural men."[158] By the 1990s "56 percent of all women [in the world] who committed suicide are Chinese and most of them are in rural areas."[159] These findings are significant because in historical and comparative terms, men are more likely to commit suicide than women. A century ago the sociologist Emile Durkheim noted that men *everywhere* committed suicide much more often than women, and that although suicide is an individual act, suicide rates reflected the conditions and experience of people living in different settings.[160] This suggests that the one-child policy in China created a situation for women that is unprecedented. According to the World Health Organization, China is the *only* country on the planet where suicide rates for women are *higher* than for men. In most countries, the suicide rates for men are several *times* greater than rates for women, and in places like Belarus and Bosnia, more than six times greater.[161] The adoption of the one-child policy, and the violence against women associated with it, has made China the exception to this universal rule.

Infant and Orphaned Girls

The social and economic pressure to have boys under the one-child policy persuaded many couples to use ultrasound machines, which were widely introduced after 1979, to identify girls so they could be aborted.[162] Many couples also drowned infant girls, and infanticide became a widespread practice, particularly during the height of the sterilization campaign during the early 1980s.[163] One Chinese woman's organization found that "in one village alone, 40 baby girls had been drowned in 1980 and 1981."[164] Both practices—abortion and infanticide—contributed to a rapidly changing sex ratio, which grew from 108.5 males for every female in 1980 to 118:100 in 2000.[165]

As an alternative, many parents took young girls to distant train or bus stations and abandoned them there, a practice known as "traveling abandonment."[166] Some scholars have estimated that "about 150,000 [girls] are abandoned each year." The regime has admitted to having only 100,000 children in orphanages, though the United Nations has counted 50,000 in one province alone.[167]

Of the children abandoned by parents—98 percent of them were girls—half of them died before being found, and the other half were placed in orphanages.[168] Chinese orphanages are poor, local institutions that local, municipal authorities, not the central government, finance. These "understaffed and underfunded" institutions were unprepared to handle the huge influx of orphaned girls that the central government's one-child policies generated, and they could not afford to provide adequate medical care for the infant girls in their custody, many of whom arrived in poor and "fragile condition." Mortality rates in Chinese orphanages during the 1980s and 1990s were "extremely high, averaging perhaps 40 to 50 percent of children and soaring to 90 percent in more remote areas."[169] These mortality rates are comparable to those in Nazi concentration camps during the Holocaust. The difference, of course, was that mortality rates in German camps were the product of design; in China they were the product of neglect. There, girls died in large numbers because orphanages could not afford to pay for the medicines they needed.

In the early 1990s the regime decided to let Americans adopt orphaned girls as a partial solution, and the number of adoptions grew from 28 in 1990 to 4,206 in 1998. US parents paid $15,000 to adopt an orphaned Chinese girl. The central government kept $12,000 of the fee and gave $3,000 to the orphanage, and the orphanage used the money to pay for medical treatment of the girls who remained in their custody.[170] As a result, the adoption fees US parents paid helped to subsidize local orphanages and reduce mortality rates among the wards. However, why the regime did not do more to assist underfunded orphanages that struggled for years to cope with the consequences of the central government's one-child policy is not clear.

Skewed Sex Ratios

The one-child policy encouraged practices—sex selection, infanticide, and abandonment—that contributed to the birth of fewer girls and more boys. By 1999 the sex ratio had risen to 118 males for every 100 females, though in some regions, where sex selection and abandonment were widely practiced, ratios reached as high as 132: 100.[171]

As we have seen, these practices adversely affected women and girls, but they also affected males, who found it increasingly difficult to find women to marry. The highly unbalanced sex ratio means that there are growing numbers "of poor rural men with no marriage prospects and huge numbers of poor rural women being kidnapped and sold as brides." Women are sometimes forcibly abducted, but more often, "girls are lured or purchased from their families in poverty-stricken areas of the Southwest, promised jobs in prosperous regions, and then transported long distances to villages in the northeast, where they are bought by poor villagers desperate for a wife and family.... The 'outside brides' are cut off from their families, while village society often supports the husband, who is seen as having legitimate rights over his purchased bride." In some places, "the shortage of marriageable women has given rise to cases of informal polyandrous unions in which the wife of one man informally services several others."[172] In 1993 the regime arrested one gang in Beijing that had abducted 1,800 women from the "pickup labor market to be sold in rural Shanxi province" and reported that nationwide, "143,000 people involved in 32,000 gangs were arrested for kidnapping more than 88,700 women and children."[173]

Birth Guerrillas and Black Children

Women and men across China resisted the imposition of the one-child policy. They evaded the system of monitoring women by disguising pregnancies and leaving the village so they could give birth to an unreported child in another setting, a strategy made easier by new immigration flows; colluding with cadre to falsify documents or engineer a false divorce so they could qualify for an exemption or to fail to report illegal births, a strategy that involved bribes; and confronting or attacking birth-planning personnel or taking revenge on them by destroying their crops, livestock, or property.[174] Widespread resistance by "birth guerrillas" who evaded the authorities and gave birth to children outside the plan resulted in the birth of as many as 135 million "black children" between 1979 and 1999.[175] The black children born without official permission have languished as "illegal persons" or "denizens," and the regime has denied them access to the social benefits of citizenship, though it is difficult to determine how many have acquired legal status when they became adults.[176]

* * *

Nonetheless, the regime defended its coercive one-child policy, arguing that population growth posed an "imminent threat" and was a "time-bomb waiting to explode."[177] The State Birth-Planning Commission warned, "If natural increase is not reduced, China's population will grow to 1.285 billion or even more by the turn of the century. One wrong move, and the game is lost.... We have to hold fast to the [one-child] policy in view of the critical situation in population growth. It is a policy in accord with the overall interest of the state. We have no other choice."[178]

Many scholars in the West agreed that the regime had no other choice and have supported the regime's one-child policies to curb population growth and prevent the "time bomb" from exploding.[179] They have argued that the end (reducing population growth) justifies the means (the one-child policy). Judith Shapiro depicted "the 'population explosion' as 'China's great nightmare" that required imposing "a draconian one-child policy."[180] Delia Davin admitted that the "human cost [of the policy] is great," but, she argued, "Against all this must be balanced the potential cost of inaction" and said that "the achievements of China's family-planning campaign are remarkable."[181] Greenhalgh, who has called herself "a constructive critic, not a hostile one," agreed, saying that "one of the most impressive accomplishments of the People's Republic of China in the last quarter of the twentieth century was to bring population within the orbit of state management."[182]

Tyrene White has argued that the "regime's determination to place tight curbs on population growth was so important that the very disturbing methodology by which China sought to achieve its aims was overlooked." Many scholars agreed with the regime that coercive policies were necessary to overcome the resistance of backward, "feudal peasants" who were reluctant to change and were unwilling or unable to reduce fertility rates voluntarily, without pressure from the state.[183]

According to Greenhalgh, "China's villagers became the object of florid discourses on rural feudalism, backwardness, and small mindedness." The regimes accused "ignorant and superstitious" rural workers of clinging to "outmoded reproductive beliefs," demonizing them as "backward elements."[184] This was the kind of language the regime had used in the 1950s to attack landlords. Many Western scholars have uncritically accepted these charges as an accurate description of rural worker behavior, much as they accepted, without question, the regime's characterization of landlords during land reform or of Mao's opponents as a new class of capitalist roaders during the Cultural Revolution. However, this characterization was not only defamatory, it was also entirely wrong.

The regime imposed the coercive one-child policy to achieve a target population of 1.2 billion in 2000. It argued that this target must be met or the "population bomb" would "explode." Nevertheless, both the 1.2 billion target and the one-child policy, which was designed to achieve it, were based on faulty assumptions and failed to take into account important social and economic developments that prevented the onset of a Malthusian crisis by the end of the century. In fact, population growth in China could have been managed *without* the imposition of the one-child policy, which exacted such a terrible price on rural households, women, and girls.

A Population Crisis?

The regime in 1978 argued that it faced the onset of a Malthusian crisis. To avert it, the regime argued that it must limit the population to no more than 1.2 billion people by the year 2000. The only way to meet this goal was to impose the one-child policy and dramatically reduce birth rates, particularly in rural areas, but this target—1.2 billion by 2000—was an *arbitrary* number. Like the goal of making twenty-one million tons of steel during the Great Leap Forward, the regime chose this number out of the blue. According to Greenhalgh, who interviewed the authorities responsible for setting this number, "the aim of the target was 'political,' ... [it] was set at a level that was *unrealistic* with the aim of creating political pressure on local birth-planning cadre to reach the lowest birthrates possible." One official "described the 1.2 billion target as an 'excessive demand' that nonetheless was desirable because it was 'effective' in creating pressure on localities to do better." The number was arbitrary, the data on which it was based was "incomplete and poor in quality," the target was intentionally inflated to create the *appearance* of a crisis, and the crisis was used to rationalize the one-child policy and pressure cadre to enforce it vigorously.[185]

But even if the target was arbitrary and unsound, there might still have been a "crisis" that required dramatic action. After all, the population in China was large and growing. The question is: was there really a "crisis"?

The answer is no. The regime did not immediately face a Malthusian crisis, certainly not one that would manifest itself or "explode" by the end of the century. This is not to say that population growth in China was not a *problem,* but rather that it was not a *crisis* of the sort that the regime portrayed. Population growth would not achieve crisis proportions during the next twenty years, or indeed during the next thirty years. Why? Because two important social and economic developments, which the regime failed to acknowledge, prevented or deferred the onset of a Malthusian crisis. First, birthrates *fell* dramatically even before the regime imposed the one-child policy, which slowed population growth, and second, food production *rose* dramatically after the regime introduced agricultural reforms.

Falling Birth Rates

During the 1960s and 1970s China experienced "one of the fastest fertility declines in recorded history . . . the number of children per woman fell from just under six to just under three."[186] In rural areas birth rates declined by more than half, from 38.9 in 1965 to 17.9 in 1979, and rural fertility rates declined from 5.35 in 1964 to 1.79 in 1978.[187] The number of women who delayed marriage until the age of twenty-three or older also increased sixfold, from 7.4 percent in 1985 to 41.4 percent in 1978, and this slowed population growth.[188]

These developments are important for several reasons. First, this decline took place *before* the regime introduced the one-child policy. Second, the decline in the period before 1978 was *larger* and *faster* than that achieved *after* the regime introduced the one-child policy: fertility rates fell by more than half in the fourteen years between 1964 and 1978, whereas they fell by less than half in the twenty years between 1980 and 2001.[189] Scholars described the decline in fertility under the one-child policy as an "awesome" achievement, even though it was less effective than the years preceding it, and by doing so they slighted the achievements rural workers made when they reduced birth rates on their own. Third, the decline in fertility and birth rates took place as a result of the private practices and *voluntary* decisions of rural households, not as a result of regime efforts to curb population growth. In fact, much of the decline in the 1960s took place when Mao *opposed* birth planning, and when he relented in the 1970s, the regime made only token efforts to reduce birth rates.

Why did rural households reduce fertility rates *voluntarily,* in the absence of government birth-control programs and without ready access to contraceptive technologies? They did so first of all in response to economic conditions in the countryside. Recall that collectivization, the Great Leap, and the famine had impoverished rural workers, killed millions, and subjected them to poor, subsistence diets. Recall too that the work-point pay system in the collectives disadvantaged households with dependents, young or old, a system that rewarded only "productive" labor in the fields and penalized "non-productive" subsistence work, much of it performed by women and dependents. The more dependents a household had, the more likely it was to be poor and hungry. Under these conditions, in which households with children were punished economically, adult couples decided to have fewer children and to delay marriage.[190] Economic stress persuaded people to have fewer children. A similar phenomenon occurred during the Great Depression. In the United States and elsewhere, fertility rates and household size dropped dramatically because households could not afford to feed extra mouths.[191] In China rural households experienced Great-Depression-like economic conditions during the 1960s and 1970s, and they likewise responded by having fewer children.[192]

The dramatic decline in fertility rates in this period may also have been a product of declining infant mortality rates. If children are more likely to survive infancy, as they did in China *after* the famine, then couples can safely reduce the number of children they have because they are more confident that the ones they have will survive.[193]

Rural people in China downsized families in the 1960s and 1970s as a survival strategy. They acted in response to *capitalist* development in China; they were not practicing a *feudal* mentality. If rural workers were still gripped by a *feudal* mentality, as the regime claimed, they would have *increased* or maintained fertility rates and family size, but they did not. Instead, they cut fertility rates by half. They acted in response to *existing* conditions. The problem for the regime was that when and if economic circumstances for rural workers *improved,* as they did after the regime reformed agriculture in 1978, rural workers might well respond to improved economic circumstances by increasing fertility rates and having more children. Perhaps the one-child policy was designed, in part, to prevent households from responding to better times by having more children. In effect, the regime introduced the one-child policy to combat the effects of the growth associated with capitalist development, not feudalism. The regime's attack on the backward, feudal character of rural workers was a libel, a way to shift the blame to the victims of the regime's no-growth development policies in the 1960s and 1970s.

Increasing Food Production

The agricultural reforms under Deng were designed to increase food production. Based on its experience in the 1950s, when land reform increased grain production from 113.2 million metric tons to 192.7 million metric tons in 1956, before collectivization was introduced, the regime could reasonably expect the 1978 reforms—which, like the earlier reforms, distributed land to farmers—to increase food production dramatically. In fact, that is what occurred. Grain production grew from 304 million metric tons in 1978 to 407 mmt in 1984. Although the growth rate of food production slowed after 1985, food production has still grown at a rate that is faster than population growth.[194] The population exceeded the target the government set, but this did *not* produce "the dreaded food crisis and the [average] diet has substantially improved" because food production has increased even *faster.*[195]

Oddly, the regime did not take growing food production into account or include it in its calculations when it set the 1.2 billion target and imposed the one-child policy in 1978. Instead, the regime minimized or ignored the impact that reform had on food production and per capita consumption. Thus, the regime's own reforms deferred the onset of a Malthusian crisis for decades, and so the regime essentially manufactured a Malthusian crisis where there was none. Because it was in charge of both agricultural and population policy, the regime was in a position to know better.

The regime was not alone in predicting a population crisis where there was none. In his 1968 book, *The Population Bomb,* Paul Ehrlich predicted a Malthusian crisis by the end of the 1970s. But the crisis failed to materialize because Ehrlich did not anticipate or appreciate the onset of two important global developments—the Sexual Revolution and the Green Revolution—both of which began in earnest about the time he was writing the book. The first development was that women with access to contraceptive technologies began to lower birth rates on their own, and not just in advanced countries but also in poor, Catholic, and Muslim countries. Chinese women did so at the same time, though without the benefit of contraceptive technologies. The second development was that farmers using Green Revolution technologies increased food production around the world. Since the 1950s world food production has outstripped world population growth as per capita food production has increased the world over.[196] Of course, this does not mean that people do not go hungry or that population growth is not a problem. Both are serious problems. But it does mean that the population crisis did not materialize as the neo-Malthusians like Ehrlich and Deng expected or when they expected it. The regime in China was the only government to adopt a set of policies based on assumptions that, in 1978, events had *already* discredited. In this regard, the regime was the one that acted in a "backward" way, applying theories from the 1960s to problems in the 1980s.

Was there an alternative to the one-child policy?

Amartya Sen, who won the Nobel Prize in economics, has argued that there was. He argued that fertility rates could be dramatically reduced without coercive measures if governments *empowered* women by providing them with better health care, education, jobs, and higher wages. For example, the fertility rates of poor, rural women in the Indian state of Kerala fell even more dramatically than they did in China under the one-child policy—and did so in the absence of coercive measures. Sen attributed this to improved health care and education and what he called "collaborative" and "participatory" government programs, and he argued that declining fertility rates were achieved without the collateral damage—infanticide, skewed sex ratios—associated with coercive policies in China.[197] Of course, this is what the regime in China did *not* do; instead the regime spent an estimated 300 billion yuan on coercive programs.[198] Could it not have achieved similar and perhaps better results if it had spent this money to *improve* women's lives rather than trying to immiserate them? Sen argued that the regime could have adopted less coercive measures—delaying marriage and allowing couples to have two children would have achieved the same reduction in population growth—and still have averted a Malthusian crisis, improved diets and economic welfare, and escaped the low-level equilibrium trap. The fact that Chinese women in the 1960s and 1970s reduced fertility rates on their own and that urban Chinese women, who received the benefits of government education, health care, and employment opportunities, also substantially reduced their fertility rates, more or less on their own (the government provided them with greater access to contraceptive technologies in the 1960s than it did to rural women), indicates that the regime need not have resorted to punitive birth control policies. As Sen argued, the "apocalyptic view" on which the one-child policy was predicated was "empirically baseless": "There is no imminent emergency that calls for a breathless response. What is called for is systematic support for people's own decisions to reduce family size through expanding education and healthcare and through economic and social development . . . the emergency mentality based on false beliefs in imminent cataclysms leads to breathless responses that are deeply counterproductive, preventing the development of rational and sustainable family planning. Coercive policies of forced birth control involve terrible social sacrifices, and there is little evidence that they are more effective in reducing birth rates than serious programs of collaborative action."[199]

* * *

During the first decade of reform, Deng discovered how to increase food production, finance industrialization, create a cheap labor force without emptying the countryside, and reduce birth rates. Deng's reforms simultaneously spurred economic development and curbed population growth, making it possible for the regime to pry open the jaws of the low-level equilibrium trap and achieve real growth for the first time since the early 1950s. Still, the reforms did not wholly transform China. Agricultural production, after rising, reached a plateau in the late 1980s. Foreign investment, though welcome, made a relatively modest contribution to development. The economy grew at a significant but not remarkable rate, and inflation emerged as an unwelcome byproduct. But this would all change in the 1990s. A series of political and economic developments both in China and around the world would transform China during the 1990s, making it one of the largest, fastest growing economies on the planet.

Chapter Six

Dictatorship, Democracy, and Tiananmen Square

"We do not fear spilling blood and we do not fear international reaction."
Deng Xiaoping, April 25, 1989

During the 1980s foreign investors made a modest contribution to economic development in China, but this changed in the 1990s. During this time foreign businesses made massive investments in China, providing more capital to China than to any other country in the world, surpassing even the United States in 2004. Whereas foreign businesses had invested only US$1 billion in China during all of 1984, they poured US$1 billion into China each *week* in 2003.[1] This flood of foreign capital fueled double-digit rates of economic growth in China during the 1990s and early 2000s. At the current pace, China, now the world's sixth largest economy, "will become the largest economy in the world" by the year 2015, according to Kenneth Arrow, a Nobel laureate in economics.[2]

This leads us to ask: why did global investment patterns shift so dramatically?

Foreign investors migrated to China for two reasons. First, during the late 1980s the regime in China created a large, cheap labor force, devalued the currency, and reasserted authoritarian rule at Tiananmen Square. These developments created a global comparative advantage in low-wage labor and low-cost goods that exerted a strong *pull* on foreign businesses, persuading a growing number of them to invest in China.

Second, a combination of economic developments—rising wages, currency appreciations, and economic crises—*pushed* businesses out of democratic and democratizing states. When they exited, foreign investors often turned to China, where wages and costs were lower. During the late 1980s and throughout the 1990s businesses increasingly invested in dictatorship, not democracies.

Tiananmen Square was a turning point. Before Tiananmen Square foreign businesses invested broadly, making modest investments in China and substantial investments in developing countries across Latin America as well as East and Southeast Asia. After Tiananmen Square they invested more narrowly, focusing selectively on China and excluding others. Events in Tiananmen Square acted like a fulcrum of change and tipped the balance toward China (see chart below). Thus, two simultaneous political developments—democratization in developing countries and the reassertion of dictatorship in China—were responsible for shifting global investment patterns, accelerating economic growth in China, and undermining it elsewhere.

This chapter examines how democratization in Taiwan and South Korea raised costs for businesses, helped *push* businesses out of these countries, and persuaded them to invest in China and other Southeast Asian countries during the late 1980s. It then shows how the reassertion of dictatorship in China, in which events at Tiananmen Square in 1989 played a central role, helped *pull* foreign investors, particularly from Taiwan and South Korea, into China.

The next chapter explains how economic crises in Japan, Mexico and Latin America, and countries across Southeast Asia *pushed* foreign investors out of democratic and democratizing states during the 1990s and early 2000s. It will also

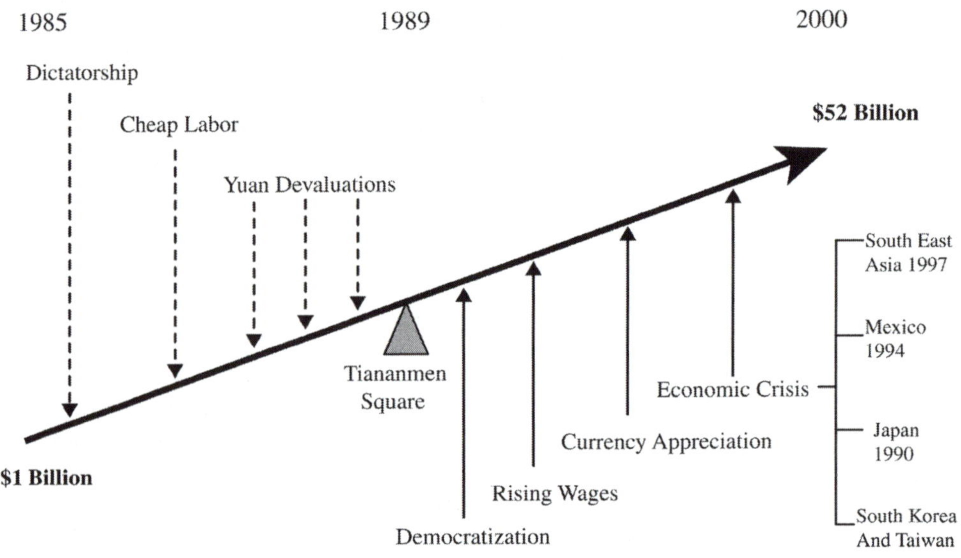

detail the steps the regime in China took to enhance its comparative advantages during this period, advantages that *pulled* foreign capital into China.

To do this, it is important first to examine the democratization of regimes in Taiwan and South Korea in the late 1980s. Democratization in these two countries had a big impact on their investment in China in the years before Tiananmen Square.

Democratization in Taiwan and South Korea

Like China, Taiwan and South Korea were ruled by one-party dictatorships for most of the postwar period. Furthermore, Taiwan and South Korea, like China, were extremely poor. In 1962 per capita income in South Korea was comparable to that in poor countries like China and Ghana; income in Taiwan was only marginally higher.[3] However, unlike China under Mao, regimes in Taiwan and South Korea quickly escaped from the low-level equilibrium trap and achieved rapid rates of growth. Economists celebrated their achievements as "economic miracles." Per capita income in South Korea grew from $87 a year in 1962 to $6,498 by 1991; Taiwan from $153 to $7,600 over the same period.[4]

Several external and internal developments contributed to rapid economic growth in both countries. First, Japan had colonized both Taiwan and South Korea. During the 1920s Japanese rulers developed the industrial infrastructure of both countries. "Japan [was] one of the very few imperial powers to have located heavy industries in its colonies," the historian Bruce Cumings observed. The infrastructures the Japanese built in Taiwan "provided a strong foundation for future industrialization," and in Korea the "industrial infrastructure ... was among the best developed in the third world." Although the United States stripped Japan of its colonies after World War II, close economic ties survived the war, Japanese firms provided loans and invested heavily in both countries, and when Japan began its remarkable ascent, it pulled Taiwan and South Korea along with it.[5]

Second, regimes in both countries introduced land reform. They seized land from large landowners and sold it at low prices to rural tenant farmers. In China the regime killed landlords as part of the land-reform process. However, in Taiwan and South Korea, the regimes *compensated* landlords for their land and paid them off with government bonds, a practice that converted them from a rural class that earned its income from rent to an urban class that earned its income from dividends, which cemented their political allegiance to the regime. Landownership transformed tenant farmers into small-scale proprietors and encouraged them to work harder and more efficiently, reinvest in agriculture, and increase food production dramatically. By extending landownership to rural farmers, the regime won their gratitude and established in the countryside a conservative base of political support for the government.[6]

Land reform had other important consequences. Increasing agricultural productivity created a labor surplus in rural areas, and jobless workers migrated into the cities. These migrants created the core of a large, low-paid labor force in the growing industrial sectors. Increasing food supplies also helped finance industrialization. Regimes in Taiwan and South Korea purchased surplus grain at below-world-market prices and then sold it for higher prices on export markets, using the profits to invest in industry.[7]

Third, after the Korean War erupted in 1950, the United States provided economic and military aid to both Taiwan and South Korea to support them as frontline, anticommunist states.[8] Between 1945 and 1978 the US government gave US$13 billion in aid to South Korea and US$5.6 billion to Taiwan, a sum nearly equal to the amount of US aid to *all* of Latin America (US$14.8 billion) and Africa (US$6.89 billion) during the same period.[9] Furthermore, US military forces based in South Korea provided additional economic benefits. US troops spent money to support local businesses, pumped hard currency (dollars) into the economy, and provided jobs for local workers in the military-service sector (bars, restaurants, and brothels). The US government also purchased local goods and offered military contracts to local businesses during the war in Vietnam, and firms in "Taiwan [and South Korea] eagerly seized the business opportunities provided by massive US spending related to the Vietnam War." For South Korea as much as 20 percent of its foreign exchange earnings in the late 1960s could be attributed to the Vietnam War.[10]

In addition to economic and military aid, the US government supplied both countries with large quantities of surplus grain through the PL 480 food aid program, which kept food prices and wages low in both countries. The United States also provided both countries with ready access to US markets and allowed regimes to protect their domestic industries with high tariff barriers.[11] As a result, both countries developed export-oriented manufacturing industries—run by large monopolistic *chaebols* in South Korea and small, competitive firms in Taiwan—to produce goods for US and Japanese markets. This helped both countries record double-digit rates of economic growth. According to one observer, if the United States had not been as generous in the 1950s, "Taiwan's annual GNP growth rate would have been cut by half, its per capita income would have been reduced by three-quarters, and it would have taken the island 30 more years to reach its 1964 living standards." For South Korea, which received twice as much US aid as Taiwan, US neglect would have seriously delayed its economic ascent. Without US assistance, Taiwan and South Korea would have looked a lot like China. Of course, unlike China, both countries had relatively small populations because they had been detached by partition from large, populous hinterlands. In addition, unlike China, rapid industrialization in both countries quickly lowered birth rates, making it easier for them to escape the kind of low-level equilibrium trap that beset China in this period.[12]

However, the conditions that contributed to explosive growth in Taiwan and South Korea changed abruptly in 1985. The Reagan administration's decision to devalue the dollar set in motion a series of events that led to democratization in Taiwan and South Korea.

In September 1985 the US government and its economic partners in the Group of Five (Japan, United Kingdom, France, and West Germany) agreed to devalue the dollar. Officially, the G-5, which West German Prime Minister Helmut Schmidt said consisted of "those who really matter in the world," said only that "some orderly appreciation of the main non-dollar currencies against the dollar is desirable." However, unofficially, they secretly agreed in the Plaza Accords to devalue the dollar by half over the next few years.[13]

The Reagan administration asked its partners to devalue the dollar to stem growing US trade deficits, which had climbed from US$25.3 billion in 1980 to US$122 billion in 1985. Although the bulk of the US trade deficit was a product of trade with Japan and oil-producing countries, US trade deficits with Taiwan and South Korea were significant. The US trade deficit with Taiwan had increased from US$2.3 billion in 1979 to US$16 billion in 1985, and its trade deficit with South Korea had grown to US$4.2 billion in 1985.[14]

US officials worried about trade deficits because they indicated that the United States was losing jobs to foreign competitors. The dollar devaluation was designed to correct this imbalance and stem the loss of US jobs. US officials hoped to persuade consumers in the United States to stop buying imports and instead buy American goods by changing exchange rates. The appreciation of nondollar currencies was designed to *raise* the price of imported goods in the United States, which would in turn discourage US consumers from buying expensive imports and shop instead for cheaper American goods. US officials also hoped to persuade consumers in other countries to buy American goods because the devaluation of the dollar *lowered* the price of US goods in overseas markets. If US consumers bought fewer imported goods and foreign consumers purchased more American products, US trade deficits would disappear. The Reagan administration thought the dollar devaluation would solve economic problems in the United States, but the falling value of the dollar and the rising value of other currencies actually created economic problems in Japan, Taiwan, and South Korea. During the next four years the value of the Japanese yen increased by 50 percent, the New Taiwan dollar by 30 percent, and the South Korean won by 20 percent.[15]

Devaluation and Democratization in Taiwan

In Taiwan the regime had tied the New Taiwan dollar to the yen. As the dollar devalued, the value of both the New Taiwan dollar and the yen rose sharply, though the New Taiwan dollar appreciated at a slower rate (30 percent) than the yen (50 percent). This in turn made Taiwanese exports to the United States more expensive. US consumers responded by buying fewer goods from Taiwan, and Taiwan's trade surplus shrank from $16 billion to $10 billion between 1985 and 1988.[16] Because Taiwan exported half of its manufactured goods to the United States, this development posed a serious threat to its economic future.[17]

While the currency appreciation associated with the Plaza Accords drove up the cost of Taiwanese goods, rising wages also drove up costs for businesses in Taiwan. For decades the ruling nationalist party in Taiwan had suppressed labor organizations and opposition political parties in order to keep wages low and maintain its monopoly on power.[18] However, in the early 1980s urban workers in Taiwan became more militant and conducted strikes to increase their wages, which had failed to keep pace with productivity gains and had been eroded by rising inflation during the 1970s.[19] Labor disputes rose from 700 in 1980 to 1,622 in 1985, and then to more than 2,900 in 1987 and 1988.[20] As a result of urban workers' successful strikes, "labor costs in Taiwan nearly doubled between 1984 and 1988." Currency appreciation and rising wages made Taiwanese goods more expensive and less competitive at a time when competition from other countries in East Asia was intensifying. Governments and businesses in Thailand, Malaysia, Singapore, Indonesia, and China had emulated Taiwan and South Korea and adopted export manufacturing as a development strategy. They became effective competitors because their labor costs were only a fraction of those in Taiwan and South Korea.[21] In 1988 workers earned $643 a month in Taiwan and $610 in South Korea, compared to only $209 in Indonesia, $132 in Thailand, and $129 in Malaysia.[22] During this period profits in Taiwan fell by one-third, and economic growth slowed "from around 10 percent in 1986 to 5 percent in 1990."[23]

Economic problems caused by the 1985 dollar devaluation contributed to an economic and political crisis in Taiwan during the next few years. Chiang Ching-kuo, the eldest son of Chiang Kai-shek, who had inherited the dictatorship after his father died in 1975, led the one-party regime in Taiwan.[24] Chiang Ching-kuo, seventy-seven years old in 1986, had maintained the nationalist party's grip on power by enforcing martial law, which had first been imposed in 1947, and relying on a captive legislature composed of elderly representatives.

When Chiang Kai-shek moved his government to Taiwan in 1947, he insisted that it still represented all of China. Legislators elected to the national assembly from districts on the mainland in 1947 and 1948 were given permanent seats, pending all-China elections at some future date. When legislators died, they were replaced by first, second, and even third runners-up from the 1947–1948 elections, and no new parliamentary elections were held until 1969, when the regime conducted "supplementary" elections to replace dead legislators. In 1988 the average age of legislators was eighty years, and fourteen legislators died in office each year on average between 1980 and 1986. The constituents of these antiquarian legislators derisively referred to them as the *zou rou,* or "walking dead."[25]

By the mid-1980s the government's ossified political institutions and geriatric leadership had become the object of public ridicule. Opposition groups demanded political reform. In 1986, as Taiwan's economic problems deepened, Chiang Ching-kuo began casting around for ways to transfer power to a successor after his death and create a reformed political system so that other social groups could participate in the exercise of political power while the ruling party still maintained its grip on power. Chiang evidently wanted to use political change to promote Taiwan's economic development. At the March 1986 meeting of the Central Committee of the GMD, the ruling party, Chiang broke with the past and argued that the regime should adopt a constitutional democracy. In April he appointed a task force to suggest possible reforms, such as permitting other political parties to participate, lifting martial law, and reforming parliamentary elections. In September dissident *dangwai* leaders announced the formation of the Democratic Progressive Party, a move that was then still illegal under martial law. However, Chiang told his colleagues in October that "the time is changing and so is the environment. To fit in with these changes, the GMD must adopt new concepts and new forms according to the basic spirit of the democratic and constitutional system. Only by doing so can the GMD be in line with current trends and forever be together with the public."[26]

Chiang then allowed the opposition to participate in the December 1986 elections, though restrictive electoral rules allowed them to make only marginal gains. Chiang then lifted martial law on July 15, 1987. When he died in January 1988, power passed to his designated successor, Lee Teng-hui, who subsequently promoted a slow, deliberate process of democratization—what observers have called democracy "on the installment plan."[27] The Taiwanese Supreme Court in 1990 ordered that the *zou rou* retire at the end of 1991, and in Taiwan's first general election, held in 1992, the opposition won 30 percent of the seats in parliament.[28]

Democratization in South Korea

In South Korea the economic crisis that the 1985 dollar devaluation triggered took a somewhat different course. There, unlike in Taiwan, the regime had tied the won to the dollar, largely because US soldiers based in the country pumped dollars into the economy.[29] When US officials devalued the dollar, the won appreciated by about 20 percent—not as much as Taiwan (30 percent) or Japan (50 percent), but still a significant amount given the fact that 40 percent of South Korea's exports went to the United States.[30] One South Korean executive complained that "we can't take any more [currency] appreciation."[31] However, whereas South Korean businesses were hurt *less* by currency appreciation than their counterparts in Taiwan, rising labor costs hurt them *more.*

The South Korean regime, like the one in Taiwan, had long suppressed unions and prevented workers from sharing in the economic gains businesses made during the "miracle" years. Workers were required to work long hours—the average workweek increased from 50.5 to 54.3 hours between 1975 and 1983—under dangerous conditions (Korea had the highest rate of industrial accidents in the world during this period), and they were crowded into expensive, urban housing. One study found that in 1985 "the poorest 30 percent of the population had an average of two square meters per person and three families per house. It is common for one family to live in one or two small rooms and often, three generations live together—in some cases, in one room." In Seoul, home to one-quarter of the country's population, two million people, or one-fifth of the city's residents, were squatters.[32]

Because industrial monopolies, or *chaebols,* organized workers in large-scale factories that employed thousands of people, workers developed a strong sense of collective identity and labor militancy during the late 1970s. The regime, however, violently suppressed worker protest and disbanded unions. A crackdown in 1980 resulted in the deaths of hundreds of workers and students in Kwangju.[33]

After a brief hiatus, labor militancy reemerged in 1985 and 1986, just as the won began to appreciate. Workers joined unions and increased the share of organized labor in the workforce from 14 percent in 1986 to 23 percent in 1989. Workers conducted strikes, and the number of labor disputes grew from 276 in 1986 to 3,749 in 1987. One labor economist noted that "32 percent of all manufacturing firms with 300 or more employees struck in 1987 and that 1.225 million workers were involved in strikes between June and October 1987."[34] Legal and illegal strikes forced businesses to make concessions and raise wages, despite the regime's determined efforts to arrest labor leaders and curb wage increases. Wages essentially doubled between 1984 (US$302 a month) and 1988 (US$633 a month), and by 1989 "Korean aggregate wage levels were the second highest in Asia, below only Japan."[35]

In 1987 students demanding political change joined urban workers demanding higher wages. The result was the creation of what sociologists have called a *minjung* ("the people" or "the masses"), "a broad alliance of 'alienated classes,' people alienated from power and the distribution of the fruits of economic growth." In the Korean context, the word connotes "a strong [populist] nationalist desire for economic and political independence." At the center of this minjung were student-intellectuals and workers, but small rural farmers occupied the flanks of this core alliance along with white-collar workers, many of them having converted to Christianity (about 13 percent of the population in South Korea was Protestant or Catholic).[36] In ideological terms, the minjung practiced "an eclectic blend of nationalism, Marxism, left-Catholic liberation theology, anti-dependency economic views, anti-war and anti-nuclear slogans, national reunification demands, and a Western-style peace movement."[37] From 1986 to 1988 workers conducted strikes, students set themselves on fire and burned themselves to death (there were "seventy incidents of self-immolation including some who jumped to their deaths from high buildings), and massive street demonstrations, with 300,000 people participating in protests in 20 different cities in June 1987."[38]

As a result, and combined with the appreciation of the won, rising labor costs slowed economic growth in South Korea from double to single-digit rates. The economic problems associated with rising costs and significant foreign debt (the regime had borrowed US$40 billion by 1984) worried officials in the regime. Cho Soon, South Korea's minister of economic planning, feared that "our country will collapse like some of the [indebted] Latin American countries."[39] He was referring to regimes in Argentina (1983), Uruguay (1984), Brazil (1985), and the Philippines (1986), which had fallen in recent years.[40] In 1987 political turmoil in the streets joined South Korea's economic problems, thereby creating a serious crisis for the regime.

In June 1987 Chun Doo-hwan, who had taken power in a 1980 coup following the murder-assassination of the dictator Park Chung-hee by the head of the Korean Central Intelligence Agency, appointed General Roh Tae-woo as the ruling party's candidate for president in the upcoming elections.[41] Roh evidently concluded that he needed to broaden the regime's political base and widen political participation in the electoral process if he was going to address the country's economic and political problems, much the same conclusion that Chiang had reached in Taiwan. Both Roh and Chiang saw democratization as a way to share power with the middle class and create a multiparty system dominated by a center-right party, which would restore the government's legitimacy, deflect popular protest, curb strikes, and get the economy moving again. Roh argued that "this country should develop a more mature democracy," and transformed himself from a military leader to a civilian presidential candidate.[42] Roh won the December 1987 election because the ruling party spent heavily to support him and because dissident leaders split the opposition vote. As president Roh negotiated the 1990 merger of the ruling party with two of the three major opposition parties, thereby creating a conservative "grand coalition" that brought Kim Young-sam, a former member of the opposition, to power in the 1992 elections.[43] Roh advanced democratization, which incorporated the middle class but excluded workers and students, as a way to preserve the political power of a conservative ruling class.

In 1987 and 1988 regimes in both Taiwan and South Korea democratized. They did so in response to changing economic conditions—appreciating currencies and rising labor costs—and to widespread popular demands for economic and political change. Of course, workers in both countries took advantage of democratization—the end of martial law in Taiwan, the decision to refrain from using the army to suppress worker movements in South Korea, and the decision in both countries to allow opposition parties to participate in elections—to organize unions and demand higher wages.[44] As a result, democratization raised wages at a time when currency appreciations already were driving up the price of exported goods. These developments exerted a substantial *push* on businesses to exit Taiwan and South Korea and find ways to reduce their costs. Increasingly, they turned to China and invested there. They did so because the regime in China *devalued* the yuan during this period and because it kept low wages low. Thus, businesses and investors in Taiwan and South Korea started investing in China during the late 1980s both because developments associated with democratization *pushed* them to exit and because developments associated with the reassertion of dictatorship in China *pulled* them into China. "In the late 1980s, with labor costs rising and [their] currencies appreciating, a number of labor-intensive industries [in South Korea and Taiwan] had already lost their comparative advantage, and in their efforts to survive were forced to move their production bases ... to Southeast Asia or to mainland China, leading to an increase in the proportion of Taiwanese overseas investment."[45]

Chinese Pull

During the early 1980s the regime in China used illegal migrants to create a low-wage workforce that could manufacture goods for export, much as Taiwan and South Korea had done. This development exerted an economic pull that persuaded foreign investors, mostly from the overseas Chinese communities in Hong Kong and East Asia, but not yet from Taiwan or South Korea, to invest in low-wage, labor-intensive manufacturing in China.

In 1985, when the United States and the Group of Five devalued the dollar, the yuan fell because Deng had pegged the Chinese currency to the dollar. As the dollar fell, the price of Chinese exports to the United States stayed the same and the price of Chinese exports to other countries fell sharply, depending on how much their currency appreciated in relation to the dollar/yuan.

However, the regime in China did not stop there. In 1986 the regime devalued the yuan against the dollar.[46] This devaluation then reduced the cost of goods exported to the United States and further cut the cost of goods exported to other, nondollar countries in Asia and Europe. When government officials in 1988 pointed out to Deng Xiaoping "that the low value of the US dollar raised the price of Japanese, Taiwanese, and [South] Korean exports to the United States and that this offered an excellent opportunity for China to enter the market with its cheaper labor [and cheaper currency]," Deng said that their proposal to increase Chinese exports "must be pursued with great boldness and speed, on no account can we lose this opportunity."[47] To seize this opportunity, Deng decided in 1989 to devalue the yuan again.[48] Successive devaluations in 1986 and 1989 reduced the value of the yuan by half against the dollar. This cut the price of its exports to the United States in half and slashed the price of its goods in other markets even more.

In this context, China offered a series of advantages for businesses and investors in Taiwan, South Korea, and also Japan during the late 1980s. By moving to China, businesses in Taiwan and South Korea could: first, take advantage of the dollar devaluation (goods that they produced in China and exported to the United States would cost less than the same goods produced in Taiwan or South Korea, where the currency was rising in dollar terms); second, take advantage of the devaluations of the yuan, which made goods manufactured in China cheaper still; and third, take advantage of low-cost Chinese labor, which was significantly cheaper than labor in Taiwan or South Korea, where militant workers were successfully conducting strikes and raising wages.[49]

Of course, not only cheap labor but also other incentives pulled investors in Taiwan and South Korea toward China. In 1986 Deng eliminated the practice of lifetime employment, what was sometimes called the "iron rice bowl," thus giving employers the flexibility to fire workers at will.[50] The regime also allowed employers to practice "military-like" management in Chinese factories. One scholar who did fieldwork in Chinese factories run by Taiwanese managers observed,

> Workers had to line up when walking from the factories to the dining halls; no chatting was allowed in the dining hall. Each time workers left the factory building, they were subjected to a body check to see if they had stolen anything from the factory. When they talked to Taiwanese managers, they had to stand up straight, with palms by the sides of the thighs.... Harsh scolding and shouting at workers were frequently seen and heard. The workers I talked to confirmed that the beating of disobedient workers was not unusual.... A manager claimed that he could shout at his Chinese workers and use "military-like management" without worrying about worker reaction. He emphasized that if he treated Taiwanese workers the same way, they would "protest immediately." Plus, Taiwanese workers were "too spoiled and were not willing to work overtime, and they demanded too many holidays."[51]

Consequently, pushed by rising currencies and rising wages in Taiwan and South Korea, and pulled by the Chinese regime's monetary and labor policies, which reduced the cost of producing exports manufactured in China, businesses in Taiwan and South Korea exited democratizing states in the late 1980s and migrated to China.

Taiwanese investment in China soared, increasing from "$100 million in 1987 to $1 billion in 1989, and to $2 billion in 1990."[52] By 1991 "Taiwan had surpassed the United States and Japan to become the second largest investor after

Hong Kong."[53] South Korean businesses followed suit, investing US$1 billion in China during this period.[54] This investment in turn changed the origin of many goods exported to the United States. In 1985, 50 percent of the footwear and 60 percent of the toys imported into the United States originated in Taiwan and South Korea.[55] Less than 10 percent of these goods were made in China. However, during the next ten years, as businesses shifted their production from Taiwan and South Korea to China, the origins of footwear and toys changed completely. By 1995, 50 percent of the footwear and toys the United States imported originated in China, and less than 10 percent in Taiwan and South Korea.[56]

Thus, the shift that began in the late 1980s, before Tiananmen Square, accelerated in the years after Tiananmen Square. Shifting investment patterns first affected the manufacture of shoes and toys; they later changed the origin of computers and electronics.[57]

* * *

On April 6, 1989, students gathered in Tiananmen Square, in the heart of Beijing, to commemorate the death of Hu Yaobang, a former general secretary of the Communist Party.[58] The students who occupied the square used the occasion to memorialize Hu, criticize the government, and call for the ouster of Deng Xiaoping. During the next few days thousands of other students joined the vigil and demanded wider political and economic change.[59]

The student occupation of Tiananmen Square occurred at an important historical juncture. Regimes in Taiwan, South Korea, and the Philippines had recently democratized. They had democratized, in part, because workers and students had joined forces to create a political alliance—what the South Koreans called a *minjung*—to demand political and economic change. Meanwhile, in Poland the mass-based union Solidarity had just concluded negotiations with the regime that legalized noncommunist opposition parties and scheduled elections that would allow a peaceful transfer of power on June 4.

Solidarity, like the *minjung* in South Korea, Taiwan, and the Philippines, was an alliance of workers and intellectuals. Earlier, in 1976, intellectuals who had organized the Committee for the Defense of Workers (Komitet Obrony Robotnikow, or KOR) defended workers who protested rising prices and a deepening debt crisis in Poland. In 1980 striking workers at the Gdansk shipyards invited KOR leaders to join forces, and together they created an independent federation of autonomous trade unions called Solidarity. Within a year seven million people in Poland, or nearly one fifth of the Polish population, had joined Solidarity. In October 1981 the union called for the creation of a "self-governing republic." Alarmed by this development and prodded by the Soviet Union, which threatened to intervene if the Polish government did not suppress Solidarity, the regime declared martial law and jailed union leaders. However, in April 1988 workers conducted illegal strikes to protest rising inflation and the austerity measures designed to curb that inflation, and they also demanded that the regime legalize Solidarity. As the economic situation deteriorated, the regime, led by Gen. Wojciech Jaruzelski on February 6, 1989, opened a series of Round Table meetings with union leaders that eventually legalized Solidarity and scheduled elections to facilitate an orderly transfer of power to a civilian government in June.[60]

The students in Beijing stood in the trough between two waves of global political change. A wave of democratization had just swept across Taiwan, South Korea, and the Philippines. Another wave, already visible in Poland, was forming a huge breaker that would crest in the fall. However, while the students and workers in East Asia and Eastern Europe were of one mind, demanding both political and economic reform, the students in China were of two. On the one hand, they were *for* political change and democracy, but on the other hand, they were also *against* economic reform.

The students advocated political change because they believed that access to political power should be based on merit, not privilege. In this regard, they played the role Mao assigned to "disadvantaged" students during the Cultural Revolution, when he argued for a political system based on merit, not class privilege. As Selden has argued, "The student's vision [in 1989] ... [was] centered on expanded political rights for the educated elite." Furthermore, the students drew their inspiration and language of democracy from contemporary movements in East Asia: "Many emulated the white headbands worn by South Korean dissidents and flashed the 'V' sign favored by anti-Marcos activists who had fought for the people's power in the Philippines. They quoted Martin Luther King Jr. and Mahatma Gandhi on non-violent protest and Abraham Lincoln and Patrick Henry on democracy."[61] They used this language in part because the regime had so thoroughly abused the Marxist-Maoist vocabulary for change in previous years that its terminology had lost any evocative power.

Although the students advocated expanding democracy for themselves—most of them were members of the ruling class—they did not believe it should be widely shared. An American teacher in Wuhan asked student leaders, "What do you mean when you say democracy? Do you want to give the 80 percent of the people who are out in the countryside the right to vote? The answer was, 'No, they're not ready.'"[62]

However, although "the demands of the Chinese protesters were moderate in the extreme," according to one scholar, the students nonetheless advocated democracy because they wanted to end the unchecked political power and privilege that made widespread corruption possible.[63] Lee has argued that "corruption was probably the single most important rallying point for the pro-democracy movement. Public opinion polls taken in 1988 and early 1989 showed that official corruption was consistently ranked as the number one *political* issue."[64] In a 1987 opinion poll "nearly 84 percent of the respondents from thirty cities cited corruption as the social problem that most disturbed them. A similar survey carried out [in 1988] identified 'embezzlement and bribe taking' as the most pervasive social crime."[65] As one student demonstrator explained, "'Corruption is everywhere. That is why we need democracy—to make people in power more responsible for their actions.' Another student said, 'Our goals are first, democracy, and next, an end to official profiteering.'"[66]

The students attacked corruption because it was a way to challenge the privileges of ruling class cadres who had used their official positions to enrich themselves and acquire individual wealth during the period of reform. The students taunted the regime by hanging wall posters attacking Deng Xiaoping and his children and by reciting the jingle, "Mao Zedong's son went to the front. Zhao Ziyang's [the Party's General Secretary] son speculates in color TVs. Deng Xiaoping's son demands money from everyone."[67] Finally, the students attacked corruption because they knew that the regime was vulnerable on this score. Prime Minister Li Peng admitted as much, saying that "there are phenomena of bureaucratism and corruption in the government and the popular masses and college students are dissatisfied with this," though he dismissed "their criticisms and suggestions" by arguing, "I consider this [corruption] to be normal."[68]

However, reform had invited official corruption in several ways. First, the agricultural reforms had created a two-tier price structure for food. Some food was sold at the low prices set by the state, other food at higher prices set by the market. The economist Barry Naughton argued that this system encouraged corruption because "someone in a position of power [could] benefit personally if he [gained] access to an item at the low state-set price and then [resold] it at the higher market price," a practice, he said, that had become increasingly prevalent in the late 1980s.[69] Second, the rising prices associated with reform-induced inflation and "the failure of government salaries to keep up with inflation led bureaucrats and functionaries to demand bribes to perform their duties. By 1988 bribes had begun to be routinely required to install phones or to start electrical service, and even to get mail delivered or receive medical attention."[70]

By attacking corruption, the students implicitly challenged Deng's and his associates' reassertion of privilege when they returned to power after Mao's death, along with their economic reforms, which had provided them with access to individual wealth. The students decried "corruption" because it was the kind of Maoist language that had been used successfully during the Cultural Revolution. It was a vocabulary that the reformers—many of whom, like Deng, had been attacked as "privileged" by student Red Guards during the Cultural Revolution—understood quite well and took seriously as a threat. Thus, the students simultaneously used the vocabulary of contemporary democratic movements and the language of Maoists during the Cultural Revolution to challenge the regime and demand political reform.

They were *for* democracy because they saw it as a way to end the political privileges that made corruption possible. But at the same time they were *against* economic reform. They opposed reform because it had led to inflation, which disadvantaged urban students and urban workers.

In general, the regime's economic reforms had led to inflation. Agricultural reforms increased food prices, whereas rapid industrialization increased the demand for energy and natural resources and drove up the price of energy, natural resources, and the goods—steel and consumer durables—made from them.[71] The regime's use of foreign loans and investment as well as heavy government spending to finance rapid industrialization increased the supply of money and credit. This made it possible for businesses and consumers to purchase food, energy, natural resources, and finished goods—and rising demand contributed to price inflation.[72] Rising prices also triggered panic buying and hoarding because consumers "bought durable goods as a hedge against inflation. One elderly man spent half of his savings to buy seven refrigerators and 150 kilograms of salt ... to protect his savings from inflation."[73] Hoarding led to shortages and contributed to even higher prices for scarce goods. "Rumors of further sharp increases ... precipitated panic buying and runs on banks in some cities, notably Shanghai in late July 1988."[74] As a result, inflation gathered speed in the mid-1980s, reached 19 percent in 1988, and rose to 28 percent in 1989.[75] "Unofficially," Seldon argued, "and more realistically, the inflation rate was closer to 40 percent [in 1987 and 1988]."[76]

Inflation disadvantaged urban residents because the government fixed their income from salaries and wages. Urban residents could not easily raise their wages to keep pace with rising prices, so as prices rose, they grew poorer. In 1987 the real incomes of one-fifth of urban households had declined, and by 1988 inflation reduced real incomes for more than half of all urban residents in China.[77] As one Shanghai worker complained, "I wish we could go back to Mao's day. At that time, we had no inflation and we were guaranteed a certain living standard. Now I can hardly afford to feed my family."[78]

Although inflation *eroded* the living standards of urban residents, it contributed to *rising* living standards for rural workers, who saw their incomes increase as food prices rose and who used their newfound gains to improve their homes and diets. The discriminatory effects of inflation—bad for urban workers but good for rural workers—divided the working class and created enormous resentment in urban areas. As Selden observed, "looking out from their cramped [urban] apartments at the two- and three-story mansions constructed by peasant entrepreneurs in the suburbs, workers on fixed salaries experienced declining relative status and position."[79] Because the regime could not or would not raise wages to "enable state employees to keep up with inflation," Naughton argued, "the result was profound discontent."[80] In 1986, Richard Baum observed, "only 29 percent of urban residents surveyed felt that the reforms provided equal opportunity for all; by November ... almost 75 percent of the [urban] people queried expressed dissatisfaction with rising inflation," which they attributed to the reforms.[81]

In an effort to raise wages, urban workers conducted work slowdowns and strikes, "so 200 strikes, each involving more than a thousand workers, are believed to have occurred in the first half of 1988 alone."[82] Urban workers also tried to keep up with inflation by taking multiple jobs. As Kathleen Hartford observed, "As anyone with a Chinese friend knows . . . many staved off [the threat of inflation] only by exhausting themselves moonlighting; and young people felt they faced a dead-end future of low-pay and boring work—if they could find a job at all."[83]

To curb rising inflation, in 1986 the regime adopted austerity measures: curbing bank loans, raising interest rates, rationing food for urban workers, raising taxes, and cutting spending to reduce government budget deficits and take money out of circulation.[84] However, this only made matters worse for urban residents. "The austerity programme . . . did not yield the desired results: [It] led to stagflation rather than stabilization," Marie-Claire Bergere observed. "Thus, besides being deprived of the [job] securities and guarantees they had enjoyed . . . the urban blue- and white-collar workers now also saw the benefits they had received from the [initial] economic reform threatened. Discontent and unrest spread."[85]

Therefore, while living standards for urban residents declined as a result of reform-induced inflation, ruling class cadre, who could profit from business or supplement their fixed government salaries with income from bribes, and rural workers, who could profit from the sale of agricultural goods, both made substantial gains. From the perspective of urban residents, the "corrupt" could keep up with inflation whereas "honest" workers fell behind. As Selden noted, "The fact that so many of those who were most obviously corrupt were the children of leading officials further undermined the legitimacy of the system."[86]

In economic terms, urban residents wanted to "return" to the kind of economic privileges—subsidies, housing, preferential treatment in employment—that urban workers and students had enjoyed under Mao. Many of the students who gathered in Tiananmen Square agreed with the sentiments of the Shanghai worker who said, "I wish we could go back to Mao's day. At that time we had no inflation and were guaranteed a certain living standard." Thus, the students were of two minds. They championed democracy and merit, a progressive view, and they advocated an end to economic reform and demanded a return to the economic privileges they had enjoyed under Mao, a conservative view.

Urban workers, who soon joined the students in Tiananmen Square and rallied to support them in other cities across the country, shared these views. Urban workers formed independent labor organizations, similar to Solidarity, in at least sixteen major cities.[87] This Chinese version of Poland's Solidarity or South Korea minjung was made possible because students, workers, and intellectuals all experienced the same economic problems as urban residents. They blamed these problems—corruption and inflation—on the reforms that the regime under

Deng introduced.[88] This alliance was not without difficulty: "Students bridled, for example, at a Worker's Federation open letter on May 21 that proclaimed that, as the 'most advanced class,' workers should constitute the 'backbone' of the movement."[89] Nonetheless, this interclass alliance, which consisted both of students who belonged to the party and of workers who were employed by the government or worked in industrial jobs, presented a serious challenge to the ruling class at a time when other movements in East Asia and in Eastern Europe were successfully demanding political and economic change.

The student-worker alliance then took advantage of Hu's death and Gorbachev's visit to attack "corruption," which was simultaneously a plea for political reform and a demand to end economic reform, and the alliance used it to rally support in Beijing and cities across the country.[90]

Initially, the regime allowed the demonstrators to camp out in Tiananmen Square, though officials accused them of spreading "'turmoil,' the same pejorative used to describe the Cultural Revolution."[91] Now, Deng concluded, "there are some people doing the same old thing, that is just like the rebellion faction during the Cultural Revolution. They won't be satisfied until all is chaos."[92] As weeks went by, hunger strikes, mounting protest, and the movement's "near universal support in major urban areas, including support by workers, citizens and many party members, constituted a direct threat to party rule."[93]

Finally, on May 20 the regime declared martial law and sent troops into Beijing. Li Peng defended the move: "There is no way out. You go back a step, they advance a step; you go back two steps, they advance two steps. It got to the point where there was nowhere left to go. Any further retreat, and we might just as well have handed the country over to them." However, people in the capital took to the streets and organized a massive nonviolent protest that blocked the army's progress toward Tiananmen Square. The troops balked at using force, milled around, and eventually withdrew on May 22–23.[94]

Faced with humiliation and political defeat, Deng, Peng, and other hardliners purged their opponents within the party, reorganized the leadership of the country's military forces, and, on the night of June 3 and the morning of June 4, ordered them to assault the demonstrators and clear Tiananmen Square. On the day that the regime in Poland sent citizens to the polls, the regime in China sent troops into the streets, where they murdered between 1,000 and 2,600 unarmed civilians.[95]

* * *

Why did the urban student-worker alliance in China fail to bring down the regime? After all, workers and intellectuals brought down dictatorships in East Asia and Eastern Europe during this period.

Political and economic crisis in China did not result in democratization, as it did elsewhere, for two reasons. First, the urban students and workers who joined forces in Tiananmen Square did not forge an alliance with *rural* workers in China. Unlike urban residents, rural workers in China *supported* Deng's economic reforms (though not the regime's population-control policies). The reforms had allowed them to increase their incomes, improve their diets, expand their homes, and, for the first time, actually *close* the gap between rural and urban workers, which had grown under Mao. Economic growth during the decade of reform purchased rural workers' loyalty or, at least, indifference to political events in 1989. Moreover, as "illegal" migrants to urban areas, rural workers experienced firsthand the discriminatory practices and prejudicial views of legal urban residents, who regarded them as their social inferiors.

The economic differences between rural and urban workers and intellectuals further prevented them from collaborating effectively during this critical juncture. As Selden observed, "The inability to build significant bridges outward from the cities to the rural area ... [was] the critical weakness of the democracy ... the movement remained painfully isolated from the peasant majority ... and the vast majority of the peasantry remained aloof."[96] However, Selden did not explain why this occurred: the movement's "inability to build significant bridges" was due to the fact that the waters of economic difference had swept them away.

Moreover, the urban *minjung* in China was smaller and weaker than its counterparts in East Asia or Eastern Europe. Although China's urban population was large in absolute terms—297 million in 1990—it still comprised only 26 percent of the total population. Much of this urban population was composed of recent migrants from the countryside, between 50 and 80 million in 1989, who likely did not share the economic and political views of legal urban residents. As a result, the minjung's social base in China was smaller than comparable movements elsewhere. As Singapore's Prime Minister Lee Kuan Yew observed, "Students in China have been watching on Chinese TV ... the almost nightly demonstrations of 'people power' in the Philippines and South Korea and forgot that China was a very different country."[97] China was "different" because its urban population was not as large and because its regime was more ruthless.

Second, factions of the ruling class in China did not use students and workers as proxies in a fight for power with other factions of the ruling class, as Mao had done during the Cultural Revolution.[98] There were, of course, different views about how to respond to the growing demonstrations. Party Secretary Zhao Ziyang argued that the regime should make concessions to the students, in part because he agreed that corruption was a problem that needed to be addressed. "The just demands of the students must be met," he said in a television speech. "They are by no means opposed to our fundamental system. Rather they are asking us to correct mistakes [corruption] in our work."[99]

Deng Xiaoping, a man who Nicholas Kristof described as "a five-foot, 84-year-old bridge player, [who was] probably the only world statesman with a taste for dog meat," rejected any concessions: "We do not fear spilling blood, and we do not fear the international reaction."[100] Deng and the other octogenarians in the party leadership viewed the students, whom they described as "wawa," or crybabies, as the latest incarnation of Mao's Red Guards, who were determined to turn the country away from economic reform and back to the chaos of the Cultural Revolution.[101] Deng described the demonstrations as "anti-Party, anti-socialist turmoil" and urged a quick, military solution, "using a sharp knife to cut through knotted hemp."[102]

Disagreements among leaders—some leaders counseled restraint and others argued for action—resulted in some delay and indecision. The leaders of the Thirty-eighth Army refused to order their troops to use force after martial law was declared. They may have done so to lodge their own complaints with the leadership, which had cut the military budget, reduced troop strengths, and marginalized military leaders as a way to save money and use the savings to promote industrialization during the reform years. But these kinds of differences are common among regimes in crisis. Still, neither Zhou nor other military leaders wanted to undo the economic reforms or surrender political or military power. In the case of military leaders, they may have used the crisis to enhance their power, and they were successful insofar as the regime greatly increased military spending and raised the political visibility of military leaders after Tiananmen Square. Nor did Zhou try to use the students to establish an independent political base "outside" the party, as Mao had done. (Deng and the hardliners later claimed that he had, but this was a fabrication.) The leadership only disagreed as to how to handle the demonstrators. Zhou and the concessionaires argued that the regime should seek a political, nonviolent solution to the protests, and this, as a practical matter, meant issuing a statement that the students were acting in a "patriotic" manner and that their complaints about "corruption" be taken seriously, which could have easily been done. Zhou also urged restraint because many of the students were themselves members of the party and the ruling class.

However, even modest concessions were too much for Deng, who viewed the struggle through the prism of the Cultural Revolution. "What we faced," Deng said after the massacre, "was not just some ordinary people who were misguided, but also a rebellious clique and a large quantity of the dregs of society. The key point is that they wanted to overthrow our state and the party."[103] Having reached this conclusion, Deng and the hardliners purged Zhou and the concessionaires (Zhou spent the rest of his life under house arrest), replaced army leaders, inserted fresh troops into the capital, and ordered them to crush the opposition. "This was a test," Deng said afterward, "and we passed."[104]

Thus, the regime passed the test and survived because urban and rural workers were divided and factions of the ruling class, after a brief hiatus, were united in their determination to retain power. In political terms, events in Tiananmen Square reasserted ruling-class authority and squashed the political opposition. However, it also had important economic consequences. "Perhaps this bad thing

[Tiananmen Square] will enable us to go ahead with reform and the open-door policy at a steady, better, even faster pace," Deng argued.[105] He was not entirely wrong. It turned out that events in Tiananmen Square accelerated the flow of foreign investment into China and sped the pace of economic growth during the 1990s. While the reassertion of dictatorship in China increased the pull on foreign investment, economic crises in democratic and democratizing states pushed foreign capital and foreign investment out of developing countries and into China, a development that both accelerated economic growth in China and undermined economic growth in other, democratic countries around the world.

Chapter Seven

Economic Crises in Democratizing States and the Foreign Investment Flood in China

> "China is like a sponge full of water, you just have to squeeze it hard until you get the last drop."
>
> *Taiwanese shoe manufacturer in China*[1]

During the 1990s economic crises in Japan, Mexico, and countries across Southeast Asia persuaded foreign investors to leave democratic and democratizing states and migrate to China. As in Taiwan and South Korea, currency appreciations played a key role in the migration of capital. Rising currencies created trade deficits that triggered a series of serious economic crises, which in turn convinced foreign investors to stampede for the exits. When they did, many of them headed to China.

The regime in China, meanwhile, took steps to enhance its comparative advantages. The regime repeatedly devalued its currency, ended job security, and laid off millions of workers. This raised unemployment rates and exerted a downward pressure on wages. Government policies made inexpensive Chinese goods cheaper still, thereby exerting a strong pull on foreign investors. These simultaneous developments—rising costs in democratic and democratizing states and falling costs in China—encouraged the migration of foreign capital to China. However, although the migration of global capital to China benefited the dictatorship—thus providing individual and collective wealth for the ruling class and strengthening the regime's political authority—it disadvantaged democratic and democratizing states around the world.

In some respects, the economic crises that struck democratic and democratizing states in the 1990s resembled the economic problems that beset Taiwan and South Korea during the late 1980s. As we have seen, the appreciation of the New Taiwan dollar and the South Korean won in the mid-1980s increased the cost of exports and contributed to economic problems that led to democratization in both countries. Democratization then brought an end to martial law and the suppression of worker organizations. It allowed workers to organize political parties and labor unions, conduct strikes, and demand higher wages. In South Korea, for instance, the number of labor disputes mushroomed from 276 in 1986 to 4,749 in 1987, and the number of workers participating in strikes grew from 46,941 to 1,262,285 in the same period. Striking workers successfully demanded higher wages: "Korea's average hourly manufacturing wage grew by 73.1 percent, 'the fastest growth rate in the world'" between 1990 and 1994, and Taiwan's grew by 39.4 percent in the same period.[2]

In Taiwan and South Korea democratization and currency appreciation combined to raise wages and the cost of goods produced for export markets. These developments persuaded, or "pushed," businesses to exit and instead invest in countries where wages and costs were lower. In the period *before* Tiananmen Square, investors from the overseas Chinese community, Taiwan, South Korea, and Japan invested not only in China, but also in Thailand, Indonesia, Malaysia, Singapore, and Mexico. After Tiananmen Square, however, economic crises in democratic and democratizing states—Japan in 1990, Mexico in 1994, and Southeast Asia and Russia in 1997—pushed investors to exit these regions and turn to China, where the pull of low wages and costs was strong. Pushed by economic crises and pulled by low wages and costs, investors increasingly abandoned developing countries and turned their attention to China. By the early 2000s China received more foreign investment than any other country on the planet, a development that simultaneously accelerated economic growth in China and undermined growth in democratic and democratizing states. To appreciate these developments, identifying the successive crises that persuaded investors to exit from democratic and democratizing states in the decade after Tiananmen Square is important.

1990 Crisis in Japan

In the decade before Tiananmen Square Japanese businesses used overseas Chinese intermediaries based in Hong Kong to manage their investments in China. "By doing so, they have been able to diversify risk, utilize overseas Chinese companies' personal connections and relations with other companies in China, and manage businesses in China in close liaison with their manufacturing and sales bases in Hong Kong, Taiwan, and Southeast Asian countries," according to Zhu. Much of the investment attributed to Hong Kong actually originated in Japan, though in the early 1980s these were modest amounts.[3] This changed after the 1985 Plaza Accords.

The appreciation of the yen, which accompanied the devaluation of the dollar as part of the Plaza Accords, sharply raised costs for businesses in Japan, where wages were already high. In response, Japanese businesses began investing elsewhere. Some firms invested in the United States, even though US wages were also high, because the dollar devaluation reduced the price of US assets for foreigners, because Japanese businesses operating in the United States could save on shipping costs and eliminate the costs associated with tariffs on imported goods, and because they could protect themselves from further dollar devaluations (which would increase the cost of producing goods in Japan).[4] Japanese businesses also invested in China and Southeast Asia "to take advantage of cheap labor in these countries, and to escape the pressure of the appreciating yen since the currencies of most of these countries were pegged to the U.S. dollar until about the middle of the 1990s."[5]

The rising yen persuaded Japanese businesses to invest heavily in China and Southeast Asia during the late 1980s, and "the Japanese Foreign Direct Investment outflow increased sharply from $6.4 billion in 1985 to $48 billion in 1990."[6] In the first half of the 1980s Japan invested in the "four little dragons" (Hong Kong, Singapore, South Korea, and Taiwan). However, as Taiwan and South Korea democratized and wages and costs there increased, "Japan switched its overseas investment to Thailand, Malaysia, Indonesia, and the Philippines."[7]

The appreciation of the yen pushed Japanese businesses to invest in the United States, China, and Southeast Asia in the years before Tiananmen Square. Then, in the 1990s an economic crisis in Japan and the rising value of the yen put additional pressure on Japanese firms to invest overseas, particularly in China and Southeast Asia.

In 1990 Japan experienced a severe economic crisis. During the late 1980s the government, worried that the rising yen would slow the economy, injected money and credit into the economy to stimulate growth.[8] But borrowers used the money to invest in stocks and real estate, not manufacturing. Speculative investments drove the stock market and real estate prices to astronomical heights. At one point, the value of the land under the imperial palace in Tokyo was said to be worth more than all the land in the State of California. Nevertheless, when the government raised interest rates to curb inflation in 1990s, the stock market and real estate prices collapsed. Businesses and individuals went bankrupt, and the domestic economy ground to a halt, a condition that persisted for the rest of the decade.[9] The collapse of the "bubble" reduced investment opportunities in Japan and persuaded businesses to search for profitable investments overseas.

During the early 1990s the US dollar fell and the yen rose for a second time. The yen rose from 157 to the dollar in 1990 to 83 to the dollar in 1995.[10] As the yen rose, the *New York Times* reported that "Japanese corporate executives seem shell-shocked by market trends over which they have no control." The rising costs associated with the yen forced many manufacturing industries in Japan to go out of business or move abroad, where exchange rates and labor costs were lower.[11]

As a result of economic crisis and currency appreciation, Japanese investment in China soared. Japanese firms invested about US$27 billion in China during this period, not including its investments through Hong Kong intermediaries.[12] Japanese firms also invested heavily in other Southeast Asian countries—or at least they did until the region was hit in 1997 by a crisis of its own (see below), a crisis that triggered an exodus of Japanese and other foreign investors.

In Japan the exit of businesses resulted in the loss of one million manufacturing jobs between 1992 and 1996 and another 1.25 million by the year 2000.[13] Workers at Hitachi, for example, "lost their jobs in Japan . . . as employers began relocating plants to China. 'Most of our growth is now coming from China,' Denis Rourk, general manager at the Hitachi plant in Shenzhen explained."[14]

1994 Crisis and Mexico

China was not the only destination for foreign investors in the 1990s. Although US businesses invested heavily in China, they also made substantial investments in Mexico, one of the biggest trading partners with the United States. Between 1989 and 1993 "foreign" investors, primarily from the United States, invested about US$32 billion in Mexico. Many of these "foreign" investors were actually Mexicans who had sent their capital to the United States during the debt crisis of the early 1980s and then "repatriated" their capital in the early 1990s. Because they invested dollars (not pesos) in the Mexican economy, distinguishing between US and Mexican investors is difficult, and economists treat both as "foreign" investment. In this regard, they are much like the overseas Chinese community, which exited China in the 1940s and returned to invest in China during the 1980s.[15] Foreign investors primarily purchased Mexican stocks and government bonds, which paid higher interest rates than US government bonds in this period. Only about 30 percent of the money foreign investors in Mexico spent went to finance industrial development, which created jobs and contributed to economic growth.[16] As a result, foreign investment generated only modest economic growth, and this prevented Mexico from escaping a low-level equilibrium trap of the kind that had plagued China during the Maoist period.[17] "From 1990 to 1994, the years of the 'Mexican miracle,' . . . the economy grew 2.8 percent per year. However, this was still barely ahead of population growth. . . . Where was the miracle—indeed, where was the payoff to all that ... foreign investment?" Paul Krugman, a Nobel Laureate in economics, asked.[18]

Foreign investment generated anemic economic growth and created problems that triggered a massive economic crisis, which persuaded foreign investors to exit from Mexico in 1994. The main problem was that the influx of foreign capital increased the value of the peso. Between 1989 and 1993 the peso appreciated about 20 percent against the dollar. This had two unfortunate consequences. First, the appreciation of the peso made US goods cheaper. Mexican consumers responded to the "for sale" price of US goods by going on a shopping spree, which increased US imports dramatically. Second, the rising peso made Mexican exports more expensive. It became harder for Mexican businesses to sell their goods in the United States, so Mexican exports declined. As imports grew and exports fell, Mexico's trade deficit grew to US$13.5 billion in 1993 and US$18.5 billion in 1994, largely because the appreciation of the peso changed consumer behavior on both sides of the border.[19]

Normally, large trade deficits force countries to devalue their currencies. They do this to change consumer behavior. If a currency is devalued, it makes foreign imports more expensive, leading domestic consumers to buy fewer imports, and it makes domestic exports less expensive, leading foreign consumers to buy more.[20] By importing fewer foreign goods and exporting more domestic goods, a country can eliminate its trade deficit. The Mexican government, however, refused to devalue the peso in 1993 and 1994, largely for political reasons. The leaders of the ruling Institutional Revolutionary Party (PRI) decided not to devalue the peso for two reasons. First, previous devaluations had undermined the legitimacy and standing of the party and its leaders. As former President José López Portillo said of his own experience in 1982, "The president who devalues is himself devalued." Second, the party worried that a devaluation would anger US officials, who were then in the process of ratifying the North American Free Trade Agreement (NAFTA). The appreciation of the peso had *increased* the sale of US goods to Mexico. A devaluation, however, would *curb* US exports, which would then provide ammunition to critics of the trade agreement.[21] Worried about the domestic and international repercussions of a devaluation, the Mexican leadership refrained from devaluing the peso.

Then, in 1994 a series of political and economic problems compounded the problems associated with a strong peso (trade deficits). On January 1, the day that NAFTA went into effect, the Zapatistas launched a guerrilla uprising in Chiapas.[22] This unexpected development created political instability and increased the perception of risk to foreign investors, who worried that trade deficits might eventually force the government to devalue the peso, which would then reduce the value of their investments (stocks and bonds) in Mexico. The US Federal Reserve also raised interest rates on US government bonds in the spring, which made investments in Mexican government bonds even less attractive. Then on

March 23 Luis Donaldo Colosio, the PRI's candidate for president, was assassinated at a political rally in Tijuana.[23] The assassination triggered a massive exodus of foreign investors who worried about trade deficits, revolt, the return on their investments, and political instability.[24] Foreign investors withdrew US$8 billion from Mexico in the days after Colosio's murder, and capital continued to exit as a rapid pace in the weeks that followed.[25]

As foreign investors fled the country, the government faced a difficult choice. First, it could raise interest rates on government bonds. Higher interest rates would persuade foreign investors to keep buying bonds, which the government needed to run the country. However, high interest rates would also trigger a recession and slow the economy, something the ruling party was reluctant to do in an election year. Alternatively, the government could issue bonds at a lower rate of interest but index the bond to the dollar to protect foreign investors from exchange-rate losses, and then it could use its currency reserves to defend the peso and keep it from falling.[26] Foreign investors placed considerable pressure on the government to choose the latter option. The government complied with foreign investor demands and issued bonds called *tesobonos*, which were tied to the dollar, and used their foreign currency reserves to prop up the peso.[27]

Unfortunately, the government's strategy did not stop the exodus of foreign investors. Then the assassination of the PRI's general secretary in September and the narrow election of the PRI's presidential candidate in November further contributed to a deepening political crisis.[28] Meanwhile, the government faced a growing economic crisis. The trade deficit had grown, the government was fast running out of the foreign currency needed to pay for imports, and the government realized it would have to devalue the peso. The problem was that the government now owed foreign investors US$26 billion for tesobonos. If they devalued the peso, investors would sell tesobonos. In December the government revealed that it had only US$12 billion to cover its financial liabilities (US$26 billion in tesobonos).[29] When the government finally devalued the peso in December, investors sold out and exited in droves, the peso fell like a stone, and the government faced bankruptcy.[30]

To prevent the economic collapse of its important trading partner, US officials put together a US$50 billion bailout in January 1995, providing the Mexican government with the money it needed to cover its debts, purchase essential imports, and stabilize the currency.[31] As part of the bailout, US officials forced the Mexican government to raise interest rates to persuade investors to purchase bonds. Although Mexican leaders earlier rejected this option after the Colosio assassination because they feared it would trigger a recession, they adopted it in 1995, and, as predicted, the economy sank rapidly into a recession as deep as any since the Great Depression. Hundreds of businesses went bankrupt, one million workers lost their jobs, and wages fell dramatically for workers who managed to keep their jobs.[32] Moreover, the economic crisis in Mexico spooked foreign investors in other Latin American countries, and this "contagion effect" made investors stampede for the exits, a development that adversely affected Argentina, among others.[33]

After a brief hiatus, investors returned to Mexico. They returned because the peso devalued—it fell from 3.50 pesos to the dollar in 1994 to 7.00 pesos to the dollar in 1995—and this put Mexican assets on sale to foreigners at bargain-basement prices.[34] For investors with dollars, the peso devaluation represented a two-for-one sale. The problem was that foreign investment in the late 1990s was used to purchase *existing* assets, not finance the creation of new assets, which might have created jobs and promoted economic growth.[35] Thus, instead of promoting economic development, foreign investment simply transferred Mexican businesses to foreign owners, a massive *de*nationalization project. Economic growth remained anemic, barely keeping pace with population growth.[36]

Although investors left Mexico and turned to China, many returned to Mexico. They did so not only because the fire-sale prices on Mexican assets attracted them but also because Mexico had two economic advantages that China did not yet possess. First, taxes on goods produced in Mexico and shipped to the United States were lower than the taxes on Chinese goods that were exported to the United States because NAFTA virtually eliminated tariffs on Mexican goods.[37] Second, the cost of shipping goods by truck from Mexico to the United States was cheaper than transporting goods by ship from China, and it took considerably less time.[38]

However, developments in the late 1990s eliminated these advantages. First, negotiations that resulted in China's admission to the World Trade Organization and a bilateral trade agreement between China and the United States reduced tariffs on most goods imported from China, and in 2001 eliminated the tax advantage that Mexico had briefly possessed.[39] Second, the falling cost of airfreight and a reduction in the turnaround time of ordering and producing goods in China eliminated the proximity advantage that Mexico had possessed. As the director of sourcing for an American apparel firm explained, "If I do it right, I can have goods air freighted from Asia at a lower cost than trucked in from Mexico."[40]

Finally, in the late 1990s the peso once again "increased about 20 percent in value against the U.S. dollar, and about thirty percent against Asian currencies."[41] This was the final straw. As the rising peso forced up the cost of doing business in Mexico, foreign investors exited, but this time they did *not* return; instead, they headed to China. For instance, US investment in the textile and apparel industry in Mexico fell by half between 1999 and 2002, and Taiwanese investment fell by 80 percent.[42] Whereas 47 percent of the bras women in the United States purchased came from Mexico in 2000 and only 5 percent came from China, by 2004, only 6 percent came from Mexico and 67 percent came from China.[43] In the two years after 2000 "more than 500 maquiladoras closed throughout Mexico," and some economists estimated that "Mexico lost about 400,000 jobs to China."[44] "An exodus of factories the last two years, many of them to China, has led to a wave of soul-searching among business leaders and government officials here over Mexico's ability to compete with other low-cost exporters for the United States market," the *New York Times* reported in 2002. "It's like somebody shaking you and saying, 'Wake up, the environment has changed, and you have to change strategy,' said Rolando Gonzalez Baron, president of Mexico's National Maquiladora Export Industry Council."[45]

Mexico's wake-up call came too late. The economic crisis of 1994, which was precipitated by Mexico's rising currency, resulted in the exit of many foreign investors and the loss of jobs. The appreciation of the peso in the late 1990s, together with the loss of Mexico's tax and territorial advantages, then contributed to the exit of foreign investors and the migration of export-oriented industries to China. As Krugman observed, during the early 1990s, "most of the money [from foreign investors] went to Latin America, especially Mexico: but after 1994, it increasingly went to the apparently safer economies of Southeast Asia."[46]

1997 Crisis in Southeast Asia

During the early 1990s economic crisis and the appreciation of the yen persuaded Japanese businesses to invest in China and in other Southeast Asian countries—South Korea, Malaysia, Thailand, and Indonesia.[47] The 1994 peso crisis persuaded investors in Mexico and across Latin America to exit. They joined foreign investors from around the world who purchased stocks and bonds and financed export-oriented industries in Southeast Asia, providing perhaps as much as US$211 billion to South Korea, Malaysia, Thailand, and Indonesia between 1994 and 1996.[48]

The influx of money bid up stock prices and real-estate values and, most importantly, increased the value of their currencies relative to the Japanese yen and the Chinese yuan.[49] As in Mexico, appreciating currencies made imported goods cheaper, and consumers responded to lower prices on foreign goods by going on a shopping spree, which increased imports. But appreciating currencies also made exports more expensive and slowed the sale of goods to other countries, which in turn led to trade deficits. As time went on, it became increasingly difficult for Southeast Asian countries to sell their products.[50] Tight labor markets and the ability of workers to organize in democratizing states enabled workers to demand higher wages, which increased labor costs.[51] The economic crisis and recession in Japan weakened consumer demand for imported goods in this important market. Then, in 1995 the Japanese yen fell against the dollar, from 80 in 1995 to 147 in 1998.[52] This made exports from Southeast Asia even more expensive and made imports cheaper still.[53] As imports surged and exports fell, trade deficits mounted—a dangerous development, as we have seen in Mexico. In South Korea, for example, the trade deficit grew from less than US$1 billion in 1989 to more than US$20 billion in 1996.[54]

Trade deficits usually force countries to devalue their currencies. By making imports more expensive, domestic consumers should buy fewer imports; by making exports cheaper, foreign consumers should buy more. Changed consumer behavior, both domestic and foreign, should then restore trade balances. However, instead of devaluing their currencies, officials in Southeast Asia, similar to the government in Mexico, defended their currencies to keep them "strong" and, in the process, depleted their reserves of hard currencies.

As in Mexico, foreign investors in Southeast Asia were not amused. They worried that rising trade deficits and falling currency reserves would eventually force governments to devalue their currencies. If that occurred, foreign investors would see the value of their assets decline, so they sold their assets, withdrew their money, and exited the country *before* that happened. The abrupt departure of about US$105 billion in 1996 and 1997 led to the collapse of stock, bond, and real estate markets and depleted the hard-currency savings that these countries had stockpiled during the early 1990s.[55]

The crisis first erupted in Thailand in July 1997. The government announced that it would devalue the baht, which promptly sank like a rock.[56] Investors cashed out and stampeded for the exits, and the government ran out of foreign currency reserves. In August it asked the International Monetary Fund for help, asking it to provide the money it needed to pay for essential imports (food and fuel). As in Mexico—where US officials demanded that the government raise interest rates to persuade investors to return—the IMF insisted that the Thai government raise interest rates. But high interest rates triggered a massive recession (as it had in Mexico) that forced businesses into bankruptcy and drove workers from their jobs.

Moreover, the crisis quickly spread to other Southeast Asian countries. In December the IMF spent US$57 billion to bail out South Korea, about what the United States had spent to rescue Mexico.[57] The South Korean economy stalled, and unemployment rose to levels not seen since the end of the Korean War.[58] Economic crisis then engulfed Indonesia and Malaysia and then hammered Brazil and Russia.[59] The contagion spread because these countries all encountered similar problems.[60] The massive influx of foreign investment in the 1990s increased the value of currencies and led to trade deficits. When it became apparent that governments would have to devalue their currencies, foreign investors rushed for the exits. This created another set of problems that led to the bankruptcy of businesses and governments, the onset of recession, and a severe economic crisis, what one South Korean official described as "bone-carving pain."[61]

Governments in Southeast Asia devalued their currencies to restore trade balances and reassure foreign investors. The value of South Korean, Thai, and

Indonesian currencies fell between 36 and 72 percent by the end of 1998.[62] As in Mexico, devaluations put their assets on sale to foreign investors, whom some economists described as "bottom fishers."[63] Foreign investors returned to purchase assets, as they had in Mexico, but "almost none [of this investment] went into new ventures."[64] Instead, the governments used this investment to deliver domestic firms and assets into foreign hands.[65] Moreover, there was a lot less investment in Southeast Asian countries after the crisis than there was during the go-go years of the early 1990s.[66] Overall, the 1997–1998 economic crisis in Southeast Asia resulted in the exit of roughly US$100 billion.[67] Although foreign investors "returned" to Southeast Asia, many of them turned to China, and the gap between investment in China and other countries in Southeast Asia grew even wider.[68]

Chinese Initiatives, Foreign Gifts

Although economic crises pushed investors out of countries in Southeast Asia and Latin America during the 1990s, the regime in China took two steps to increase its comparative advantages and strengthen its pull on foreign investors. First, it repeatedly devalued the yuan against the dollar. The yuan fell in steps from 4 yuan to the dollar in 1989, to 6:1 in 1993—a 50 percent decline—and then to 8:1 in 1994.[69] Successive devaluations made Chinese goods, which were already inexpensive, cheaper still on foreign markets. Although economic crises forced governments in other countries to devalue their currencies, which then lowered the price of their goods on foreign markets, they did not match the aggressive Chinese price cuts. The regime, like Wal-Mart, stayed ahead of its competitors by using devaluations to slash prices. The regime could pursue this aggressive price-cutting policy because it could set the value of the yuan without interference. The regime did not permit domestic or foreign businesses to buy and sell yuan or convert yuan into dollars or other hard currencies without a government license.[70] By keeping the yuan unconvertible, the regime, not the market, set the value of the currency. Although this protected the Chinese economy from the kind of currency fluctuations that afflicted other countries in the 1990s, it also gave China an unfair advantage in its competition with other countries. The flood of foreign investment into China should have driven up the value of the yuan, making Chinese exports *more*, not *less* expensive than goods produced by China's competitors in Latin American and Southeast Asia.

The Chinese regime's manipulation of exchange rates therefore disadvantaged other countries. Governments in other countries could not manipulate exchange rates to their advantage because the United States and international monetary institutions insisted that they allow currency markets to determine exchange rates and threatened to punish them if they did not. However, US leaders made an exception for Chinese practices. Why they did so is the subject of the next chapter. Governments in developing countries could take modest steps to set favorable exchange rates, but they ran the risk of encouraging capital flight and the exit of foreign investors if they strayed from market-based rates.

During the 1990s, the regime in China took a second step to increase its comparative advantage: It suppressed the wages of domestic workers. The suppression of independent trade unions and the massacre of students and workers at Tiananmen Square in 1989 prevented workers from demanding higher wages or political reform (which might have made organizing unions that could demand higher wages easier) as their contemporaries had done in Taiwan, South Korea, and the Philippines. In economic terms, the regime used repression to put a lid on the wages of Chinese workers.

Then, during the early 1990s the regime began privatizing domestic manufacturing industries that produced goods for Chinese markets, selling off most of the large, state-owned firms and closing thousands of other, small, money-losing businesses.[71] Then in 1997 the regime announced plans to sell "more than 10,000 of China's 13,000 large and medium-sized enterprises." Although regime officials insisted that "the share-holding system has nothing to do with privatization," the transfer of state assets to private hands, typically to business managers connected to the party, resulted in large-scale privatization.[72] Wang Zhongyu, Minister of the State Economic and Trade Commission, defended this policy by saying, "We must have a system where the strong survive and the weak fail. That is the lesson of the market economy."[73]

The regime's decision to privatize state firms, merge enterprises, close unprofitable firms, and "shed the state's burden of money-losing businesses" resulted in massive job loss, what the Chinese called *xia gang*, which means to "step down from one's post." The phrase is meant to evoke memories of the Cultural Revolution, when Mao sent workers "down to the countryside" (*xia xiang*) for a period of involuntary exile.[74] In 1993 the railway system laid off 1.1 million workers, the textile industry 1.2 million workers, the coal industry 400,000 workers, and the government more than 8 million employees, and a "disproportionate number of the laid-off workers were women."[75]

During this period, officials urged factory managers to "break the three 'irons'—the iron salary, meaning inflexible wages; the iron chair, or permanent jobs for officials ... and the iron rice bowl, or lifetime jobs for ordinary laborers."[76]

As a result, the privatization and consolidation of state-run firms and the determination to cut wages and job guarantees led to massive job loss and rising unemployment. In China rising unemployment made it possible for employers to reduce wages and make low wages even lower still. In response, the number of factory disputes tripled between 1993 and 1994, and workers conducted more than 6,000 illegal strikes in 1993 and participated in more than 200 riots, many of them erupting as "protests against layoffs and unpaid wages in cash-starved state industries."[77]

Consequently, by suppressing exchange rates and workers' wages, the regime strengthened its comparative advantages. At the same time, the regime received two important economic gifts from abroad: the return of Hong Kong (and Macao) in 1997 and admission to the World Trade Organization in 2001.

In 1984 the British government agreed to return Hong Kong to China in 1997. When it did, the regime acquired the center of finance in Southeast Asia; cemented its financial ties to the overseas Chinese community, which supplied about one-half of all the foreign investment in China; and received an advanced, sophisticated financial infrastructure that could contribute to economic development in the mainland.[78] As the *New York Times* observed on the eve of the takeover, "The flow of Chinese companies into Hong Kong seeking [its] expertise, [capital], and services ... promises to turn Hong Kong into the Manhattan of the Middle Kingdom."[79]

Then, in 2001 the Bush administration finalized an agreement admitting China to the World Trade Organization and concluded a bilateral agreement with China that lowered US tariffs and restrictions on Chinese imports.[80] In one fell swoop, US officials eliminated the kind of advantages that trade agreements had previously provided to their democratic trading partners. As we have seen, this particularly disadvantaged Mexico, contributing to the migration of foreign investors from Mexico to China in the early 2000s.

The Foreign Investment Flood

During the 1990s democratization, rising wages, and currency appreciation triggered economic crises in Asia and Latin America that pushed or persuaded foreign investors to exit democratic and democratizing states. Although some foreign and domestic investors were persuaded to return, they did not return with the same financial commitment or determination to promote economic development. Meanwhile, the dictatorship in China took steps to improve its comparative advantages. The regime's determination to devalue the yuan and suppress wages by laying off millions of workers exerted a power pull on foreign investors and persuaded them to invest in Chinese dictatorship rather than developing democracies.

Tiananmen Square was the fulcrum of change. Although China had received some foreign investment during the first decade of reform, foreign investment soared in the decade after Tiananmen Square. For example, in 1984 China received US$1 billion in foreign direct investment. However, in 1997 China received US$45 billion in one year, and in 2003 it received foreign investment worth more than US$1 billion per *week*, fifty-two times what it had captured in 1984.[81] In 2004 China then surpassed the United States as the world's leading recipient of foreign direct investment.[82]

This flood of investment contributed to rapid economic growth in China, though there is some evidence that it was not particularly well used. As foreign investment climbed from US$10 billion in 1992 to US$40 billion in 1996, growth rates in China actually fell from 15 percent in 1992 to 10 percent in 1996 and to single digit rates in the late 1990s.[83] Some economists have observed that China has made relatively inefficient use of the capital that it received.[84] A senior government official admitted in 1998 that "local government officials might be fabricating numbers or investing in useless projects simply to increase the growth rate." And a *New York Times* reporter asked, "A central question is just how soundly the extra funds are being spent. How much is going to build needed roads and irrigation canals and innovative factories, as the government says . . . ? How much to build unnecessary office space and to help doomed companies that produce unsalable stockpiles, as critics claim?"[85]

However, although China may not have used foreign investment very efficiently—in part because corruption is endemic and in part because there's just too much of it to manage effectively—it has nonetheless fueled rapid growth. The global migration of foreign capital has simultaneously *promoted* economic development in China and *undermined* it in democratic and democratizing states. During the 1990s foreign investors came to prefer China to all others. This has contributed to "selective globalization."[86] Although proponents of globalization have argued that investment would promote economic development generally, the investment that has been available worldwide has not been distributed widely; instead, it has been selectively disbursed. China has become its primary destination. Selective globalization has contributed to *diverging* economic conditions, not to *converging* economic fortunes.

Foreign investors have lavished their wealth on China and neglected investments in democratic and democratizing states. In 1996, for example, global businesses invested US$42 billion in China but only US$6 billion in Mexico and US$2 billion in Russia. India, with nearly one billion people, received less than US$3 billion from foreign investors in 1996, a paltry $3 per person.[87]

One might argue that foreign investors turned to China during the last twenty years not because they *preferred* China but because they were *allergic* to economic crises in other countries where said crises put their investments at risk. However, that would not explain why foreign businesses have not made significant investments in India.

Like China, India has a huge population of poor, hard-working people who are desperate for work. In India 350 million people earn less than US$1 a day.[88] Like China, a reform-minded government in India decided in the early 1990s to adopt economic policies that were designed to attract "foreign" investors (both from other countries and from the overseas Indian community) who could finance development. The government lowered tariff barriers, opened the economy to foreign trade, and devalued the currency (the rupee) by 22 percent against the dollar to make its goods cheaper on export markets.[89] Like China, India had a huge supply of low-wage labor. Moreover, India had one "comparative advantage" that China could not easily match: 34 million Indian workers speak proficient English, which is one of India's official languages.[90]

Many US firms took advantage of low-wage, well-educated, English-speaking Indian workers to outsource US service-industry jobs—computer software, accounting, customer support, insurance claims, and call-service centers—to India, where workers conduct business and communicate in English with customers in the United States. In the early 2000s US firms providing these services employed about one million workers in India.[91]

In economic terms, India could match or surpass China's advantage in low-wage labor and low-cost goods, but it has not persuaded foreign investors to choose India over China, except in the relatively small, English-speaking service sector. Not by a long shot. Between 1991 and 2004 foreign businesses annually invested between ten and twenty-five times as much in China as they did in India.[92] The question is: why?

Businesses chose China over India not because wages are lower in China but because in China the dictatorship can *prevent* them from rising. By contrast, India is a democracy, where even low-wage workers can demand and get higher wages. Workers in India can do so because they can migrate freely, organize collectively, and change jobs in search of higher wages or better working conditions. Workers in China cannot migrate legally without permission, and if they do, they are treated as illegal aliens in their own country. Furthermore, they cannot organize independent unions, risking assault or arrest if they do, as the events in Tiananmen Square demonstrated.

Workers in India can demand and get higher wages because India is a democracy. That is exactly what has happened in the English-speaking, outsourcing service sector. Foreign and domestic businesses in this sector compete for the best workers, and workers can search for the best opportunities. As a result, wage increases have been the most common method of attracting and retaining employees. For example, "Wipro, the big outsourcing company, gave its 24,000 employees in India an average raise of 10 percent [in 2003]."[93]

Not only do workers in India have the right to migrate and organize, which has increased their ability to bargain effectively with domestic and foreign firms, they have also used their right to vote to obtain rights and benefits that are unavailable to workers in China. In India foreign investment in the service sector provided jobs, raised wages, and spurred economic growth in cities around the country. However, rural voters who were unhappy with the unequal distribution of opportunities and wealth threw out the ruling political party that had promoted service-industry development, and in 2004 they elected a new government that promised to redistribute the benefits of growth more widely.[94]

Foreign investors took the election results as a signal that the new government would allow workers to demand higher wages and levy taxes on businesses, as democratic governments often do, to finance benefits for workers generally.[95] Foreign investors began to exit, which resulted in a major decline in the stock market, after which foreign investment, which was never strong, slowed dramatically.[96]

This kind of development has also occurred in neighboring Bangladesh, where the cost of labor is "only half of what China is, and maybe less than that."[97] But in Bangladesh, as in India, workers regularly conduct strikes, or *hartals*, that push wages up and drive business managers crazy. Not surprisingly, foreign businesses prefer to invest in China, where strikes are rare, rather than in Bangladesh, where wages are lower but strikes are more common.

Given a choice, foreign investors would rather employ low-wage workers in China, where the dictatorship can keep both wages and exchange rates from rising, than hire workers in a democracy, like India or Bangladesh, where workers can raise wages and markets can drive up exchange rates. In India, too, foreign investment has driven up exchange rates, much as it did in Mexico and Southeast Asia in the 1990s.[98]

In conclusion, during the 1990s foreign investors exited democratic and democratizing states, where wages and exchange rates were rising, and turned to China, where the regime consolidated a global comparative advantage in low-wage labor and low-cost goods. This advantage resulted in a flood of foreign investment in China. It came initially from investors in the overseas Chinese community, from South Korea and Taiwan, and then from Latin America and Southeast Asia, Japan, and the United States. This unprecedented surge of foreign investment promoted rapid economic growth in China. However, it also effectively undermined economic development in these and other democratic countries, like India and Bangladesh, which were starved or deprived of the capital they needed to grow.

Chapter Eight

US Accommodation and the China Market

> "The rich world has ganged up on China. It is a mistake for the United States to try to impair the Chinese economy by pushing Beijing to raise the yuan's value."
>
> *Stephen S. Roach, chief economist, Morgan Stanley (China paid US$5 billion for a 9.9 percent stake of Morgan Stanley in 2007.)*

US officials and American businesses have provided the regime with substantial political and economic benefits in the years since Nixon traveled to China. US officials recognized the regime and facilitated its entry into the United Nations, where it secured a permanent seat on the Security Council. US officials also recognized the regime's claims to Taiwan and downgraded political and military relations with its former ally. Admission to the United Nations allowed the regime to secure loans and economic assistance worth more than US$40 billion from the World Bank and the International Monetary Fund.[1] The World Bank contributed to fund projects in China even though the regime had amassed more than US$2.4 trillion in foreign reserves by 2007.[2] US presidents from both parties promoted the regime's admission to the World Trade Organization in 2001, which gave China even greater access to US and world markets. US officials then lifted the decades-long quotas on textile imports. Analysts have predicted that the Chinese will capture more than 50 percent of the US market, thereby closing 1,300 textile plants and eliminating 600,000 jobs in the United States in coming years.[3]

US officials have also encouraged American businesses to invest in China. In 2008 the Bush administration "announced $14 billion in new business deals [US investment in China] on the eve of high-level economic talks to ease tensions between the two countries."[4] US firms have responded to this invitation by investing about US$66 billion in China, most of it in the years since Tiananmen Square, making the United States the second largest source of direct foreign investment in China after the overseas Chinese community.[5]

US firms that invested in China have become vocal supporters of the regime. During the 2008 Beijing Olympics, McDonald's ran "Cheer for China" television ads, and Pepsi "painted its familiar blue cans red [as part of] a limited edition 'Go Red for China' promotion." As one Western advertising executive argued, "reinforcing your image, aligning yourself with the China dream, and aligning yourself with China entering the world stage" was essential if global businesses wanted to succeed in the Chinese market.[6]

During the 1970s and 1980s US officials from both parties provided political and economic benefits to China because they wanted to enroll the regime in an alliance against the Soviet Union, which US policymakers regarded as the principal threat to US interests during the Cold War.[7] This strategic political justification for US accommodation with China disappeared after the collapse of communist countries in Eastern Europe in 1989 and the Soviet Union in 1992.[8] Since then US policymakers and private investors have argued that US support for the regime would promote two important economic and political developments. First, US investment in and trade with China would allow US firms to capture large and growing markets in China, which would be good for the US economy. As US Trade Representative Charlene Barchefsky explained, US support for the regime "will open the world's largest nation to our goods, our farm products and services in a way we have not seen in the modern era."[9] Second, economic development in China, assisted by the United States, would eventually, inevitably promote democracy, an argument that will be examined in the next chapter.

The prospect of capturing Chinese markets has enthralled policymakers. President Bill Clinton described his efforts to admit China to the World Trade Organization as an "opportunity that comes along once in a generation."[10] Clinton was so taken with the idea that he abandoned US efforts to link US assistance to China with improvements in the regime's treatment of human rights, a dubious diplomatic strategy he described as "delinking" or "comprehensive engagement."[11] President George W. Bush subsequently admitted China to the World Trade Organization and gave the regime most-favored-nation status without requiring it to adopt the free-market policies required of other postcommunist and democratizing states during the 1980s and 1990s.[12]

Although US policymakers and private investors have used the prospect of capturing Chinese markets to justify their political and economic support for the regime, investment in China has *not* enabled them to seize Chinese markets. Just the opposite is true. Instead, Chinese firms are capturing *US* markets: "The United States is buying $6 worth of goods from China for every $1 worth of goods it ships to China." As Matthew Crabbe, director of a market research firm observed, "The only U.S. produced items that I can think of that exist in large quantities in China are dollar bills."[13]

The annual US trade deficit with China grew from zero in 1983 to US$268 billion in 2008.[14] One observer put it this way:

> Huge container ships stream into [Seattle] every day loaded with clothes and shoes, furniture and video games, electronics and airplane parts made in Asia. On their return trip, those same ships often cross the Pacific half empty, bearing chemicals, meat, grain, and engines, and routinely stuffed with hay or scrap paper. "This is what the nation's trade imbalance looks like," said Mark Knudsen, the deputy director of the Port of Seattle. "We've got so much empty cargo space, it pays to ship over hay for Chinese animals or scrap paper to be recycled into packaging for Barbie dolls."[15]

The trade figures show that US firms have *not* captured Chinese markets. Instead, Chinese firms and US firms based in China have captured US markets. The regime has allowed foreign firms to produce goods for *foreign* markets, and by 2000 "foreign-invested firms ... were responsible for almost one-half of all China's exports."[16] Nevertheless, US and foreign firms have been unable to capture *domestic* markets in China. Why? Because the regime has adopted aggressive mercantilist policies that benefit Chinese firms and disadvantage foreign firms. These policies were designed to reserve nascent markets in China for domestic Chinese firms that are linked to the state and tied to the ruling class.

Mercantilism in China

Adam Smith, author of *The Wealth of Nations,* and his successors opposed the "mercantilist" economic policies practiced by eighteenth-century states.[17] Although classical economists have disagreed about the merits of particular policies, they agreed that mercantilist practices were generally an obstacle to economic development. They opposed mercantilism for two reasons. First, they believed that the "protectionist" policies mercantilist states adopted promoted monopoly and undermined competition. They regarded monopoly as an evil because it stifled innovation and opportunity for other businesses and because it forced consumers to pay more for goods that monopolies produced than they would if a number of firms produced goods under competitive conditions. (Consumers who, in Boston, dumped into the harbor tea belonging to the English East India Company, then one of the world's largest monopolies, shared this view.)

Second, they argued that mercantilist states adopted "bullionist" policies designed to acquire and retain bullion (gold and silver), which promoted hoarding behavior.[18] Smith argued that the hoarding of bullion was misguided because it restricted the supply of money in circulation and that this inhibited economic activity and constrained economic growth. He argued that the hoarding of bullion made countries poorer, not richer—a counter-intuitive view at the time—and said that the wealth of a nation was *not* to be found in its hoard of gold but in the economic activity of its citizens, particularly of its consumers. By spending their coin, not hoarding it, consumers could call into existence an army of competitive merchants and manufacturers who would profit from the sale of low-cost goods to consumers. This, he argued, was where the "real" wealth of a nation was to be found.[19]

Like eighteenth-century mercantilist states, the regime in China has adopted policies that promote "protection" for domestic firms and the "hoarding" of foreign exchange, which is the "bullion" of the modern era. These policies promote domestic Chinese firms, which are tied to the state and/or the ruling class, and disadvantage foreign firms, who have found it difficult to compete effectively in China's domestic markets. The economist Nicholas Lardy observed that although many foreign businesses have worked hard "to break into a potentially lucrative [Chinese market] in the 1990s, [they] have been disappointed."[20] The fact that Google, "an internet Goliath with $22 billion in revenues and some of the smartest people on the planet, is getting clobbered in China," where a regime-supported domestic firm has bested it, leading it to consider abandoning the Chinese market entirely, shows the difficulty foreign firms face when they try to capture Chinese markets.[21]

Why have US and foreign firms generally failed to capture Chinese markets? The first part of the answer is that the regime has adopted a series of "protectionist" land, labor, capital, technology, and regulatory policies that provide domestic firms with advantages that foreign firms cannot obtain.

Land

The central government and local officials have condemned and seized land in rural and urban areas and then sold or leased it to domestic firms at prices that are unavailable to foreign firms. "In rural areas, at least 65 million peasants lost farmland between 1990 and 2003, and many failed to receive favorable compensation," and in the cities, "urban citizens are forced to move elsewhere without reasonable compensation."[22] This practice has triggered widespread protests—disputes over the loss of land have been a leading cause of petitions submitted to government officials between 1996 and 2003—and in one case it led to the deaths of thirty villagers who, in 2005, were protesting against government plans to seize village lands for a wind-power plant in Dongzhou.[23]

By awarding prime land at rock-bottom prices to domestic firms, the regime has provided benefit to domestic firms that foreign firms cannot match. For example, "the government supports the [auto] industry by allowing [Chinese] automakers the choicest land, near deepwater ports. The site for the Geeley factory here in Ningho, for instance, is just 600 yards from the docks."[24]

Labor

The regime allows domestic firms to hire "illegal" migrant workers, but it prevents foreign firms from doing so. They must hire workers with *hukou,* legal permission to live in the cities where they work.[25] This is just one of a number of advantages the regime's labor policies provide to domestic firms. Domestic firms can pay their employees lower wages than foreign firms. They commonly withhold and garnish the wages of their workers to prevent them from leaving and often defer or refuse to pay their employees for work they have performed. Domestic firms treat their employees more harshly than foreign firms—demand longer hours, overtime, and fewer vacations—because illegal migrants have no legal protection or political recourse, and firms can have them dismissed, arrested, and deported from the city if they complain, organize, or go on strike. Some observers have noted that Chinese firms have relatively few managers, which reduces their costs. According to Ted Fishman, "Despite the enormous number of workers in Chinese factories, the ranks of managers are remarkably thin by Western standards. Depending on the work, you might see 15 managers for 5,000 workers, an indication of how incredibly well *self-managed* they are."

Low levels of management can be attributed in part to "self-discipline," which may be a product of the fact that "culturally, the Chinese put a high premium on not losing face, [which in manufacturing] translated into not making mistakes on the production line." But it is also a product of the fact that illegal migrant and legal resident workers have few rights. Workers are disciplined by managers, a coercive state, and other, unemployed workers. As Fishman notes, "For every worker disinclined or unable to apply himself with energy and concentration, there is always another poor Chinese worker willing to escape the farm or adrift in the so-called floating population of the unemployed, willing to take his place."[26] As Prasenjit Duara, a professor of Chinese history at the University of Chicago has argued, "The Communists made the workforce docile and organized labor to be a managed entity that would be continuously mobilized," and this has helped firms keep management costs low. What's more, management enforces a "military" discipline on workers. Supervisors are allowed to verbally and physically abuse employees and have often used managers trained in the army. The Chinese automaker Geeley "not only does not have to worry about unions, it even hires drill sergeants from the People's Liberation Army to improve discipline."[27]

Capital

The regime provides domestic firms with low-interest loans to build factories and finance their business. As Lardy says, "China gives firms access to credit from state-owned banks at interest rates that are fixed by the state and also carry other conditions that may differ from those that would obtain in a market-oriented financial system."[28] The interest on loans that state-run banks provide to domestic Chinese firms was set at 5.31 percent in 1995, and many loans have been "issued at or below the regulated rate of 5.3 percent, often with little regard for the credit histories of the borrower," according to the *New York Times.* This is considerably lower than the rates foreign corporations pay when they borrow from Western banks to finance expansion and operations.[29]

How can the regime offer loans to domestic firms at below-market rates? It can do so because it raises capital from two sources: domestic consumers and foreign investors. First, the "interest rate on savings accounts is legally limited to 2.25 percent," so households that deposit money in state-run banks earn very little on their deposits.[30] The "banking system channels these funds as investment into industrial firms," for the most part, to "the least productive portion of the industrial economy, the state-owned enterprises."[31] For many years, the regime "beggared its own citizens, keeping . . . bank deposit interest rates artificially low" to support domestic firms. . . . In essence, the government is subsidizing business investment at the expense of household income."[32]

The regime does not permit banks to use household savings to extend credit and make loans to Chinese consumers, as Western banks do, but instead "requires them to channel a significant part of their lending [to domestic firms] in support of state policy objectives."[33] During the 1990s "about two-thirds of the loans made by the entire banking sector went to state-operated enterprises. Only about 10 percent was provided to TVEs, private firms, and foreign joint ventures."[34] As we will see below, the regime's reluctance to allow the banks to lend money to Chinese consumers has important and adverse consequences for the growth of Chinese markets. The savings that Chinese households deposited created a large supply of inexpensive capital for domestic firms—a source of capital that foreign firms cannot access.

Second, the regime requires foreign investors to deposit the foreign exchange they use to finance their businesses with the regime. The regime then imposes obstacles for foreign firms to access their hard currency deposits and requires them to conduct their business in yuan, at the official exchange rate, which the government sets. The regime then lends the foreign exchange foreign firms deposit to domestic businesses and allows them to use it to purchase the foreign imports (raw materials and machinery) they need to run their businesses. Foreign direct investment "is being converted into yuan, pumping up the money supply, and allowing China's banks to lend more and more [to domestic firms]."[35] Of course, the regime allows foreign investors to reclaim their foreign exchange, but it delays and restricts their access to hard-currency accounts. The regime claims it does so to prevent rapid movements of foreign exchange, or "capital flight," from disrupting the economy, as it did during crises in Mexico and Southeast Asia, but in the meantime it can use the money during the "float." The regime uses other people's money—foreign investor's money—to provide cheap credit and foreign exchange to domestic firms at low rates. In effect, foreign investors have helped finance their Chinese competitors.

Moreover, the regime regularly allows Chinese firms to delay or avoid repayment of the loans from state-run banks. According to the *New York Times,* "Companies setting up shop in China face domestic manufactures that consistently undercut them by building factories at practically no cost, borrowing the money cheaply from state-owned Chinese banks and using various strategies to avoid repayment."[36] Credit agencies "estimate that banks in China are unable to collect timely payments of interest and principal on more than 40 percent of their loans," and, as a result, "most state banks are bankrupt by western accounting standards."[37]

Because the regime allows banks to carry nonperforming loans on their books, the real interest rates many Chinese firms pay for capital are reduced to zero. Moreover, "because real domestic interest rates were until recently consistently *negative,* credit demand far outstripped supply and bank lending was generally based on bureaucratic rationing through lending quotas rather than a careful assessment of credit worthiness. The intermarriage of politics and finance thus provided officials in both local governments and banks plenty of opportunities for patronage and corruption."[38] Consequently, Chinese firms can obtain capital that is cheaper than capital made available to foreign firms, thereby giving them an important advantage in their competition with foreign firms.[39]

By providing low- to no-interest capital to domestic firms, the regime has encouraged the creation of excess capacity in many industries: steel, autos, and, more recently, solar panels. "Overheated investment in steel is no accident," a Chinese government editorial complained. "It's just a prominent example of reckless investment and low-quality excess development in some industries and regions."[40] Li Junfeng, a secretary general of the regime's Renewable Energy Industry Association, offered this assessment of the regime's easy credit policy: "The problem is we have so many stupid enterprises." For instance, in the solar industry the bids domestic firms make to build a solar power plant in China were "so low [that] the government rejected [them because they were] likely to result in losses for whatever state-owned bank that lent the money to build it."[41]

Cheap capital, the proliferation of "stupid enterprises," and the resulting overcapacity in many Chinese industries have driven down prices and reduced the profitability of domestic Chinese firms. According to Lardy, "By 1998, the pretax profit [for Chinese firms] . . . was only 5 percent. This is well below rates of return achieved in advanced industrial economies, not to mention emerging markets, where such returns are commonly higher. The pretax rate of return on capital in U.S. manufacturing firms in the 1990s, for example, averaged 11 percent."[42]

Foreign firms have found competing with domestic Chinese firms that are supported by the regime's cheap-capital and loan-forgiveness policies difficult. Chinese firms have routinely sold their goods at prices *below* the cost of producing them, thus enabling these firms to capture markets both in China and abroad. For example, the head of China's largest solar panel maker told a reporter that Suntech sold its products at below the marginal cost in the United States in order to build its market share and admitted that the company had lost money between 2005 and 2009, though "after his admission was published, he recanted his remarks."[43]

Technology

The regime has demanded that foreign firms transfer their technology to the government and domestic firms in exchange for the opportunity to enter the market or produce goods in China. "Coerced technology transfer from foreign firms as a condition for Foreign Direct Investment and trade licenses" has provided domestic firms with technologies that would be extremely difficult or prohibitively expensive to acquire on their own.[44] This has allowed them to save money on research and development, which is a significant cost of production for the foreign firms that developed the technology.

Of course, foreign firms are aware of this. When Volkswagen began producing cars in China during the 1980s, it "used dated technology in the cars it sold [in China]," which prevented the regime from acquiring more advanced technology. Determined to change this, "the Chinese government asked multinational automakers in the 1990s which one of them would offer the most advanced technology in exchange for the right to enter the market and build a factory in Shanghai. General Motors won the contest and brought its latest robots and automotive designs to China."[45] Of course, "winning" this contest was a dubious honor. Chinese automakers, with US technology in hand, subsequently captured a growing share of the domestic market, a pattern that has been repeated in steel, chemical, pharmaceutical, computer, and a host of other industries.[46] "I have never seen the foreign business sentiment as pessimistic as it is right now [in 2010]," said James McGregor, a consultant in Beijing. "There's a sense that China is saying, 'We have your technology and your capital—and now we have control of the market.'"[47]

The regime has also allowed domestic firms to steal the technology that they cannot legally obtain through the government's coercive technology-transfer program. In 1998 the regime estimated that domestic firms stole "between $19 and $24 billion" in pirated and counterfeit goods on Chinese markets, and the National Association of Manufacturers "estimated that between 10 and 30 percent of China's GDP" came from piracy and counterfeiting.[48]

The theft of technology and "intellectual property" has been ubiquitous in China. Chinese firms published bootleg versions of the last three installments of the Harry Potter series *before* J. K. Rowling had even finished writing them. Five of every six Yamaha motorcycles sold in China are counterfeit, and almost all of the cigarettes sold as foreign brands are counterfeits produced by "licensed cigarette factories within China."[49] Designs for iPhone prototypes were stolen from Apple's factory in Szenshen and a "HiPhone" quickly appeared for sale on the streets. "If you're outsourcing to China . . . there's a bounty on every design," the manager of a consulting firm in China explained.[50]

Chinese partners of foreign firms often "divert the output [of a factory] without the knowledge of the foreign investor or will run another line [on the side] using the same designs or equipment."[51] Danone, a French food-processing company, accused its domestic partner, Wahaha, "of secretly operating a parallel company that mirrored the joint venture operations with virtually identical products and siphoned off as much as $100 million from the partnership." After a long, unsuccessful legal battle, Danone sold its operations in China to Wahaha, which had grown into a "$2 billion beverage behemoth and one of China's best-known brands," and exited the China market.[52]

Chinese firms have even faked entire companies. One Chinese firm "set up what amounted to a parallel NEC brand with links to a network of more than 50 electronics factories in mainland China, Hong Kong and Taiwan" and "attempted to hijack the entire brand. It is not a single case of a factory knocking off a branded product. Many of them had been given bogus paperwork that they say gives them the right to do it."[53] Another Chinese firm for many years manufactured and sold pirated "Microsoft" products worth more than US$2 billion.[54]

The production of counterfeit and pirated goods has had important economic consequences, and it has created real problems for defrauded consumers. Chinese drug counterfeiting led to the deaths of "19 Americans and hundreds of allergic reactions after manufacturers used an inexpensive chemical as a substitute for heparin," and the use of a "cheap counterfeit ingredient" in a cold medicine produced in China killed nearly 120 people in Panama and disabled hundreds more.[55] Consumers who have purchased counterfeit HiPhones have been severely burned when their fake phones burst into flames. The regime warned consumers that "their radiation usually exceeds the limit" and admitted that "faulty mobile phones were the No. 1 consumer complaint" in 2008.[56] The regime found that "nearly a fifth of the [Chinese made] food and consumer goods [sold in China] were . . . substandard or tainted" and posed a serious threat to consumers. Experts say that "aggressive and opportunistic entrepreneurs take advantage of the country's chronically weak enforcement of regulations, choosing to blend fake ingredients into products; to sign contracts agreeing to sell one product only to later switch the raw materials for something cheaper; and to doctor, adulterate, or even color foods to make them look fresher or more appetizing, when in fact they might be old or stale."[57]

Not content simply to steal foreign technologies, Chinese firms, likely with assistance from the regime, have launched cyber attacks on foreign firms and nongovernmental organizations, seeking to break into the e-mail accounts of Chinese human rights activists, dissidents, and their supporters—Google most recently, in 2009, but also Yahoo and Doctors without Borders in 2004.[58] Canadian researchers "discovered that digital documents had been stolen via the Internet from hundreds of government and private organizations around the world from computer systems based in China."[59]

Executives at Google have considered leaving China, where they have fallen behind Baidu, a Chinese firm that dominates the search engine market in China.[60] Baidu has captured a larger share of the market—63 percent to Google's 33 percent—in part because the regime allowed it to offer pirated music software to consumers, which gave it an important edge over Google, which could not do so.[61]

Chinese domestic firms' pervasive theft of foreign technology would not be possible without the regime's support. In fact, the regime has regularly used the army to conduct espionage against foreign civilian businesses—hacking into their computers, breaking into their hotel rooms, and compromising individuals in an effort to force their cooperation with Chinese authorities.[62] The regime has been unwilling to enforce antipiracy laws even though it has enormous police powers at its disposal, and "ineffective enforcement has allowed counterfeiting to emerge as the main source of income for many midsized towns and, sometimes, for entire counties ... [and] allowed whole sectors of the economy to become addicted to piracy."[63] The regime allows producers of black-market "*shanzhai*" phones to advertise their products on infomercials on state-run TV, in which counterfeiters ask consumers to "Buy *shanzhai* to show your love of our country."[64]

Thus, the regime's technology-acquisition policies, both legal and illegal, provide significant economic advantages to domestic firms while simultaneously inflicting considerable damage on foreign firms and domestic consumers.

Regulatory Regime

The regime subjects foreign firms to an extensive system of regulation, licensing, and red tape. For instance, it requires foreign firms to "operate in China through locally-owned firms, creating a cumbersome ownership structure that limits their flexibility," and it restricts foreign firms in some industries, such as the auto industry, from owning a majority stake in joint ventures.[65] In 2008 the regime introduced a new "anti-monopoly" law designed to prevent foreign companies from acquiring Chinese firms, and it used this to block Coca-Cola's bid to buy Huiyuan, a Chinese beverage maker, for US$2.4 billion.[66]

The regime reneged on its promise to open the government procurement process to foreign firms that bid on contracts, a commitment China made when it joined the WTO in 2001, and the regime "banned all local, municipal, and national government agencies from buying imported goods except in cases where no local substitute exists."[67] This enabled it to "steer contracts to Chinese-owned firms."[68] For instance, as part of its efforts to develop a solar industry, the regime has promoted the construction of wind and solar plants. "When the government took bids for 25 large contracts to supply wind turbines, every contract was won by one of seven domestic companies. All six multinationals that submitted bids were disqualified on various technical grounds," the *New York Times* reported. The government's rigged bidding practices enabled domestic wind-turbine producers, who were assisted by "low-interest loans from state-owned banks," to capture "almost three-quarters of the domestic market, compared with a quarter for European and American companies—the reverse of the ratio four years ago."[69] Furthermore, the regime has not only prevented government agencies from buying goods from foreign firms, it has discouraged domestic retailers from displaying or selling foreign goods in their shops.[70] The regulatory burdens imposed by the regime on foreign firms have not been imposed on domestic firms, thereby allowing them to reduce the costs associated with regulation.

The regime has provided domestic firms with numerous advantages—inexpensive land, labor, capital, technology, and less-burdensome regulations—that foreign firms cannot obtain, and it then subjected foreign firms to policies and practices—piracy and theft—that disadvantage businesses and harm consumers. The regime's intervention on behalf of domestic firms, what economic historians have described as "protectionist" mercantilism, has enabled domestic firms to wrest Chinese markets from foreign firms. In recent years, the fact that the prospect of US firms capturing the China market is a mirage has become clear. The prospect of winning Chinese markets has receded despite the massive investments and determined efforts of US and foreign firms.

Chinese Consumers: Savers Not Spenders

Government policies have restricted foreign firms' ability to access or capture Chinese markets. They have also restricted the *size* of the domestic market and inhibited its growth. Although China has millions of potential consumers, the regime's policies have persuaded them to save, even hoard, their money, rather than spend it. This means that consumer demand in China is weaker, and the market, in real terms, is smaller than many people imagine.

During the 1990s the regime shredded the social safety net for education, health care, and retirement benefits that it had long provided to urban residents, and it eliminated the three "irons"—steady wages, permanent jobs, and lifetime employment—that protected Chinese workers.[71] The regime eliminated many services that it had long provided for free or demanded fees for services that it still offered.[72] "People dare not to spend more because of the underdevelopment of the social welfare system," one Chinese official explained. "They save for good reason: at least one-fourth of the population has no health insurance at all, according to official estimates. Hundreds of millions face crippling bills for treatment of serious illnesses that are not covered by rudimentary insurance programs. Public pensions cover less than one-third of workers. An estimated 130 million migrant workers are not protected by unemployment insurance."[73]

The decline of public social services has had several important consequences. First, "the inadequacy of the social safety net forces the Chinese to engage in 'precautionary savings,' buffering themselves against disaster."[74] Chinese households now "save 25 percent of their income because the social safety net for education, health care, and retirement benefits has disappeared over the course of China's market reforms."[75] Households have to hoard their savings and put large sums of money aside to pay for weddings, health care emergencies, education for their children, and retirement, particularly if they are one-child families with daughters, which means they have to forego the assistance that male children might provide in old age.[76]

Chinese households might save less and spend more if the regime made consumer credit available so consumers could borrow money to cover big expenditures. However, the regime has long discouraged consumer lending—a policy that dates back to the 1950s—because it wanted to use workers' savings to finance industrialization and provide cheap capital to domestic firms (see above). Consumers can sometimes borrow money from informal lenders, but the interest rates or "curb rates" lenders charged are high, 20 percent and up.[77] Consumers have found great difficulty obtaining loans to finance major purchases, and 95 percent of the consumers who buy cars in China pay cash.[78]

The regime has not only refused to make credit available to Chinese households, but it has also barred foreign banks from providing financial services and credit—regardless that it agreed to do so as part of the WTO accession agreement—because that would divert money from state-run banks and the firms that depend on the cheap credit they provide.

As a result, Chinese households have become strong savers but weak consumers. "Chinese households set aside a quarter of their disposable income and, collectively, consumers and institutions put away $2.5 trillion every year. And in the past ten years, consumption has actually fallen as a share of GDP." As the economist James Surowiecki has argued, "If Americans are addicted to living beyond their means, the Chinese are too adept at living below theirs."[79]

By forcing households to hoard their savings rather than spend it, the regime has restricted the size of the market in China and inhibited its growth.[80] The Chinese market, it turns out, has not been as large or as promising as it might be. As Keynes notes, the propensity to save is strong. What's more, the regime's policies in recent years have made this proclivity stronger still. Hoarding behavior acts as a constraint on the market in China and limits its potential, particularly for foreign firms.

The Dollar Hoard

Like Chinese consumers, the regime hoards its treasure. Its monetary policy, which reduced the value of the yuan against the dollar by 70 to 80 percent between 1978 and 1995, created growing trade surpluses and generated foreign exchange earnings for domestic and foreign firms based in China.[81] However, whereas the regime encouraged foreign firms to invest in China and produce goods for export, it adopted policies that make it extremely difficult for them to withdraw their capital or make off with their foreign exchange, primarily dollars, that they earned from trade. The regime required firms to "surrender 100 percent of their foreign exchange earnings to the government" and placed "tight limitations on the rights of individuals to hold foreign currency and strict controls on the outflow of currency."[82] The regime gradually eased some of these restrictions but nonetheless maintains policies that encouraged the entry and prevented the exit of foreign exchange.[83] This approach is consistent with the mercantilist practices of states in the seventeenth and eighteenth centuries, when states took steps to increase the flow of bullion into their countries and restrict its exit.[84] Like them, the Chinese regime's mercantilist practices have enabled it to amass huge reserves of foreign exchange, most of it in dollars, which is the modern form of gold. In China, "many people refer to the dollar as *mei jin* or 'American gold.'"[85]

In 1971 the regime possessed only US$167 million in foreign exchange. At the beginning of the reform period in the late 1970s, Deng Xiaoping announced plans to increase the regime's foreign exchange reserves: "'Comrades, just imagine!' he enthused. 'One day we may have a foreign exchange reserve as big as $10 billion!' Silence fell on the audience, because that figure seemed so improbable. After a long pause, Deng went on to tell the unconvinced crowd, "Comrades, just imagine! With 10 billion American gold, how much China can do!'"[86]

The regime set out to meet Deng's goal and succeeded beyond his wildest dreams. The regime's foreign exchange reserves increased slowly during the 1980s, then "soared from $21 billion to $51.6 billion by 1994, and to $73.6 billion by the end of 1995."[87] Its hoard grew to US$150 billion in 2000, US$700 billion in 2005, and then to more than US$2.4 trillion in 2010.[88] Because the regime acquired most of its foreign exchange from trade with the United States, dollars made up almost two-thirds of its reserves. The regime used the dollars it acquired to buy US treasuries, about $1.5 trillion by 2009.[89]

Thus, the regime in China has created a vast hoard of American treasure, a practice consistent with the mercantilist agenda, which was to hoard bullion. "Of the mercantilist concepts, one of the most basic was bullionism, or as some modern French writers prefer to call it, chryshendonism," one economic historian has written. A French economist explained that chryshendonism is the "belief that all happiness lies in gold."[90]

Adam Smith and the classical economists criticized the determination to hoard bullion as misguided. They argued that by hoarding gold, people restricted the amount of capital that could be used to finance economic growth.[91] Although this was a problem, it was not *entirely* misguided. As Immanuel Wallerstein pointed out, the accumulation of bullion reduced interest rates on the capital that was available. As he put it, "Bullion cheapened money."[92] The flow of gold and silver into the United Provinces, for example, "created and sustained low interest rates, ... which attracted further flows," and low interest rates then stimulated other kinds of investment that contributed to economic growth.[93]

In the case of China, the regime's determination to hoard "American gold" rather than spend it has provided two important economic benefits. First, by hoarding dollars (and other foreign exchange), the regime can borrow against it and make capital available to domestic firms at extremely low, even negative interest rates (see above). To paraphrase Wallerstein, "Dollars cheapen capital in China." In addition, because the regime uses its dollars to purchase the US treasuries that are issued to cover budget deficits in the United States, this practice also "cheapens capital in the United States." As the *New York Times* reported, "China's demand for American bonds has helped reduce rates for other [US] borrowers."[94] Consequently, by providing low-cost capital to domestic firms, which foreign firms cannot obtain, the regime has helped domestic firms capture markets in China. In a general sense, the regime's "hoarding" behavior assists its "protectionist" policies and indirectly fuels economic growth, Adam Smith's critique of bullionism notwithstanding.

Second, the regime uses its hoard of dollars to blackmail the United States. US officials have long demanded that the regime abandon the monetary policies that devalued the yuan against the dollar and then kept it at an artificially low rate. In 2004 John Snow, the Treasury Secretary under Bush, "threatened to hold China's 'feet to the fire' if it did not relax the yuan's decade-long peg of 8.28 to the dollar and let it float so that Chinese exports would not enjoy such a huge price advantage in the American market."[95] Timothy Geithner, Snow's successor in the Obama administration, charged that the regime "manipulated" its currency to the detriment of American firms and workers.[96] US officials have argued that if the regime allowed the yuan to appreciate against the dollar, as it would if global markets, not the regime, set exchange rates, the Chinese would sell fewer goods in America, US firms would sell more goods in China, and the US trade deficit with China would shrink.

Although Chinese officials have repeatedly promised in the last decade to reform their monetary policies and allow market forces to set exchange rates, they have not done so.[97] Moreover, they have regularly threatened to sell their hoard of US treasuries whenever US complaints have become too loud or insistent, and in 2009 they cut their purchases of US securities to signal their willingness to carry out this threat.[98]

If the regime liquidated its dollar hoard and sold US treasuries, the US government would likely have to raise interest rates to sell the treasuries it needed to cover large and growing US budget deficits, now more than $1 trillion annually. Higher interest rates could deepen and prolong the recession in the United States, something that US officials are understandably reluctant to do. Therefore, they have avoided forcing the issue of exchange rates. Paul Krugman, a Nobel-prize winning economist, has argued that the Chinese threat is not as serious as US officials imagine. "Right now the world is awash in cheap money. So if China were to start selling dollars, there's no reason to think it would significantly raise US interest rates. It would probably weaken the dollar against other currencies—but that would be good, not bad, for U.S. competitiveness and employment. So if the Chinese do dump dollars, we should send them a thank you note."[99] This, as yet, is a minority view, not the official US position. Consequently, the Chinese threat to sell its hoard of dollars has allowed the regime to maintain mercantilist monetary policies that advantage firms in China and disadvantage US firms.

By hoarding dollars, the regime has resisted US demands that it abandon its mercantilist monetary and protectionist trade policies and allow the market to operate effectively. Of course, if the regime abandoned its monetary policy and allowed the dollar to devalue against the yuan, the devaluation of the dollar would reduce the value of its dollar-based hoard and slow the sale of Chinese goods in US markets, something that Chinese officials are understandably reluctant to allow.[100] In fact, they have repeatedly expressed worry about the "safety" of the dollar and asked US officials to reassure them that US budget deficits will *not* "weaken the dollar and put at risk China's vast holding of Treasury securities and other dollar-based assets. China holds an estimated $1.5 trillion in such securities, making it the U.S.'s largest creditor."[101]

However, although the regime's hoarding behavior has provided it with important economic benefits, it has also created two serious problems. First, whereas the regime had used much of its foreign exchange earnings to buy dollar-based securities, it also created a sovereign investment agency in 2002 and directed it to use some of this money, about US$200 billion, to acquire "'strategic assets'—mines, oil fields, whole companies—around the world" and, more recently, to shore up the finances of domestic Chinese banks.[102] Critics have argued that the regime *could* have used some of its hoard of foreign exchange to invest in social spending, to improve health care and education. "China has huge amounts of foreign reserves; why doesn't the government put more of it into education?" one Chinese critic asked.[103] If it did so, it would encourage domestic consumers to save less and spend more, provide domestic jobs, improve the standard of living for rural and urban workers, and *expand* the domestic market, which would benefit domestic and, perhaps, foreign firms. But instead of using foreign exchange to make social investments, the regime has used it to make investments in industry, which has been the regime's single-minded purpose since 1949. It turns out that Adam Smith and the other critics of mercantilism were partially right: the hoarding of bullion has limited the growth of the market and disadvantaged consumers in important ways.

Second, by providing huge amounts of low- to no-interest capital to domestic banks and businesses, the regime has encouraged domestic firms and state officials to squander investment and create assets that they cannot productively use or deploy. They have invested heavily in commercial real estate and businesses where overcapacity has led to low or negative rates of profit.[104] "The investment binge, like any bubble, could produce unneeded factories and underused highways and power plants, weakening the financial sector. 'If China keeps relying on cheap capital to generate growth, sooner or later it will face a major crisis," Xu Xianonian, a Chinese economist warned. "Right now, the economy is afflicted by the curse of diminishing returns." No other country invests as much of its resources in fixed assets—roads, bridges, office towers, factories, and power plants—and some economists say China has become dangerously dependent on an investment boom that cannot be sustained."[105] Heavy investment has bid up the price of assets—particularly of real estate and corporate stocks—thereby creating a "bubble" of the sort that plagued economies in Japan (1990), Mexico (1994), Southeast Asia (1997), and the United States (2008).[106]

China has channeled a growing percentage of investments into real estate, from 3 percent of all investment in 1986 to 20 percent in 2005, and this contributed to the formation of a bubble. In 2005 Shanghai built "more towers with space for living and working than there is space in all the office buildings in New York City." Shanghai has 4,000 skyscrapers, "twice as many as New York, and the regime has plans to build 1,000 more."[107] This building boom has bid up the price of land, and 1,000-square-foot apartments in Shanghai sell for $70,000, thirty-five times the average per capita income, which is "wildly out of line with the historical levels of three to four times annual income."[108] Rising real estate prices drew domestic and foreign investors into the market, and new investment has driven up prices. "The developers of many of these new buildings ... don't even want tenants," a Japanese economist observed. "They are just building the buildings to sell to some other company at a higher price."[109] Eventually, of course, the price that owners need to recoup their investment will exceed the number of people able to buy or rent the space, which could puncture the bubble, as it did in Japan in 1990 and the United States in 2008.

The emergence of bubbles in real estate, stock, and other Chinese markets has the potential to create serious economic problems, as it did, for example when a bubble in the Chinese wild tea market burst in 2009 and ruined the investors who purchased Pu'er tea. Speculators in southwest China drove up the price of Pu'er tea from US$15 to $150 a pound, and farmers doubled production "before tumbling far below its pre-boom levels. "Most of us are ruined," Fu Wei, a tea trader admitted. "A lot of people behaved like idiots."[110]

If China experienced a serious structural adjustment—for example, if exchange rates changed and the yuan appreciated against the dollar—a whole new set of problems could emerge that would not only puncture asset bubbles but also trigger a recession and dramatically slow economic growth. A dramatic change in exchange rates would reduce exports from China, and this would trigger widespread unemployment in the country's export industries and reduce consumer demand. The value of China's hoard of dollars would fall, which would increase the cost of capital and force interest rates to rise. Chinese firms that financed their businesses with cheap credit would have to pay more at a time when consumer demand was falling, which could force many of them into bankruptcy and threaten the banks with insolvency. Businesses and banks would try to sell their assets to recover loans, but the glut of assets for sale on the market would reduce their value, and prices could collapse. Under these conditions, what Paul Krugman described as a "Wile E. Coyote moment" (the moment when the cartoon character finds himself running in midair over a chasm), foreign investors might decide to slow investment in China or withdraw altogether, and this could slow economic growth.[111] "If, in the wake of a growth slowdown ... domestic savers could lose confidence and attempt to withdraw their deposits, China could, warned Lardy, face 'a financial meltdown.'"[112]

Recently there has been some evidence that investors think that some sort of structural adjustment may occur in China: investors withdrew US$240 billion from China during the last quarter of 2009.[113] One Wall Street investor, James Chanos, warned that "China's hyper stimulated economy is heading for a crash, rather than the sustained boom that most economists predict." He "suspects that Beijing is cooking its books, faking, among other things, its eye-popping growth rates of more than 8 percent," and he has staked out positions in the market that "short" China, betting that its real estate bubble will soon burst.[114] Whatever the real number, the Chinese economy has slowed: "After growing nearly 12 percent [in 2007] China's economy grew by about 9 percent in 2008, and [perhaps] as little as 5 percent [in 2009]."[115] As Chanos warned, "Bubbles are best identified by credit excesses ... and there's no bigger credit excess than in China."[116]

Although a serious structural adjustment might trigger a severe economic crisis in China, there has been little evidence to suggest that an exchange rate adjustment is likely in coming years, largely because US officials have been unwilling or unable to alter the regime's mercantilist exchange-rate policies. Still, as Krugman has argued, "If something cannot go on forever, it has to stop."[117]

US Firms and China

The regime in China has adopted mercantilist policies that have posed difficulty for foreign firms to capture markets in China. Why, then, have US and other foreign firms invested so heavily in China?

They invest in China not because they expect to capture Chinese markets but because they use China to capture markets in the United States.

US firms have invested in China because they can produce low-wage, low-cost goods in China and export them to the United States, where they sell these goods to high-wage consumers. Recall that US and foreign firms and their Chinese affiliates produce nearly 60 percent of China's exports.[118] This development has created a powerful economic constituency in the United States that supports the regime's participation in the World Trade Organization, endorses political efforts to accommodate the regime, and *opposes* US efforts to alter exchange rates. They oppose any yuan appreciation because that would make the goods that US firms produce in China more expensive and thus more difficult to sell in the United States. The regime in China has successfully resisted US pressure to abandon its mercantilist policies in part because it has enlisted the aid of important business allies in the United States.

The US firms that produce goods in China for export to the United States are a diverse group, composed of large multinationals and small start-up shops in retail and manufacturing. Wal-Mart, the world's largest retail firm, imports more than 10 percent of all the goods imported into the United States from China.[119] Another US retailer, "Li and Feng, arranges the manufacture of $6.1 billion worth of clothes for mall store chains like Kohl's, American Eagle Outfitters, and Restoration Hardware."[120]

However, whereas US multinationals have dominated the production of exports from China, small start-up firms, such as the children's pajama business run by Philip Chigos and Mary Domenico out of their two-bedroom apartment in San Francisco, also organize the production of export industries in China. "We'd love to say, 'made in the U.S.A.' and use American textiles and production," Mr. Chigos said, "but we don't want to sell our pajamas for $120." Although the couple has never been to China and admits that they are unclear about the location of Suqian City, where their clothes will be made, Ms. Domenico says that "with the technology available, we'll never touch the product."[121]

Although US firms that manufacture autos, aircraft, computers, and apparel have long produced goods for US markets in China, small-scale manufacturing firms have joined them in recent years, such as Cochran's, a tombstone company in Barre, Vermont, which imports black granite headstones from China and engraves them for customers, dead and alive, in the United States. "If we weren't doing this," Peter Burke, a Cochran manager explained, "we wouldn't be doing so good right now. Everyone's saying, 'China's bad, it's hurting us,' [but] it's not."[122] Thus, the emergence of a large and diverse coalition of pro-China businesses in the United States has created what Oded Shenkar calls a "fault line separating those U.S. industries and firms who see themselves primarily as beneficiaries of an increasing China trade and investment and those who see themselves as victims of China's ascent."[123]

US firms that produce goods in China have argued that trade with China has provided US consumers with cheap goods that enable them to improve their standard of living, what might be called the "Wal-Mart effect." They have described efforts to curb the Chinese regime's mercantilist practices, particularly its exchange-rate policies, as "protectionist" and argued that efforts to raise the value of the yuan would raise prices for US consumers. In 2005, for example, US retailers who import clothes from China went to court to block Bush administration efforts to limit imports from China, arguing that these measures "would raise the prices of clothing for American consumers."[124] They have portrayed US firms' efforts that have asked the government to stem the flood of textiles, steel, and other goods from China as backward. Stephen S. Roach, chief economist at Morgan Stanley, argued that China should not be forced to change its exchange rate policies: "The rich world has ganged up on China. It is a mistake for the United States to try to impair the Chinese economy by pushing Beijing to raise the yuan's value."[125] In 2007 China paid US$5 billion for a 9.9 percent stake in Morgan Stanley, using dollars earned from the regime's protectionist policies.[126]

Ironically, US firms who do business in China, along with their supporters like Stanley Roach, have used the language of Adam Smith to *defend* Chinese mercantilism and portray themselves and the regime as "free traders" that are battling backward "protectionists" in the United States.

The consortium of US firms that do business in China has an important advantage in its contest with US firms that do not produce goods in China. Pro-China firms have only to argue that US officials *continue* their longstanding policy of accommodation and preserve the status quo. This has placed the onus on US firms who are adversely affected by Chinese/US imports to *change* government policy, which is a much more difficult task. "It's like running in a 100-yard dash against a [US-China] team that starts on the 50-yard line," Bill Hickey, a steel industry executive complained. "My employees are being slaughtered by unfair competition," he said, a development he blamed on Chinese "currency manipulation."[127] The steel industry shut down seventeen of the twenty-nine blast furnaces in the United States in 2008, and by 2009 imported steel, increasingly from China, had captured 30 percent of the US market.[128]

By investing in China, US firms have contributed to job loss in the United States. Economists estimate that two to three million US jobs in manufacturing were lost to China between 2001 and 2004, about one million jobs were lost for each $5 billion in imports from China, which was about one-sixth of all the manufacturing jobs in the United States.[129] A study by the University of California at Berkeley identified another "14 million American jobs at risk in the near term" from the outsourcing of manufacturing and service jobs to China and India.[130] The loss of US jobs has contributed to rising unemployment, and the threat of job loss has exerted a downward pressure on wages, even in industries where jobs remain. Workers at Safeway stores in California agreed to freeze wages after Safeway "insisted that it needed to hold down costs to compete with Wal-Mart," the largest importer of cheap goods from China. "We tried to get weekly pay increases, but the company wouldn't do it," Laurie Piazza, a cashier explained. "I think Wal-Mart has a lot to do with this. They're setting the model."[131]

Of course, while US investment in China has contributed to stagnant wages in the United States, other developments have also kept US wages from rising. Since 1981, about the time that US firms started investing in China, stock prices in the United States have risen sharply. The Dow Jones Industrial Average rose from 777 in 1982 to 14,000 in 2008. As prices rose, US firms reorganized their businesses to increase profits and payouts, as dividends, to shareholders who demanded that returns keep pace with rising stock prices. Firms merged with other businesses to increase efficiency and shed workers, introduced new technology to increase productivity, and relocated or outsourced jobs to other countries where wages were cheaper, particularly to China in the 1990s and 2000s, as we have seen. As a result, they substantially increased productivity and profits: "From 1974 to 1995, productivity grew at about 1.4 percent a year. Productivity growth in the United States accelerated to about 2.5 percent a year from 1995 to 2000. Since then, productivity has grown a bit over 3 percent a year, and averaged 3.5 percent between 2002 and 2005."[132] Growing productivity then helped US firms increase their profits: annual corporate profits quadrupled, from less than $200 billion to $736 billion between 1983 and 1996.[133]

Under these conditions, it might be possible to share productivity and profitability gains with workers and pay them *higher* wages. However, US firms were increasingly reluctant to share these gains with workers. Instead, they have allocated a greater share of profits to managers and shareholders, paying huge salaries, bonuses, and stock options to managers and dividends and interest to shareholders. Workers have found it difficult to maintain or raise wages in an environment in which job loss from mergers, new technologies, or outsourcing and de-unionization has been an ongoing feature of corporate reorganization in the United States. Wages have declined for the majority of American workers, despite working harder, longer, and more efficiently.[134] Median household income has declined, and workers' share of the Gross Domestic Product fell 2.5 percent between 2000 and 2005.[135] "You have the lower-half of the wage distribution in the United States that has not experienced income gains for a long time now," Barry Bosworth, a Brookings Institution economist, observed.[136]

Although the wages of US workers have stagnated, US firms that invest in China have argued that the import of low-cost goods from China has enabled American workers to "Live Better," as Wal-Mart's slogan says. But the gains to US workers from shopping for discounts at Wal-Mart have been small. As the economist Paul A. Samuelson explained, "Being able to purchase groceries 20 percent cheaper at Wal-Mart does not necessarily make up for the wage losses."[137] Moreover, these modest savings have been offset, for most US workers, by the rising cost of health care, energy, housing, and education.[138] By 1998 for the first time since the Great Depression, the savings rate of US workers had fallen to zero, and "almost a fifth of American adults have a net worth of zero or less."[139] Moreover, workers could no longer count on the transfer of wealth from families who had acquired savings during the 1950s and 1960s: the value of the median inheritance, which consists of the wealth transferred from one generation of workers to the next, fell from $42,167 in 1965 to $29,221 in 2005.[140] By reorganizing business and suppressing wages, US firms increased profits. But this created two problems: it undermined the living standards of US workers, and it restricted the growth of the US market, which undermined businesses—both in China and in the United States—that produced goods for US consumers. The fact that US workers were tapped out placed the growth of the US economy in jeopardy.

During the 2000s government officials and private banks advanced a solution to these problems: give US workers *credit* in lieu of a raise. As the former IMF economist, Raghuram Rajan, explained, "With the purchasing power of many middle-class households lagging behind the cost of living, there was an urgent demand for credit. The financial industry, with encouragement from the government [which kept interest rates low and capital inexpensive], responded by supplying home-equity loans, subprime mortgages, and auto loans."[141]

With cheap, borrowed money in their pockets, US consumers bought new homes. This increased the demand for houses and bid up real estate prices. Eventually, the supply of affordable houses exceeded the demand, the amount of debt that consumers could carry reached its limit—the average household owes $84,911 on their mortgage, $14,414 on auto and school loans, $10,062 on home equity loans, and $8,565 on their credit cards—and their inability to raise their wages limited their ability to obtain credit or repay debt.[142] These developments contributed to consumer bankruptcy, the collapse of real estate prices, the wholesale destruction of financial institutions that had extended credit, and a massive

$1 trillion-plus government bailout. The expansion of US industry in China was not wholly, or even primarily responsible for these developments; however, US investment in China did contribute to the suppression of wages in the United States, which was a key development in the crisis of the late 2000s. Any account of the crisis would have to include a discussion of the role played by Chinese mercantilism as well as US officials and private firms that have assisted it.

Chapter Nine

Democracy Deterred

> "So you dirt-poor trash think you can oppose the city government? You don't have a chance in hell. You're crazy! Your heads are filled with sand!"
>
> *Ji Shengrong, a government official in Sanchawan*

US policymakers and many China scholars have argued that the regime in China will eventually, inevitably democratize. It will do so, they argue, because dictatorship is incompatible with capitalist markets, because political and economic engagement with the wider world will promote the spread of democratic values in China, or because an emerging middle class will demand political change. "China is in the middle of a historic transition to capitalism and ultimately democracy," Jonathan Adelman argued in 2001. The political scientist Larry Diamond asserted that "sooner or later, economic development will generate growing pressures for China to make a definitive regime change to democracy." Zheng Youngxian argued that "capitalism is generating a Chinese bourgeoisie," which he described as "a class with teeth," one that would eventually demand its share of political power.[1] "While democratic reform may not in *all* cases be an inevitable outcome of economic reform," Doug Guthrie argued in 2006, "it is, at this point, an *inevitability* in China."[2] He went on to argue that China was in the midst of a "Quiet Revolution."[3] In 1992 Steven Levine wrote, "China is a weak, if not yet disintegrating state."[4] Merle Goldman argued in 1995 that "China could no longer be described as a strictly authoritarian or totalitarian country" and suggested it might be described as "fragmented authoritarianism" or, after Harry Harding, "consultative authoritarianism."[5]

Still, describing the twenty years since Tiananmen Square or the thirty years since Deng initiated economic reforms as a time when China made a "transition" to democracy would be difficult. Too many years have passed without significant political change. As Kellee Tsai observed, "China has not undergone a democratic transition, and its capitalists show no evidence of mobilizing to demand democracy." Bruce Dickson agrees: "The argument that the Chinese Communist Party can ultimately be the agent for gradual and peaceful change in China . . . that democratization in China will follow the transformation path, is not based on any tangible evidence."[6] In addition, Edward Friedman, a China scholar at the University of Wisconsin, has argued that many people in the West have been clinging to the misguided notion that China's economic development would quickly lead to political liberalization: "It is clear that what matters most to the CCP is the survival of the regime and their monopoly on power."[7]

Instead of moving toward democracy, the regime has moved away from it. In 2004 Hu Jintao said that multiparty democracy was a "blind alley for China."[8] Party officials at different times have rejected the idea that China might someday adopt a multiparty political system, a separation of powers, a bicameral legislature, an independent judiciary, a Western-style legal system, or the "U.S. human rights concept."[9]

So why hasn't China democratized, as many observers predicted?

The regime has been able to deter democracy for two reasons. First, it expanded and consolidated the ruling class. This enabled the regime to acquire new sources of wealth and power, which has made it stronger today than it was in 1989 or 1978. Second, it has effectively divided the working class and deployed a coercive apparatus that has made it extremely difficult for workers in China to challenge the regime's authority.

Unite and Prosper

In 1978 the ruling class consisted almost exclusively of communist party members and government bureaucrats. The party, the state, and the ruling class were virtually synonymous. During the reform period that followed, the regime mobilized this class to promote economic development, but it also encouraged the participation of "entrepreneurs," drawn from different social groups, and eventually allowed them to join the ruling class, a development that expanded, enriched, and strengthened the regime. However, this process, which might be described as a ruling-class strategy to "unite and prosper," was a difficult one, largely because bureaucrats and entrepreneurs might have obstructed or derailed the process of economic development.

Class Mobilization and Corruption

When Deng introduced the reforms, he needed to mobilize the bureaucracy and persuade it to enforce the labor-migration and population-control policies that were essential to the success of the project (provide a cheap supply of labor for industry and, by curbing population growth, allow the country to escape the low-level equilibrium trap) as well as to promote state-run and privately owned firms' capital accumulation. The problem for the regime was that the bureaucracy might *resist* its directives, as they had under Mao in the early 1960s. They might do so because taking action might expose them to risk, a real concern for bureaucrats subjected to the harrowing campaigns of the Cultural Revolution. They might also resist because they had little incentive to comply with the new directives—the regime essentially asked them to increase their workload without increasing their salaries—and they might resist because the regime's new policies were unpopular, and working people under their authority might direct their anger at the bureaucrats responsible for enforcing the new policies. To overcome the bureaucracy's resistance to the reform project, Deng offered bureaucrats an incentive. He gave them the opportunity to use their offices to secure not just *collective* wealth, which they had long enjoyed, but also, for the first time, the chance to obtain *individual* wealth. By allowing bureaucrats to engage in corrupt practices—kickbacks, skimming, bribes, embezzlement, what are collectively known as *guanxi* in China—the regime provided bureaucrats with the incentives they needed to perform their duties, enforce new and difficult policies, and promote the reforms.

Of course, the problem in China, as in most developing countries, was that the bureaucrats might use the power and privilege associated with their offices—their license to steal, as it were—to divert government resources into their own pockets and impose excessive demands or "taxes" on businesses. The first could raise the "overhead" costs of government administration and make government spending *less* effective. The second could impose burdensome taxes on businesses that might deprive them of the profits they needed to finance expansion and promote economic growth. If corrupt bureaucrats imposed taxes that were too high, they might throttle economic development in its infancy. "At the enterprise level, appropriation, embezzlement, or negligence by officials can deprive a firm of its life support in the worst case and create financial chaos."[10] This is what has occurred in many countries across Africa, Asia, the Middle East, Latin America, and the former Soviet Union.

Governments in some countries have dealt with the problems associated with corrupt and stifling bureaucracies by privatizing state assets, transferring them to private entrepreneurs, and severing the connection between state bureaucracy and private enterprise, as occurred in Latin America after the debt crisis of the early 1980s and in Eastern Europe and the former Soviet Union after 1989. Although this strategy eliminated, at a stroke, the bureaucracy, it created another set of problems. The new entrepreneurs, many of them former bureaucrats who claimed an inside track on the privatization process, essentially looted the assets of privatized firms, laid off workers, and invested their assets abroad. The flight of capital deprived firms of the money they needed to grow and, importantly, reduced the state's control over economic development.[11] Many democratic governments watched helplessly as private entrepreneurs stripped businesses of assets and fled abroad with the loot. "Communist ruling elites in the former Soviet Union were able to use their institutional privileges [to] exploit the loopholes in property rights laws to steal public assets in the privatization process."[12]

Although states wanted to rid the economy of a burdensome bureaucracy, they still had an interest in providing employment, promoting economic development, collecting taxes from this activity, and using the revenues to provide social services.[13] In Russia Vladimir Putin "solved" this problem by attacking and jailing prominent "oligarchs"—the former bureaucrats, now entrepreneurs, who had enriched themselves when Boris Yeltsin privatized state assets. Putin then reclaimed the government's stake in private business by insisting on a "partnership" with the oligarchs. The partial "nationalization" of Russian businesses in the 2000s reversed the wholesale privatization of government assets in the 1990s, a development that won Putin "broad approval."[14]

Some of these problems have been evident in China, but corruption in China has not had the same kind of crippling effect on economic development that it had in Russia and in many other countries. The regime in China has been able to minimize the costs of bureaucratic corruption because it took a more methodical approach to privatization and because it found a way to use different groups—bureaucrats and entrepreneurs—to restrain each other's behavior.

In China the regime did not abruptly privatize state assets, as governments did in many other countries. Instead, it privatized state assets slowly during the reform period. It moved fairly quickly to privatize land for rural workers, though it has never fully ceded control of land to private users (essentially, the regime provides long-term leases to rural workers). It privatized state-run businesses much more slowly, and the regime allowed businesses to fail only in the 1990s, when private firms could replace them. The regime privatized cautiously and slowly because it wanted to avoid the problems associated with the abrupt transfer of assets and because it wanted to retain control over the "private" firms that emerged.

When he undertook reform, Deng faced two problems: first, how to give bureaucrats the opportunity to profit from reform without making administrative, overhead costs (embezzlement) prohibitive and without throttling emerging businesses with excessive taxes (bribery and kickbacks); and second, how to persuade entrepreneurs in state-run and, increasingly, private businesses to reinvest profits and remain faithful to the regime's economic development objectives rather than using their authority to loot companies and abscond abroad with the money.[15] The regime solved both problems by insisting on a "partnership" between "bureaucrats" and "entrepreneurs," an alliance in which each partner would *encourage* and *discipline* the other.[16]

To some extent, the regime returned to the economic practices of the 1950s, when it allowed the domestic bourgeoisie to manage "nationalized" businesses (firms that the regime had seized from the bourgeoisie), though the regime had insisted that the bourgeoisie operate under the supervision of party bureaucrats. The difference in the 1980s and 1990s was that when the regime renewed this practice, it did so with "privatized" businesses (state-run firms that the regime transferred slowly to private hands). In addition, it did so with personnel drawn from different social backgrounds. The "new" entrepreneurs consisted of three groups: first, bureaucrats (cadre with good and bad class backgrounds) who moved "over," much like the bureaucrats who became entrepreneurs in Russia; second, survivors of the "old bourgeoisie" (workers with bourgeois-identified backgrounds) who reasserted themselves; and third, members of the rural and urban working class who seized the chance to get rich. These new groups expanded the ruling class and diversified its social character.

Why did the regime embed party bureaucrats in state-run and private firms? Because the regime wanted to give bureaucrats a material interest in the economic *success* of the business. The regime reasoned that if bureaucrats had a stake in the *profits* of a business, they would resist the temptation to impose excessive and burdensome taxes (bribes and kickbacks) on firms that might undermine its ability to accumulate capital.[17] As Tsai has argued, "Cadres in many rural localities had a vested interest in allowing profitable businesses to operate and contribute to local revenues."[18]

How would this partnership assist entrepreneurs? By taking on, as partners, bureaucrats who worked for the government, entrepreneurs could obtain access to government resources, to the land, labor, capital, and technology that the regime made available to entrepreneurs as part of its privatization/economic development agenda: "Corruption ... enabled less-privileged groups to gain access to the economy and government services."[19] Taking on bureaucrats as partners and shareholders was a small price for entrepreneurs to pay for access to cheap capital and other government resources. "Putting up with annoying cadres is just part of what it takes to be an individual entrepreneur," one businessman explained. "In other words," Tsai has argued, "private entrepreneurs benefit from bureaucratic protection and favors, while cadre benefit materially from providing such services ... [and] it is clear that strong ties often exist between cadres and entrepreneurs."[20] Of course, having accepted party bureaucrats as partners and shareholders, entrepreneurs would then have to be mindful of the state's larger economic interests, which were to promote the reinvestment of profits and the expansion of industry. As a result, "China has avoided the state capture ... that plagued ... Russia's transition to the market."[21]

By insisting on a partnership between corrupt bureaucrats and profiteering entrepreneurs, the regime effectively *encouraged* (provided incentives for the enthusiastic participation of each group) and *restrained* the behavior of each. Bureaucrats could tax businesses, but not too much. As one bureaucrat said of his relations with a private, foreign entrepreneur, "If we charge him too much, our country might lose the precious foreign capital to a neighboring country." According to one businessman in China, "A constant drizzle" of bribes to bureaucrats was a more effective way of doing business than a "big shower."[22] Entrepreneurs could devote themselves to profit making, provided they reinvested profits for the common good. "Local graft was permitted [by the regime] so long as it was pro-growth. Elites from business and government joined together in mutually beneficial ways and in return for these opportunities gratefully gave their loyalties to [the regime]," Barry Naughton has argued.[23] Over time, the two social groups—bureaucrats and entrepreneurs—have forged close political and economic ties. These "bureau-preneurs" have effectively created an expanded ruling class with access to new sources of both wealth and power.[24] "Corruption is the glue that keeps the party stuck together," Minxin Pei concluded.[25]

The regime made it possible for bureaucrats to *prosper* in the new, reformed economy. "In limited ways, some forms of corruption may be helping sustain the reform strategy of continuing party dominance in the midst of economic change," one scholar has argued.[26] If it had not done so, the bureaucrats might have taxed businesses more heavily and obstructed economic growth or failed to enforce the policies that were essential to the success of reform. Essentially, the regime gave bureaucrats the opportunity to profit from *privilege*. "Corruption helped to act as a solvent for the uncompromising issue of ideology and interests by turning *potential* opponents of reform [bureaucrats] into participants."[27]

At the same time, the regime made it possible for entrepreneurs to profit from privatization, but it kept them tied to the regime's political and economic objectives. Initially, the regime gave entrepreneurs the opportunity to advance economically, to seek upward mobility based on their *merit*. Eventually, however, it opened the door to *political* opportunity, and in 2001 it allowed "entrepreneurs" to join the party and ascend its ranks.

The regime's strategy knit together two factions of the ruling class that had been at odds during the Cultural Revolution: party cadre who defended power based on "privilege" (Deng), and those who supported power based on "merit" (Mao). By allowing bureaucrats and entrepreneurs to acquire individual wealth derived from both "privilege" (corruption) and "merit" (profit), the regime *united* the ruling class, assuaged its two contentious factions, and made the regime a larger, richer, and more formidable social, economic, and political force.

Of course, this strategy has incurred important economic, social, and political costs. The regime reported in 2009 that bureaucrats misused or embezzled about US$35 billion during each of the previous five years, and one Chinese scholar estimated that 80 percent of government officials were corrupt.[28] Economists estimated that entrepreneurs took US$65–85 billion out of China between 1978 and 1995.[29] Illegal capital flight has ranged from US$10 billion to as much as US$40 billion annually during the 2000s, according to some economists, which suggests that the looting associated with privatization in Russia has also occurred in China.[30] Although these costs are substantial and burdensome, they have not been so high as to significantly slow economic growth in China, according to most economists.[31]

Corruption has also imposed indirect costs on government agencies and state-run businesses. In 1998 bureaucrats and entrepreneurs spent about Y150 billion on feasting and gift giving in order to develop, consolidate, or advance partnerships between bureaucrats and entrepreneurs, a sum equal to "more than half of [China's] annual budget for education." The dining and wining expenses charged to government agencies and businesses often included "karaoke sing-alongs, ballroom dancing (and the hiring of female dance partners), and hors d'oeuvre." These activities were not only expensive but extremely time consuming. One researcher estimated that bureaucrats and entrepreneurs spent one hundred hours a month, or two-and-a-half weeks per month (on an eight-hour-day schedule) on feasting and gift giving, and "the efficiency loss to production and public administration may well be in the hundreds of billions of yuan, if measurable at all."[32] In this sense, corruption has undermined public agencies' efficiency and private businesses' productivity.

Corruption may also have undermined the effectiveness of the military. According to the *New York Times,* in 1998 Jiang Zemin ordered the army to "relinquish its sprawling multi-billion dollar commercial empire," which generated about US$602 million in profits and taxes annually, "saying it was the only way to combat an epidemic of smuggling, which the army dominates."[33] Zemin warned, "The army must no longer be in business. Otherwise, this tool of the proletarian dictatorship will collapse."[34]

Corrupt practices also impose costs on foreign firms doing business in China. They are expected not only to develop quanxi networks and partner with corrupt officials, who impose informal taxes on business activity, but also to engage in corrupt practices in their own countries, where such behavior is often illegal. For example, US firms that want to sell equipment in China are expected to provide prospective Chinese buyers with free trips to the United States, where they spend one day visiting the supplier's factory and several days in New York and Las Vegas, where they are given the opportunity to gamble and be entertained. "A U.S. equipment supplier [reported] that a free trip to visit the supplier abroad has been part of the deals he negotiated with his Chinese customers. It has been built into the system as a routine, and his company has had a long-term contract with a travel agent who arranged all the trips for his Chinese customers."[35]

More recently, Chinese bureaucrats and entrepreneurs have asked their domestic and/or foreign partners to pay for their children's tuition and education in the United States as the price of doing business.[36] "Money, in the form of 'tuition donations,' has become the standard method by which, and often the only way, parents can get their children into schools of their choice."[37] Chinese bureaucrats and entrepreneurs also use "overseas educational expenses . . . to launder illegally acquired incomes," a kind of capital flight in which children carry their parent's wealth overseas.[38] How many of the 64,000 Chinese students who studied at US universities in 2002–2003 were financed by corrupt bureaucrats, entrepreneurs, and foreign firms? This is difficult to say. Whatever the number, US universities participate, knowingly or unknowingly, in the corrupt practices of the ruling class in China.

Corruption has also incurred significant political costs. People in China who have paid taxes to corrupt officials, who tried to compete in business with entrepreneurs who have partnered with bureaucrats, who have been denied access to public services or education, and who have witnessed the upward mobility of people based on privilege, not merit, have come to resent corrupt bureaucrats and profiteering entrepreneurs, particularly because their activities violate the principle of "equality" that the "communist" regime has long promoted. As a result, corruption has undermined the regime's political legitimacy.

Of course, the regime has denounced corruption and campaigned against it. Although some scholars like Guthrie have argued that guanxi has declined in importance in recent years, most observers agree with Yan Sen, who has argued that "while the incentives and opportunities [for corruption] have multiplied over time, the disincentives against it have progressively weakened over the course of economic liberalization and administrative decentralization."[39] Polls showing that foreign businesses regard China as *more* corrupt in the 2000s than it was in the 1990s support the view that corruption has gotten worse.[40] A World Bank report said, "that the countries worldwide that rate *below* China [as being worse than China] in controlling corruption dropped from 58.7 in 1996 to 42.3 in 2000," meaning that corruption in China got worse, not better.[41]

The regime disciplines, jails, and even executes its own officials for corruption, though the percentage of officials who are charged with crimes is very small compared to the number who are reprimanded.[42] Of the seventy-five million reports of corruption citizens have filed (an astonishing number), the party disciplined only 1 percent, 789,300, and prosecuted only 37,492 in criminal courts.[43] The regime also rotates cadre to prevent them from becoming too entrenched in office, but "the unintended effect . . . is to turn these officials, literally, into roving bandits . . . [who are motivated] to cash in their political investments quickly."[44]

Nevertheless, although the regime has disciplined bureaucrats who violate corrupt "norms" and has worked to keep their avarice in check by embedding them in profit-making firms, that corruption is not an aberration but a key feature of its development policy is clear.

Could the regime eventually "professionalize" the bureaucracy along Weberian lines so that it derived its income from salary, not graft, and eliminate the economic "privileges" associated with office? Perhaps. But that would risk antagonizing the bureaucrats who have been responsible for maintaining and enforcing "order." It is doubtful that the regime would take steps to undermine the support of the bureaucracy (as Mao did during the Cultural Revolution) or risk reigniting the conflict between factions of the ruling class: the party of privilege (bureaucrats) and the party of merit (entrepreneurs).

A New Middle Class?

Many scholars have argued that the reforms created a new middle class, which consists of between seventy-five and one hundred million members.[45] "China's middle class, non-existent 30 years ago, is large and growing quickly," John Frisbie and Michael Overmyer have argued.[46] Scholars regard this as a significant development for two reasons: First, "this affluent and highly educated social class [has] power and interests [that are] separate and distinct from those of the state."[47] Second, "this new class could serve as the social base for China's democracy movement."[48]

The idea that the new middle class will become a force for political change in China is based on the theoretical expectations of Seymour Martin Lipset and other political scientists who have argued that economic development and the growth of a middle class in other settings contributed to democratization.[49] Based on these theories, Shaohua Hu predicted that China would democratize by 2011, and Carl Rowen predicted it would become democratic by 2015.[50]

They are mistaken. The class that has emerged in China during the reform period is not a new *middle* class but an expanded *ruling* class, and it is a force for *continuity* (dictatorship) not *change* (democracy).

Until the reforms in 1978, the ruling class was virtually synonymous with the communist party, which had grown from three million members in 1948 to thirty-seven million members in 1979, a more than a tenfold increase.[51] Membership in the party nearly doubled during the reform period, from thirty-seven million in 1978 to seventy-three million by 2002, which is more people than live in California (thirty-seven million), Texas (twenty-four million), and Illinois (twelve million) combined.[52] During this period the percentage of party members identified as "workers and peasants" declined, from 63 percent in 1994 to only 45 percent in 2002, and the percentage of entrepreneurs or "red capitalists" increased from 13 percent in 1993 to nearly 30 percent in 2003.[53] The party also increased the number of college-educated cadre. In 2001 "one-third of college students nationwide had applied for party membership."[54]

Of course, the party probably overstates the number of "workers and peasants" in the party. Many of the party members who became entrepreneurs retained their identity as members of other classes (as "workers and peasants") that had been assigned to their parents in the 1940s and 1950s, and their offspring then inherited these class identities as part of the regime's racialized view of class. As a result, many people in the party are listed on party rolls as workers or peasants even though they have not been workers or peasants for decades.

Since the regime introduced the reforms, party members have partnered with entrepreneurs who had not been party members or members of the ruling class in state-run and private firms. Some of these entrepreneurs from different social classes (old bourgeois-identified workers and new rural and urban workers) joined the party after Jiang Zemin lifted the ban on entrepreneurs in 2001. As Jiang explained, "like a big furnace, the party can melt out all sorts of nonproletarian ideas and unify its whole thinking on Marxist theory and the party's program and line. Today, in admitting the outstanding elements of other strata [entrepreneurs with different social origins] into the party ... we will surely be able to preserve the ideology of the party members [and the ruling class]."[55]

Taken together, these two groups—the 73 million party members and a roughly equal number of nonparty entrepreneurs—combined to create a ruling class consisting of about 120 to 140 million people in the 2000s. There is some overlap between these two groups because about one-third of party members are "entrepreneurs." This is the same number of people that scholars describe as belonging to the "new middle class." To this number one might also add a small but important group: the wealthy overseas Chinese entrepreneurs who have taken up residence in China and participate as informal or de facto members of the ruling class even though they are not Chinese citizens.[56] (This is not uncommon. In other countries, wealthy foreigners—people like Rupert Murdoch in the United States—often participate as members of the ruling class.)

This new, expanded ruling class, numbering about 120 to 140 million people, accounts for roughly 10 percent of the population and controls about 45 percent of China's wealth.[57] These figures are consistent with the demographic size and economic wealth that ruling classes in many other countries claim. It is comparable to Spain, Japan, and South Korea—though not the United States, where the top 10 percent owns 69.8 percent of the wealth.[58]

Consequently, the so-called "new middle class" is, in fact, an expanded *ruling* class. Although some scholars still describe it as a "middle class," they argue that it is *not* a force for social change and democracy. For example, Dorothy J. Solinger, who calls it a "middle class," has argued that "Politically, most indications are that the middle class and even more so the wealthy are wedded to, and benefit from the current status quo [dictatorship]."[59] David S. Goodman has argued that "the new middle class, far from being alienated from the party-state or seeking their own political voice, appears to be operating in close proximity ... [and] depend heavily on the party-state."[60] Maurice Meisner agrees: "This state-created bourgeoisie ... was largely drawn from the ranks of the Communist Party and was wholly dependent on the party."[61] As a result, "China's capitalists are pragmatic and creative, but they are not budding democrats ... should democratization occur in China, it will not be led by a disgruntled hoard of private entrepreneurs."[62] David Brooks described the ruling class this way: "The Communist Party is basically a gigantic Skull and Bones. It is one of the social networks its members use to hold wealth together.... Once it seemed that economic growth would create an independent middle class, but now it is clear that the different parts of society have been assimilated into the state/enterprise establishment."[63]

This development has not been unique to China. Owen Lattimore has argued that "those who rule ... hang onto the best of what is left of the old order, and at the same time take the best of what is offered by the new, [leading in time] to considerable diversification."[64] As Wallerstein said, "We are back to the practice of an emerging capitalist class recruited from varying social backgrounds."[65] In China the "selectorate," the term Susan Shirk used to describe the leadership of the regime—which is "composed of the three major elements: the roughly 300 members of the Central Committee, several dozen Communist Party elders, and the top officers of the PLA"—has fused the "best" of the old order (communist party bureaucrats) together with "the best of what is offered by the new order" (entrepreneurs drawn from ruling- and working-class backgrounds). By joining these two groups, the regime has created an expanded ruling class that is closely tied to the selectorate and is a force for its defense.[66]

Thus, the regime has grown stronger in the years since Tiananmen Square because it has expanded and consolidated a prosperous ruling class. It has also grown stronger because it has successfully divided and suppressed the working class.

Divide and Conquer

During the Maoist period, the regime eliminated landlords, bourgeois entrepreneurs, and rural proprietors as social classes and created deep divisions between rural and urban workers. In the thirty years since Deng introduced reforms, the regime has worked to divide and subdivide the working class. For instance, it has used the hukou system to divide rural migrants from urban workers in the cities. In 2004 the government reported that migrant workers in the cities were owed US$43 billion in unpaid wages and "some have remained unpaid for up to 10 years."[67] One Chinese writer described migrant workers as a new class, characterized by the "three have nots: people with no land, no jobs, and no access to national income insurance."[68]

The regime's one-child policy intensified gender divisions in the household, largely to the detriment of women and girls, and the gap between male and female wages has grown: "The female disadvantage in income increased from a 15 percent deficit compared with men in the mid-1980s, to a 20-percent deficit by 1993, and to a 25-percent deficit in 2000."[69] This gap increases with age. In

1988, women over fifty-five "earned 72 percent as much as men of the same age, whereas by 1995, women earned only 42 percent as much as men."[70]

The regime's agricultural policies briefly narrowed the gap between rural and urban households in the 1980s, from 2.30 to 1 in 1980 to 1.7 to 1 in 1984, but it started growing again in 1984, reached 1980 levels in 1994, and grew to 3.21 to 1 by 1994.[71]

During the 1990s the regime's slow-motion privatization of public land and state-run businesses resulted in the loss of land, health care, and jobs for tens of millions of rural and urban workers. Government officials' privatization of public land in rural areas resulted in the loss of land for between seventy and one hundred million farmers.[72] As a result, "China has more unemployed people in rural areas than the entire American workforce, and many are migrating to the cities in search of work, providing a check on wages."[73]

The regime also "shifted public health resources away from rural areas toward the cities," a development that "opened a yawning gap between health care in the cities and rural areas where the former system of free clinics has disintegrated."[74] In 1970 85 percent of rural workers had health insurance, but by 2003 "less than 20 percent of them were insured."[75]

Further, the privatization of state-run businesses, which began in earnest in 1997, resulted in massive layoffs.[76] The regime's National Bureau of Statistics reported that "nearly 31 percent of those employed in the state sector [in 1997] were cut (from 100.4 million to 76.4 million)" during the next four years.[77] Naughton argued that "half of public enterprise workers were let go."[78] Solinger has said that "internal reports and scholarly papers have put the tally [of laid-off workers] as high as 60 million."[79] Despite the rapid rate of economic growth, the rate of unemployment rose to between 10 and 16 percent during the 2000s, and "the Chinese are still firing eight or nine million workers a year [during the 2000s] as part of their reforming of state-owned enterprises, and those workers don't have a safety net—much less a wage."[80]

The massive job losses associated with privatization created, for the first time, a "reserve army of the unemployed," which some experts believe may number "as many as 200 million … in a country of 1.3 billion." This development divided rural and urban workers into two new categories: the employed and the unemployed. Joseph Fewsmith, a China scholar at Boston University, told the *New York Times* that "China's workers have already borne the brunt of every cycle of modern Chinese history." Citing a frequent Chinese observation, he said, "They didn't get enough to eat during the famines of the Great Leap Forward. They didn't get an education because of the Cultural Revolution. And they are getting laid off because of the economic reforms."[81]

Region, status, income, gender, and employment divide the working class. These divisions have weakened the working class and strengthened the ruling class. One measure of the regime's growing power is social inequality, which has grown dramatically since 1978. In the years since 1978 "the income gap between rich and poor is growing faster than anywhere else on earth," and though China was "one of the world's most egalitarian societies in the 1970s, China in the 1980s and 1990s became one of the most unequal countries . . . among developing countries generally."[82] Naughton has argued that "there may be no other case where a society's income distribution has deteriorated so much, so fast."[83] The Gini Index, which is used to measure inequality (with 1 meaning the highest inequality and 0 total equality), went from 0.16 (one of the lowest in the world) in 1980 to 0.30 in 1990, which means that it is "about as bad as in the Philippines and Bolivia, two countries known historically for extreme inequalities and steep class divisions."[84] Put another way, in 1990 the income of the richest 20 percent of the population in China was 4.2 times as big as the income of the bottom 20 percent; by 1998 it had grown to 9.6 times as big.[85]

Growing inequality suggests that the struggle between the ruling class and the working class is extremely one-sided and that the ruling class has used the reforms to make enormous gains at the expense of the working class. The regime has defended growing inequality by saying, after Simon Kuznets, that it is a temporary phenomenon. Kuznets, an American economist, argued in the 1950s that economic development *initially* increased economic inequality, but that it *later* reduced inequality.[86] "Let some get rich first," Deng argued in the early days of reform, suggesting that others would eventually follow. Later, officials argued that economic growth would lead, in a series of stages, to eventual equality: "Prosperity to some, to most, then to all."[87] However, thirty years have gone by since the reforms were introduced, and income inequality has steadily grown. The first stage—during which time some will get rich first—has become a permanent condition.

Why hasn't the first stage (growing inequality) led to a second state (declining inequality), as Kuznets predicted? It has not done so for a simple reason. In general, ruling classes never *share* their gains, redistribute their wealth, and reduce economic inequality unless people or the state insist that they do. People in democratic states sometimes demand that ruling classes share their wealth, as they did in the United States and in Western Europe after World War II. However, the ruling classes in dictatorships never voluntarily share their wealth unless, of course, they are forced from power. In China the state has not been a force for economic equality—though during the Maoist period it was a force for widespread misery, which is a cruel kind of "equality"—and a divided and subdivided working class has been unable to insist on the redistribution of economic or political power.

Of course, workers have challenged the regime and demanded change. In the years since Tiananmen Square, they have submitted petitions, staged individual protests, organized strikes, and participated in violent, large-scale riots. In 2000 individuals and groups submitted ten million petitions to government officials, twice as many as they had in 1995.[88] Officials recorded 8,700 protests and riots in 1993, 32,000 in 1999, 58,000 in 2000, 87,000 in 2005, and 90,000 in 2006, a tenfold increase.[89] In 2003 three million people participated in antigovernment protests.[90] Most of the protesters "were farmers, laid-off workers, and victims of official corruption, who blocked roads, swarmed government offices, even immolated themselves in Tiananmen Square . . . to demand social justice."[91]

Rural workers have staged protests on a wide range of issues. In 2006 farmers in Panlong staged a sit-in after government officials cheated residents out of their land. Police assaulted the villagers and killed two of them, including a thirteen-year-old girl.[92] In 2007 three thousand villagers from several towns in Southwest China "stormed government offices, overturned vehicles, and burned offices" after local officials mounted an unusually "intensive campaign to enforce strict population-control measures, including forced abortions."[93]

Further, several hundred residents near a lead- and zinc-smelting plant near Beijing blocked traffic, stoned trucks entering the plant, and fought with police after learning that 615 of the 731 children in two nearby villages had tested positive for lead poisoning.[94] Parents near another smelting plant staged violent protests after finding that 1,354 children had tested positive for lead poisoning.[95] Parents who lost their children when an earthquake destroyed poorly constructed schools in Sichuan Province on May 12, 2008, conducted protests and commemorations for more than a year.[96]

Large-scale riots, involving thousands of demonstrators and scores of deaths, erupted in Tibet in March 2008 and in the capital city of Xinjiang in July 2009.[97] In both cases workers in ethnic minority communities, angry about being displaced by migrants who belonged to China's ethnic majority, attacked immigrants and burned and looted businesses owned by Han migrants.[98] In 2005 police fired on demonstrators opposed to the construction of a power plant in Dongzhou and killed twenty or more of them.[99]

Rural and urban workers in China have mounted energetic protests against the regime in recent years. Although the number of protests and participants has grown, they have had an extremely difficult time achieving economic gains or political change. "The workers' seething discontent over the lack of rule of law, cadre accountability, and party discipline are palpable, but remains an *unaggregated* impulse," Ching Kwan Lee has argued.[100] The spontaneous protests that have emerged rarely spread and did not long endure. To that extent, they resemble the kind of spontaneous protests "primitive rebels" made in the period before workers organized permanent organizations—trade unions and political parties—that helped workers spread and sustain campaigns against ruling classes and states. Eric Hobsbawm used the term "primitive rebel" to describe people who mounted protest without the benefit of permanent organizations.[101]

The protests workers mounted in China have been isolated and episodic for several reasons. First, successful protest would require at least some *parts* of a divided and subdivided working class to unify. However, for that to occur, workers would have to reach across sweeping economic, geographical, and social divides; communicate effectively with different groups; enlist them in a common cause; and create some kind of organizing network or social structure to cement these bonds and sustain a movement over time. These are all extraordinarily difficult things to do under the regime in China. Workers cannot communicate with sympathetic workers through the trade unions, which are corrupt organizations run by officials, and are prevented from organizing economic or political, or religious associations outside the party. Most workers cannot communicate through the Internet because they don't own computers. In 2004 China had ninety-four million Internet users, most of them likely members of the ruling class.[102] In any case, the government has managed to monitor, control, and disable the Internet to prevent workers from communicating, as it did in Xinjiang and Tibet after the riots in 2008 and 2009. "Nearly six months after grueling rioting [in] Xinjiang, Chinese authorities gingerly began to lift an Internet blackout ... allowing partial access to a pair of official news sites."[103] Tamara Shie has argued that "Arguments for the emancipatory power of the Internet are merely utopian political rhetoric."[104] Under these conditions, without permanent organizations or means of communication, workers' ability to organize, spread, or sustain antigovernment protest has been difficult.

Second, workers who stage protests in China have been unable to articulate a language for change. The regime's political campaigns have so debased the vocabulary of class struggle and social change that it has become virtually impossible to use. As Lee observed, "workers have started to shy away from class-based identities, portraying themselves during protest actions as weak and deprived groups (*ruoshi qunti*) rather than as working class or proletariat."[105] Unfortunately, this kind of language, which portrays workers as *victims,* may invite sympathy but does little to build solidarity because sympathizers may be understandably reluctant to *become* victims themselves, which might occur if they joined with victimized workers.

Third, the regime has labored to keep protests isolated and episodic by co-opting workers. The regime has deployed several strategies to co-opt workers in recent years. Officials paid hush money to parents whose children were killed in the Sichuan earthquake—offering "$8,800 in cash and a per parent pension plan of nearly $5,600"—lifted the one-child policy so that parents could try to replace dead or injured children, sent fertility specialists to assist them, and promised to investigate shoddy construction practices and hold local officials responsible for negligence.[106]

The regime sometimes agreed to meet worker demands, as it did in 2009, when it decided not to privatize a state-run steel mill after thirty thousand workers mounted furious protests and beat a company executive to death.[107] The regime also replaced and sometimes jailed local officials who had incurred the wrath of demonstrators. The regime fired two government leaders after "254 villagers died . . . when their homes were engulfed by a cascade of muddy iron ore waste from the reservoir of an unlicensed mine" in Shanxi Province in 2008.[108] What's more, "The Central government in Beijing [fired] 25 local officials and [put] 22 of them under criminal investigation" after they conspired to cover up a coalmine fire that killed 35 men in Zhonglou.[109] When the government acts in this fashion, "the central government is seen as an ally of the protestors—as long as it punishes corrupt lower-level officials—[and makes] a show of stepping in and taking action."[110]

Of course, if these strategies fail to co-opt demonstrators, officials warn them not to continue their efforts. When elderly women in Sanchawan led protests against a land grab and blocked construction, police and construction workers surrounded the women while a government official harangued them through a megaphone: "So you dirt-poor trash think you can oppose the city government?" Ji Shengrong shouted. "You don't have a chance in hell! You're crazy! Your heads are filled with sand!" Police first arrested the demonstrators and then jailed and beat sympathizers, demanding that they identify leaders of the protest. One man, Zhang Baohua, was repeatedly beaten and kicked during a four-day interrogation.[111]

Government officials who had grown impatient with the ongoing protests and commemorations grieving parents organized after the Sichuan earthquake warned parents not to organize a month-long mourning ceremony, arrested hundreds of parents who participated in commemorations, and charged a prominent supporter who had investigated shoddy construction practices with illegal possession of state secrets.[112]

Coerce and Deter

The regime has deployed a cruel and lethal coercive apparatus to prevent workers and citizens from challenging its authority, claiming constitutional or human rights, or demanding the redistribution of economic wealth or political power.

In China the constitution grants citizens the right to petition the government for redress, a practice that dates from the prerevolutionary period.[113] In 2005 citizens submitted 12.7 million petitions on behalf of individuals or groups, up from 10 million in 2004.[114] However, most of these petitions were ignored, and "only 0.2 percent of the petitions filed received a response."[115] As the number of petitions has grown, the regime has taken steps to discourage workers from submitting petitions and to punish them if they do. Petitioners who have traveled to Beijing have been arrested by police: "We have organized several petition sweeps," a Beijing police official admitted. "Now we are seeing fewer petitioners than before."[116] "Retrievers," the nearly ten thousand bounty hunters who local officials pay between $140 and $300 to keep petitioners from successfully filing their complaints, also abduct petitioners.[117] The bounty hunters have seized petitioners and imprisoned them in secret "black jails." Secret prisons "have sprouted in recent years partly because top leaders have put more pressure on local officials to reduce the number of petitioners in Beijing. Two of the largest holding pens . . . can handle thousands of detainees who are funneled to smaller detention centers. . . . Officially, these jails do not exist."[118] The retrievers confiscate petitioner's cell phones and identity cards and hold them incommunicado, for days, weeks, or months. "When you're taken to a black jail, no one knows where you are and you are totally vulnerable," Wang Songhan, a researcher reported.[119] Inmates have reported that their captors have robbed, beaten, raped, and tortured them.[120] After serving indeterminate sentences, petitioners are deported back to their homes, often escorted by the bounty hunters who are paid to make sure their petitioners leave town. One man made ten trips to Beijing, each one ending in his detention in a black jail. "I know my life is in danger," Wang Shixiang explained, "but I just can't swallow this injustice."[121]

The extrajuridical treatment of petitioners who seek to exercise constitution-guaranteed "rights" demonstrates that the regime cares little for constitutional government or the rule of law. In fact, the regime has long deployed an extralegal system of forced labor in "reeducation camps," which date back to the 1950s. One survivor, Xianhui Yang, now a novelist, said that in his camp, which held 3,000 political prisoners between 1957 and 1961, all but 500 of the inmates died, mostly from starvation.[122] Although observers believe that the regime has fewer reeducation camps today than it did during the Maoist period, today "at least 220,000 people are serving 'reeducation through labor' sentences—one-to-three-year terms that are meted out by the police and [and nonjudicial panels] without trial."[123]

The regime has used forced-labor camps to punish political dissidents, out-of-favor party members, and members of targeted social classes (landlords, intellectuals), ethnic groups (recently in Tibet and Xinjiang), and religious groups (Falun Gong, Buddhists, and Christians).[124] The regimes ten-year campaign against Falun Gong resulted in the arrest and detention of eight thousand practitioners and the deaths of at least one hundred, according to human rights experts. Bu Dongwei, a Falun Gong adherent, "who spent three years in a labor camp, said he was forced to share a room with about thirty people, most of them petty thieves and drug addicts who were encouraged to abuse the Falun Gong detainees."[125]

Individuals, family members, and members of proscribed social classes have been arrested and sentenced to labor camps without trial, outside the legal system, and on an arbitrary basis for long periods of time, during which they are tortured and abused as well as exploited as unpaid convict labor.

Of course, the regime also maintains a "legal" system—if it can be called that—which is used to arrest, try, and punish "criminals," though this includes not only street criminals but also people who have committed political or ideology infractions (see above). The legal system relies not only on paid government officials in the policy, judiciary, and prisons but also on a huge network of "largely uncompensated work by millions of non-professional citizen security activists ... citizens who, driven by fear or ambition, are ready to do the government's bidding," citizens who use their eyes and ears to spy on their neighbors.[126] "You have to be careful because informers are everywhere," a Uighur man told a *New York Times* reporter. "I would not trust anyone if I were you."[127] Officials also hire bounty hunters and thugs to abduct petitioners, assault protestors, and intimidate journalists.[128]

Officials order police to conduct sweeps and arrest people without cause, and the police rely on torture to extract information and confessions. A UN report in 2005 "condemned the 'widespread' use of torture in Chinese law enforcement" and said that "police and prison guards are pushed to extract admissions of guilt and are rarely punished for using electric shock, sleep deprivation, and submersion in water or sewage, among other techniques the U.N. Commission on Human Rights considers torture, to obtain them."[129] In one case, "the police intentionally locked up [an inmate] with tuberculosis patients until he became infected."[130] The regime admitted that 115 prisoners died as a result of torture in 1993 and 126 in 1994, a figure that likely understates the actual number.[131]

The defendants in Chinese courts are often denied access to legal counsel, and if defendants do have representation, legal authorities regularly threaten their lawyers. In 2009 authorities "threatened to delay or deny the renewal of legal licenses for 18 top civil rights lawyers, escalating the use of a tactic they have used to put pressure on lawyers they consider troublemakers." Other lawyers have been attacked by thugs, and arrested, beaten, and jailed by police.[132] "Defense attorneys can be held responsible if their client commits perjury," and this can be used to disbar lawyers.[133]

The judiciary is corrupt and acts at the behest of party and government officials. The regime commissioned a survey that found that 39 percent of respondents said that corruption in the judiciary was "quite serious."[134] The US State Department reported that, "in practice, the judiciary was not independent. It received policy guidance from both the government and the CCP, whose leaders used a wide variety of means to direct courts on verdicts and sentences."[135] The journalist Zhang Weiguo "reported that while in prison, he was told that, whatever the evidence in his case might be, 'it will be up to the leaders at a higher level to determine the nature of your case.'"[136] In criminal trials "only one in seven defendants reportedly had legal representation," the US State Department noted, and in some political cases "defendants and lawyers were not allowed to *speak* during trials."[137]

Judges allowed prosecutors to read witness statements, "which neither the defendants nor his lawyer had the opportunity to question," and "the percentage of witnesses who came to court in criminal cases was less than 10 percent and as low as one percent in some courts." The presumption of *guilt* and the absence of lawyers and witnesses, allowed the judiciary to conduct speedy trials and obtain high conviction rates: "The conviction rate for first-instance criminal cases was above 99 percent in 2006," the State Department reported.[138]

Furthermore, the regime executes thousands of people each year. In the late 1990s the regime annually executed an estimated 15,000 people. Since then, "the number of executions began dropping in 2001—not long after Beijing was chosen as the site of the 2008 Summer Olympics." In 2006 "reports in the state media put the number of executions at 8,000," and the regime "handed down 7,000 death sentences in 2009."[139] Still, China executes "more people every year than all other nations combined, by some Chinese estimates, up to 10,000 a year," though some scholars "have put the annual number as high as 15,000" in 2005.[140]

People in China are executed "for even relatively minor crimes [such as tax evasion, embezzlement, prostitution, and drug trafficking], and on occasion for no crime at all," James Seymour has argued. "Perfunctory trials and a meaningless appeals process result in many wrongful executions."[141] In 2009 the regime executed a mentally ill British citizen after a trial that lasted only thirty minutes. The man, Akmal Shaikh, "was apparently so delusional during an appeals hearing ... that the judges could not help but laugh out loud."[142]

After conducting speedy trials and cursory appeals, the regime executes convicts, either by firing squad or by a shot with a small caliber pistol to the back of the head, and frequently harvests their organs for use in the medical transplant market.[143] A small-caliber weapon is used to minimize splatter that might besmirch the executioner and to preserve the body so that its organs can be harvested.[144] According to Chinese government statistics, as much as 65 percent of the 10,000 organs used for transplants in China in 2009 "were taken from death-row inmates after their executions."[145] This system no doubt provides incentives for the regime to condemn some prisoners as a way to meet the demand for organs.[146]

Of course, many people are executed for crimes they did not commit. The regime executes some people simply to make an example. In 2007 the regime "executed its former top food and drug regulator [Zheng Xiaoyu] ... for taking bribes to approve untested medicine, as the Beijing leadership scrambled to show that it was serious about improving the safety of Chinese products." To underscore this, officials held a news conference "to emphasize their determination to cut down on fake and counterfeit food and medicine."[147] Essentially, the regime used Zheng's death as part of a public relations campaign, a deeply cynical project.

Two years later the regime executed two men for selling milk contaminated with melamine, doing so as part of a public relations campaign to demonstrate its commitment to product safety. Keep in mind that a legal system that gave them no real opportunity to defend themselves and offered no reliable evidence that they were responsible for the crime convicted these men. One woman whose son fell ill after drinking contaminated milk said of the verdicts, "I feel sorry for them, but they were just scapegoats. The ones who should take responsibility are the government."[148]

Taken together, the regime's willingness to deploy such loathsome practices, without regard for the rights of its citizens, has made protest and dissent extremely difficult and dangerous. For example, in 2010 the Nobel Peace Prize was awarded to Chinese dissident Liu Xiaobo. The regime arrested him in 2008 and, in 2009, sentenced him to eleven years in prison for cowriting a call for human rights in China.[149] The regime described the Nobel committee as "clowns," denounced the award as a "political farce," and accused the committee of "open support of illegal criminal activities in China."[150] Chinese authorities hastily organized a competing "peace" prize and awarded it to a Taiwanese politician, but he refused to attend the charade or accept the US$15,000 prize.[151] The regime also enlisted its diplomats in a Nobel Prize counteroffensive and persuaded or coerced a number of countries—Serbia, Morocco, Pakistan, Venezuela, Afghanistan, Columbia, Ukraine, Algeria, Cuba, Egypt, Iran, Iraq, Kazakhstan, Russia, Saudi Arabia, Sudan, Tunisia, Vietnam, and the Philippines—to boycott the ceremony in Oslo.[152] At the ceremony, "for the first time since 1935, when the laureate Carl von Ossietsky languished in a [German] concentration camp and Hitler forbade any sympathizers to attend ... no relative or representative of the winner [Liu Xiaobo] was present to accept the award." In his absence, a statement made by Liu Xiaobo to the court in China was read: "I have no hatred. Hatred can eat away at a person's intelligence and conscience.... Freedom of expression is the foundation of human rights, the source of humanity and the mother of truth.... I hope I will be the last victim ... [of] China's endless literary inquisitions."[153]

Unfortunately, Liu Xiaobo will not be the regime's "last victim"; instead, the regime's ongoing practices—arbitrary arrest, extralegal imprisonment, torture, prearranged trials without due process, juridical murder and organ harvesting—have consolidated its power and deflected demands for a redistribution of wealth and power in China. Indeed, China's economic success has emboldened its leadership not only to imprison and torture its own citizens but also to demean the advocates of human rights around the world.

Conclusion

> "The fact that Google cannot exist in China clearly indicates that China's path as a rising power is going in a direction different from what the world expected and that many Chinese were hoping for."
>
> *Xiao Qiang, China Internet project, U.C. Berkeley*[1]

When the Chinese Communist Party seized power in 1949, it moved aggressively to accumulate the capital it needed to finance industrial development and provide collective wealth for its members. The regime described this process as a "stage" that would lead inevitably to "socialism." But its policies never contributed meaningfully to socialism; instead, the accumulation of capital was a "stage" in the development of *capitalism,* albeit one that failed to generate any real economic growth during the next thirty years.

To accumulate the capital it required, the new ruling class destroyed rural landlords, dispossessed the urban bourgeoisie, seized the assets of rural proprietors, drove the survivors of these classes into a growing rural and urban working class, and demanded that they all work harder for fewer rewards. During the 1950s the regime justified its attacks on other classes by arguing that proprietors, large or small, engaged in backward "feudal" behaviors—hoarding wealth and consuming the available surplus, rather than investing it—that prevented the regime from investing the surplus in industrial development and modernization. By seizing the assets of rural and urban workers, restricting their income-producing activities, curbing their consumption, reducing their living standards to subsistence levels or below, and demanding that they increase their workloads and redouble their efforts, the regime accumulated the capital it needed to finance industrial development during the Great Leap Forward. However, the regime's mismanagement of China's financial, human, agricultural, and industrial resources during the Great

Leap squandered the capital it extracted from proprietors and workers, condemned millions of people to death from famine, and reduced the rest of the rural and urban working class to penury and misery. Mao's simultaneous decision to abandon the regime's modest population-control policies meant that a growing population consumed the meager economic gains made during the 1960s and 1970s. As a result, China was caught in a low-level equilibrium trap, which prevented the regime from generating any real economic growth for a generation.

Still, women's voluntary efforts to reduce birth rates, which they practiced in defiance of government policy, helped slow the *pace* of population growth in the 1960s and 1970s. In fact, their voluntary efforts did more to curb population growth than the regime's coercive one-child policies that were subsequently introduced. Women's unappreciated efforts to downsize their families in the 1960s made it possible for China to escape from the low-level equilibrium trap in the 1980s.

During the 1960s Mao invited the slightly disadvantaged members of the ruling class to attack their betters, a strategy designed to shore up his sagging position as the leader of the regime and make the party-state bureaucracy more responsive to his whims and edicts. He masked this agenda by describing the Great Proletarian Cultural Revolution as a titanic struggle between two different and antagonistic classes: proletarian and bourgeois-bureaucratic, but this was a fiction. Mao's analysis of the class struggle was based on his own arbitrary, self-serving, and superficial definitions of class, which enabled him to frame the conflict to his advantage. The Cultural Revolution was not, in fact, a struggle between two different classes, but instead a contest between two factions within the *same* ruling class. Faction fighting and tumultuous purges prevented the regime from advancing economic development during this period and failed to produce any meaningful *political* change. The only tangible political result of this so-called "Revolution" was the expansion of a bureaucracy devoted to Mao.

In the 1970s US recognition of China, Mao's death, and the return to power of the ruling-class faction led by Deng Xiaoping, which had largely been displaced during the Cultural Revolution, made it possible for the regime to adopt a set of "reforms" that promoted real economic growth for the first time. The regime used the *hukou* system to control rural-to-urban migration and the one-child policy to curb population growth. It returned control of agricultural production to rural producers, which encouraged them to increase food production, and it used foreign debt and investment to provide the capital it needed to finance industrial development. These policies, which involved both the reassertion of "control" *and* the "devolution" of authority, further slowed population growth and stimulated the economy, thus enabling China to escape the low-level equilibrium trap that had long prevented economic growth.

Could the regime have escaped the low-level equilibrium trap on its own? No. The regime could not squeeze enough capital from impoverished workers to finance rapid industrialization. Instead, foreign investors played a central role, providing the capital that the regime—and Chinese workers—could not.

To attract foreign investors, the regime adopted labor and monetary policies that enabled firms to produce low-wage and low-cost goods in China, and it used its police powers to prevent Chinese workers from demanding higher wages. During the 1980s these policies exerted a powerful "pull" on foreign investors, particularly members of the overseas Chinese community.

In the late 1980s and throughout the 1990s investors from around the world joined investors from the overseas Chinese community. Various kinds of economic crises that persuaded investors to exit "pushed" many of these investors out of democratic and democratizing countries. Then, the regime's low-wage and low-cost policies encouraged these investors to invest in China. Although *economic globalization* was associated with *political democratization* in the 1970s and 1980s, globalization in the 1990s and 2000s has been associated with a flood of investment in China, which contributed to dictatorship, not democratization. After 1989 foreign investors abandoned democratizing states in droves and invested in China, where the dictatorship reasserted itself by slaughtering workers in Tiananmen Square and creating a stable, low-wage, low-cost environment for foreign investors and the domestic ruling class.

The affinity of capital for dictatorship in China has been problematic because the discriminatory pattern of selective investment in China undermined the economic prospects of workers and many businesses in democratic and democratizing states around the world. Moreover, because the corrupt ruling class has captured the gains economic growth has made in China, growing social and economic inequality has also disadvantaged rural and urban workers in China.

Since 1971 the United States has provided crucial political and economic assistance to the regime. US officials and private investors have long argued that economic assistance and political "engagement" would open Chinese markets to US goods and promote democratization in China. Neither has occurred. There are two reasons for this.

First, the regime has adopted mercantilist policies that disadvantage foreign businesses and reserve the domestic market for Chinese firms. Second, the corrupt ruling class has forged close economic ties with domestic and foreign firms, which has in turn allowed it to acquire collective and individual wealth. It has used that wealth to expand the ruling class and consolidate its political power, and it has used its authority to divide and subdue rural and urban workers in China. The growing wealth and power of the ruling class has made it *less* likely that China will democratize any time soon. Despite this, US officials, firms that invest in China, and scholars in academic and public policy institutions have continued to defend the regime, excuse its ruthless policies, and champion the prospects for market capture and democratization. They describe critics of the US government's pro-China trade policies as "protectionists" and portray themselves as defenders of "free trade," despite the fact that the regime is the one that practices protectionist mercantilist policies and peddles "unfree" labor to foreign investors. They excuse the regime's long-standing and continuing abuse not only of economic classes and ethnic minorities in Tibet and Xinjiang but also of women and girls who are the victims of the regime's coercive one-child policies; of migrant workers who are treated like illegal immigrants in their own country; of workers who domestic and foreign firms exploit in prisonlike sweatshops; and of the billion-plus denizens in China who are deprived of constitutional and civil rights, subjected to arbitrary arrest and detention, often in secret jails, deprived of due process in a meaningful "legal" system, and subjected to punishment and death. For decades the evasions and denials of pro-China policymakers, investors, and academics in the United States have provided aid and comfort to the regime.

* * *

The dictatorship failed to promote economic growth during its first thirty years in power. However, during the last thirty years, the regime, supported by massive foreign investment, has achieved rapid rates of economic growth. Still, continued economic development in China is not inevitable. Individual states and the world economy experience periodic downturns. [See chart, Appendix II, p. 191] These downturns, or "B-phases," grow out of problems that emerge during periods of growth. Back in the 1980s, for example, most economists predicted that Japan would become the world's biggest economy, this based on its long record of economic growth during the postwar period. But an economic crisis in 1990, which was a byproduct of rapid growth and inflationary real estate prices, slowed Japan's ascent, and Japan failed to reach the summit of the world economy. Today, economists claim that China will soon become the world's largest economy, but this should be viewed with caution, if not skepticism. In recent years several problems have emerged that might slow or obstruct China's economic ascent: first, the hoarding behavior of Chinese workers, second, the corrupt behavior of the Chinese ruling class, and third, the fickle behavior of foreign investors.

Hoarding Behavior

The "hoarding" behavior of Chinese workers may slow or restrict the development of the domestic market in China. The regime has long suppressed the wages of rural and urban workers. Workers not only have to subsist on meager wages, but they also have to save what they can to provide for their future and protect themselves from misfortune. The regime no longer provides workers with job security, unemployment insurance, health care, pensions, or social security, and it refuses to provide them with financial services (decent interest on savings deposits) or credit that they might use to pay for weddings, invest in small business, build a home, or pay for unexpected medical or funeral expenses. Workers cannot rely on government resources, so they must rely on themselves and keep ready cash in hand. Consequently, Chinese workers "save" whatever they can. But workers' determination to save or "hoard" their resources means that they are poor consumers, and their collective behavior threatens to undermine the growth of the domestic market.

The domestic market in China has grown in recent years, largely because the 120 million members of the ruling class, who have acquired individual wealth, have become avid consumers. Although this is a fairly large market, it is limited by the fact that it depends on the ruling class's spending, a group that is fixed in number and does not include the vast rural and urban working class, who cannot afford to participate in the market as consumers. Growing social inequality in China—the fact that the ruling class has captured most of the wealth associated with economic growth and denied the benefits of growth to Chinese workers—may become an obstacle to developing the domestic market in China, a market that foreign investors have dreamed in vain of capturing. The domestic market might continue to grow if the regime redistributed the wealth in China by providing workers with collective wealth in the form of health care, education, and pensions. In addition, the regime might redistribute wealth by providing workers with individual wealth in the form of higher wages, interest on savings, and the provision of low-cost credit. The first strategy might reduce worker anxiety and persuade workers that they need not hoard their savings. The second approach might give workers the means to participate in the market as consumers, albeit thrifty ones. Of course, the regime seems determined not to redistribute its collective or individual wealth. Why would it do so unless workers forcefully demanded a greater share? Nevertheless, if the regime does not redistribute wealth, the growth of the domestic market will be restricted in important ways, and this could seriously slow economic development in China.

Corrupt Practices

The ruling class has engaged in several kinds of behavior that may adversely affect economic development in China. Since 1978 the ruling class has used state resources, inexpensive credit, and foreign investment to create a profusion of domestic firms that have excess capacity and earn low rates of profit. Many of these industrial and financial firms are technically bankrupt. The state supports them because they provide collective and individual wealth to the members of the ruling class. They remain in business only because the state directly or indirectly supports them. As one official admitted, "The problem is that we have so many stupid enterprises."[2]

The creation of a vast and inefficient business infrastructure is a waste of resources and an economic burden, which may slow economic growth in the future. However, if the regime eliminated all the "stupid" businesses in China, bankrupt firms would lay off workers, and this could contribute to an economic downturn.

The ruling class has not only invested heavily in "stupid" businesses, but its members have also invested heavily in commercial and residential real estate, which has lead to a building boom and soaring real estate prices. However, the price inflation in real estate may have created a "bubble" of the sort that emerged in Japan in the late 1980s and in the United States in 2008. A price deflation could trigger widespread bankruptcy and ruin financial institutions, which could slow economic growth in China.

As we have seen, the ruling class practices corruption on a vast scale. In fact, corruption is a central component of the regime's development strategy. It is designed to tie bureaucrats to the economic fortunes of business enterprises so they do not overburden firms with taxes and regulation and also to tie entrepreneurs to the state so they adhere to the regime's developmentalist agenda. Although this partnership has been a force for development, it has imposed informal taxes on foreign and domestic firms. These taxes raise the real cost of doing business in China and undermine the economic advantages the regime's low-wage, low-cost policies provides. If the cost of corruption rises or becomes more apparent, China may become less attractive to foreign investors. Unless it is checked, corruption may undermine economic development. Again, for the regime to curb corruption without antagonizing its own members would be difficult, particularly in the bureaucracy, which relies on it as a source of wealth and power.

Fickle Foreign Investors

Foreign investors may act in ways that undermine economic growth. China depends heavily on the flood of capital provided by foreign investors, now averaging about US$1 billion a week. But foreign investors are a fickle group, as we have seen during crises in Southeast Asia and Latin America. They might slow investment or exit China if the costs of doing business in China rose substantially. Rising wages, a substantial appreciation of the yuan, and rising corruption could increase costs and discourage foreign investors. There is some evidence that some or all of these things might occur.

In the spring of 2010 workers at factories financed by foreign investors—Honda and Foxconn Technologies—organized protests and demanded higher wages. "The cost of doing business in China is going up," the *New York Times* reported.[3] Another *Times* article reported, "New pressure to raise pay and improve labor conditions, coming in part from the Chinese government, is likely to raise the cost of doing business in China and could induce some companies to shift production elsewhere."[4]

If wages rose sharply, foreign investors might slow their investment in China or divert it to other low-wage countries, but although wages have risen in a few settings, whether the regime will permit across-the-board wage increases is unclear. Perhaps the regime has allowed, even encouraged workers at *foreign* firms to demand higher wages as part of a government strategy to increase costs for foreign firms and make them less competitive in Chinese markets. If that were true, rising wages in the foreign sector, like other mercantilist policies the regime has adopted, would disadvantage foreign firms and help reserve the domestic market for *domestic* firms linked to the regime. Given its past behavior, that the regime would let a large-scale, independent labor movement demand higher wages from domestic firms that are run by party bureaucrats and entrepreneurs in the ruling class is unlikely. Still, rising wages in the foreign sector, where goods are produced for export, might raise costs and slow foreign investment in China.

A sharp appreciation of the yuan would also raise the cost of doing business in China for firms that export goods to other countries. As we have seen, the regime has long kept the yuan at an arbitrarily low rate against the dollar, which has made its exports cheap on global markets. Although US officials have sometimes urged the regime to abandon this mercantilist practice, they have not demanded change, in part because US firms that export goods from China do *not* want exchange rates to change and in part because US officials fear that the Chinese might slow their purchase of US Treasuries if exchange rates changed (a sharp appreciation of the yuan would reduce the real value of the US$2 trillion the regime has hoarded). However, in recent years a growing number of US firms that these policies have disadvantaged have persuaded some legislators to demand that the US Treasury Department condemn the regime's mercantilist monetary policies, label China a "currency manipulator," and take steps to force the regime to alter exchange rates.[5] In June 2010 senators criticized Treasury Secretary Timothy Geithner's approach to China's monetary policies. As one senator remarked, "If the current state of our Chinese currency negotiations has a theme song, it would be Maxine Nightingale's rhythm-and-blues hit, 'Right Back Where We Started From.'"[6]

Although the regime will likely not drastically alter its monetary policies any time soon, particularly in the absence of a concerted US effort to demand real change, new exchange rates would increase the cost structure for foreign investors in China. They might respond to change by slowing the pace of their investment in China.

Foreign investors have also begun to reassess the costs associated with corruption. Endemic corruption, the widespread theft of technology, patents and copyrights, the regulatory burdens imposed on foreign corporations, censorship, and government-sponsored attacks on firms such as Google have indirectly raised the cost and risk associated with doing business in China. Google, one of the first firms to reassess its investments in China in the wake of government attacks on its private accounts, concluded that the cost of trying to do business in China was too high. Whether other foreign firms will reach the same kind of conclusion and exit is unclear, but foreign firms are alert to the behavior of other firms. If other firms follow Google's lead, investment patterns might change quickly and dramatically.

Foreign investors often engage in herdlike behavior, but they are not a homogeneous or single-minded group. Much of the foreign investment in China belongs to the overseas Chinese community. Some of them have been incorporated, more or less, into China's ruling class, on an unofficial basis. Given their close ties with the regime, how much "solidarity" overseas Chinese investors might practice in the face of rising costs and the departure of other foreign investors is not clear. Would they stick with the regime or would they abandon China and follow the herd? These are difficult questions to answer in advance.

Any one of these developments—rising wages, a currency appreciation, rising corruption—might increase the cost of doing business in China, slow the pace of foreign investment, reduce the rate of economic growth, and trigger an economic crisis or downturn for the first time in decades. Of course, if China were to experience an *economic* crisis, there is no guarantee that this would create a *political* crisis for the regime or contribute to democratization. It might instead lead to reactionary change. How the regime might respond to an economic crisis is anybody's guess. It might strengthen the regime's mercantilist economic policies and its residual Maoist political inclinations, which might lead to a search for domestic scapegoats who could then be blamed for the crisis, attacked, and purged. A crisis might also divide and weaken the ruling class and give workers an opportunity to demand economic and political change.

* * *

China is run by a cruel, corrupt, mercantilist dictatorship. Its policies and practices harm rural and urban workers in China and undermine workers and businesses in democratic and democratizing countries around the world. The regime's mercantilist policies thwart the kind of collective decision making that market-based institutions can provide, and its abusive and self-serving political practices stifle the kind of collective decision making that representative, democratic political institutions can provide. In China, that greater economic and political freedom—marketization and democratization—would benefit not only workers in China but also workers around the world is obvious.

Nonetheless, seeing how either development might occur is difficult. I say this for two reasons. First, the internal forces for change in China are weak. An expanded, consolidated, and wealthy ruling class has captured much of China's new wealth for itself and used state resources to divide the working class, punish dissent, and prevent workers from demanding a greater share of economic wealth and political power.

Second, the external forces for change are weak. Government officials in the United States, together with foreign investors and their intellectual supporters in the academic and public policy communities, have long accommodated the regime, excused its mercantilist economic policies and its abusive political practices, helped raise its political stature, provided it with economic opportunities, and bestowed it with massive amounts of foreign aid and investment. They have been reluctant to exert any serious economic or political pressure on the regime, largely because an important sector of US industry *opposes* any changes that might adversely affect their ability to do business in China. In the absence of foreign pressure, the regime has little incentive to change its behavior.

Still, this might change if workers, businesses, and government officials in the United States and in other democratic countries demanded economic and political change in China. Perhaps this book will contribute to that effort.

Appendix I

Model of Low-Level Equilibrium Trap

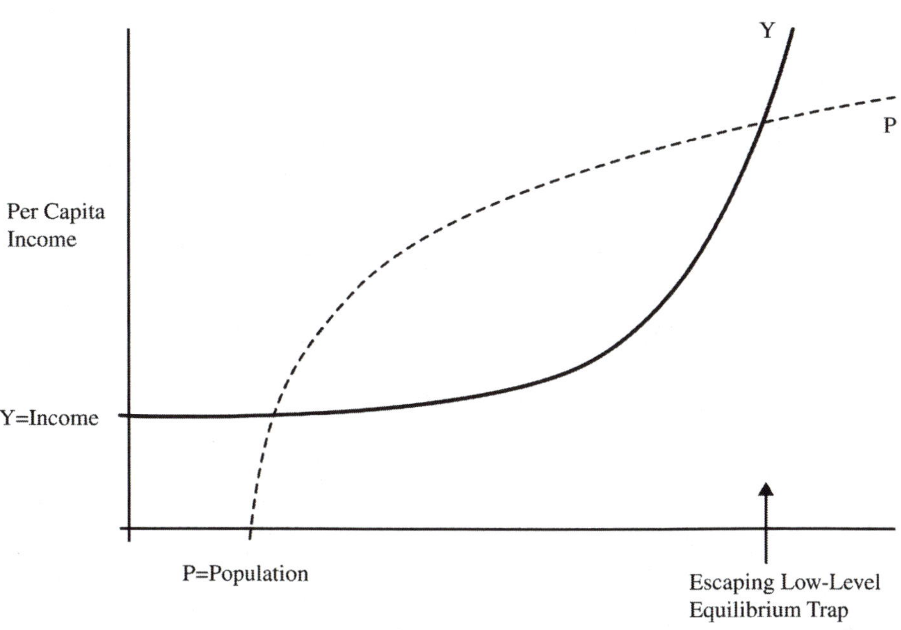

Appendix II

Long Wave of Economic Development in China

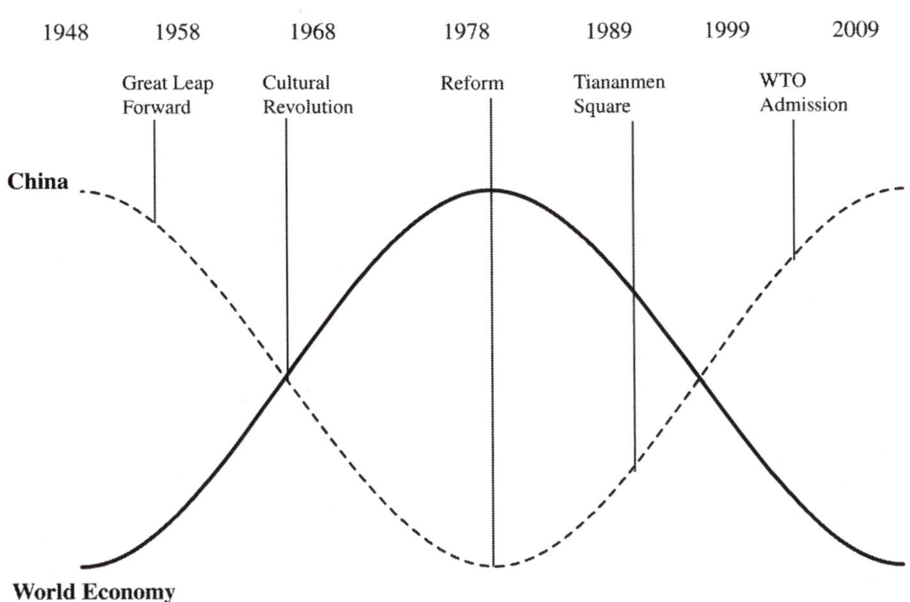

Notes

Preface

1. Theda Skocpol, *States and Social Revolutions: A Comparative Analysis of France, Russia, and China* (Cambridge: Cambridge University Press, 1979), xi.

2. Maurice Meisner, "China's Communist Revolution," *Current History* (September 1999), 245.

3. Robert Schaeffer, *Warpaths: The Politics of Partition* (New York: Hill and Wang, 1990); Robert K. Schaeffer, *Power to the People: Democratization Around the World* (Boulder, CO: Westview Press, 1997); Robert K. Schaeffer, *Understanding Globalization: The Social Consequences of Political, Economic and Environmental Change* (Lanham, MD: Rowman and Littlefield, 1997, 2003, 2005, 2009); and Torry D. Dickinson and Robert K. Schaeffer, *Fast Forward: Work, Gender and Protest in a Changing World* (Lanham, MD: Rowman and Littlefield, 2001).

4. Robert Schaeffer, "The Entelechies of Mercantilism," *Scandinavian Economic History Review* XXIX, no. 2 (1981); Robert Schaeffer, "A Critique of the 'New Class' Theorists: Towards a Theory of Working Class in America," *Social Praxis* 4, nos. 1–2 (1978).

Chapter One

1. Roderick MacFarquhar, *The Origins of the Cultural Revolution: 2 The Great Leap Forward, 1958–1960* (New York: Columbia University Press, 1983), 324.

2. John Maynard Keynes, *The General Theory of Employment, Interest, and Money* (New York: Harcourt, Brace and World, 1964), 347, 367–68, 347–48.

3. Carl Riskin, *China's Political Economy: The Quest for Development Since 1949* (Oxford: Oxford University Press, 1987), 19.

4. Ibid., 16.

5. Maurice Meisner, *Mao's China and After: A History of the People's Republic* (New York: Free Press, 1986), 78.

6. Riskin, *China's Political Economy*, 19, 14 (emphasis added), 47.

7. Ibid., 33.

8. Scholars disagree about the term "gentry." I am using it here as a synonym for "capitalist landlords." Scholars also disagree about its size. Some say the gentry made up about 3 percent of the population; others say 4 percent. Victor D. Lippit, *Land Reform and Economic Development in China: A Study of Institutional Change and Development Finance* (White Plains, NY: International Arts and Sciences Press, 1974), 167. Scholars also disagree about the percentage of land owned by the gentry, ranging from 30 to more than 44 percent, which was the percentage of land that the communist regime seized and redistributed during land reform. See Meisner, *Mao's China*, 203; Riskin, *China's Political Economy*, 50.

9. Lippit, *Land Reform*, 46–49; Riskin, *China's Political Economy*, 26.

10. Riskin, Ibid., 25. Rich peasants, merchants, and widows also made credit available in rural settings. Geoffrey Shillinglaw, "Land Reform and Peasant Mobilization in Southern China, 1947–1950," in *Agrarian Reform and Agrarian Reformism: Studies of Peru, Chile, China and India*, ed. David Lehmann (London: Faber and Faber, 1974), 131.

11. Lippit, *Land Reform*, 121.

12. Theda Skocpol, *States and Social Revolutions: A Comparative Analysis of France, Russia, and China* (Cambridge: Cambridge University Press, 1979), 68.

13. Lippit, *Land Reform*, 5.

14. Meisner, *Mao's China*, 103.

15. Riskin, *China's Political Economy*, 17.

16. Keynes, *The General Theory*, 347–48.

17. Riskin, *China's Political Economy*, 48.

18. Meisner, *Mao's China*, 104.

19. John Wong, *Land Reform in the People's Republic of China: Institutional Transformation in Agriculture* (New York: Praeger, 1973), 92–93; Shillinglaw, "Land Reform," 137–38.

20. Wong, *Land Reform*, 94, 93.

21. Shillinglaw, "Land Reform," 141, 150, 142.

22. Ibid., 94.

23. Meisner, *Mao's China*, 81, 82, 106–08; Riskin, *China's Political Economy*, 52.

24. Laurel Bossen, *Chinese Women and Rural Development: Sixty Years of Change in Lu Village, Yunnan* (Lanham, MD: Rowman and Littlefield, 2002), 90.

25. Meisner, *Mao's China*, 108.

26. Bossen, *Chinese Women*, 90; Meisner, *Mao's China*, 108.

27. Lippit, *Land Reform*, 122; Meisner, *Mao's China*, 108.

28. Riskin, *China's Political Economy*, 50.

29. Meisner, *Mao's China*, 108. The regime encouraged poor farmers to pool their resources—sharing draft animals and machinery—and work cooperatively on water projects and soil conservation so they could increase productivity, and by 1954 "58 percent of China's farm households had joined mutual aid teams." Lippit, *Land Reform*, 169; Mark Selden, *The Political Economy of Chinese Development* (Armonk, NY: M. E. Sharpe, 1993), 75.

30. Riskin, *China's Political Economy*, 21.

31. Jack Grey and Patrick Cavendish, *Chinese Communism in Crisis: Mao and the Cultural Revolution* (New York: Frederick A. Praeger, 1968), 26 (emphasis added). The regime used violence in some instances. When it took over Shanghai, the regime arrested thousands of counter-revolutionaries and executed a number of them at "six public execu-

tion grounds." Most of the people arrested, executed, or imprisoned were GMD officials or members of triad gangs and secret societies who collaborated with the GMD, though, no doubt, there were members of the urban bourgeoisie among them. One source said that "more than 200,000 people lost their lives in Shanghai during the first five years of CCP rule and another 640,000 went to jail or labor camps," but the source notes that these figures "seem high and are difficult to prove." Lynn T. White III, *Policies of Chaos: The Organizational Causes of Violence in China's Cultural Revolution* (Princeton, NJ: Princeton University Press, 1989), 94n28.

32. White, *Policies of Chaos,*108–09.

33. Riskin, *China's Political Economy,* 97; White, *Policies of Chaos,* 110.

34. Riskin, *China's Political Economy,* 42, 45.

35. Ibid., 46; Elizabeth J. Perry, *Challenging the Mandate of Heaven: Social Protest and State Power in China* (Armonk, NY: M. E. Sharpe, 2002), 211.

36. White, *Policies of Chaos,* 110.

37. Riskin, *China's Political Economy,* 39.

38. George T. Crane, "The Taiwanese Ascent: System, State, and Movement in the World-Economy," in *Ascent and Decline in the World-System,* ed. Edward Friedman (Beverly Hills, CA: SAGE, 1982), 97–98. Like the communist party, the GMD was capable of violence. When the inhabitants of Taiwan protested when the GMD imposed nationalist rule on the island, the regime killed ten to twenty thousand members of the opposition in 1947. Selden, *Political Economy,* 115. However, they did not resort to violence when they introduced land reform in Taiwan.

39. Selden, Ibid., 117.

40. Riskin, *China's Political Economy,* 69.

41. Shillinglaw, "Land Reform," 143 (emphasis added).

42. Frantz Fanon, *The Wretched of the Earth* (New York: Grove Press, 1963), 147, 35; Albert Memmi, *The Colonizer and the Colonized* (Boston: Beacon Press, 1965), 151.

43. Meisner, *Mao's China,* 107.

Chapter Two

1. Carl Riskin, *China's Political Economy: The Quest for Development Since 1949* (Oxford: Oxford University Press, 1987), 110; Maurice Meisner, *Mao's China and After: A History of the People's Republic* (New York: Free Press, 1986), 100.

2. Mark Selden, *The Political Economy of Chinese Development* (Armonk, NY: M. E. Sharpe, 1993), 72; Riskin, *China's Political Economy,* 54.

3. Selden, *Political Economy,* 11.

4. Penny Kane, *Famine in China, 1959–61: Demographic and Social Implications* (Houndsmills, UK: MacMillan Press, 1988), 46.

5. Ibid., 45.

6. Riskin, *China's Political Economy,* 69.

7. Selden, *Political Economy,* 83.

8. Riskin, *China's Political Economy,* 57.

9. Ibid., 87.

10. Selden, *Political Economy,* 13.

11. Ibid., 85.

12. Ibid., 88, 87, 92 (emphasis added), 58.

13. Riskin, *China's Political Economy,* 88–89.

14. Kane, *Famine in China,* 51.

15. Riskin, *China's Political Economy,* 92.

16. Elisabeth Croll, *Women and Rural Development in China: Production and Reproduction* (Geneva: International Labor Office, 1985), 21.

17. Ibid., 40.

18. Ibid., 37 (emphasis added); Selden, *Political Economy,* 139, see chart.

19. Riskin, *China's Political Economy,* 94.

20. Croll, *Women and Rural Development,* 21; Gail Hershatter, *Women in China's Long Twentieth Century* (Berkeley: University of California Press, 2007), 62.

21. Croll, *Women and Rural Development,* 38–39.

22. Selden, *Political Economy,* 144, 140.

23. Croll, *Women and Rural Development,* 42; Riskin, *China's Political Economy,* 121.

24. Kenneth Pomeranz, "Women's Work, Family, and Economic Development in Europe and East Asia: Long-term Trajectories and Contemporary Comparisons," in *The Resurgence of East Asia: 500, 150, and 50 Year Perspectives,* ed. Giovanni Arrichi, Takeshi Hamashita, and Mark Selden (London: Routledge, 2003), 150; Selden, *Political Economy,* 123.

25. Selden, Ibid., 123–24.

26. Laurel Bossen, *Chinese Women and Rural Development: Sixty Years of Change in Lu Village, Yunnan* (Lanham, MD: Rowman and Littlefield, 2002), 104–05.

27. Roderick MacFarquhar, *The Origins of the Cultural Revolution: 2 The Great Leap Forward,* 1958–1960 (New York: Columbia University Press, 1983), 138.

28. Bossen, *Chinese Women,* 131.

29. Ibid., 129.

30. Selden, *Political Economy,* 78–80.

31. Riskin, *China's Political Economy,* 124.

32. Elisabeth Croll, *Chinese Women Since Mao* (London: Zed Books, 1983), 1.

33. Croll, *Women and Rural Development,* 10.

34. Hershatter, *Women,* 25.

35. Riskin, *China's Political Economy,* 170–71; MacFarquhar, *Origins of the Cultural Revolution,* 150; Tyrene White, *China's Longest Campaign: Birth Planning in the People's Republic, 1949–2005* (Ithaca, NY: Cornell University Press, 2006), 28–29.

36. Riskin, *China's Political Economy,* 119; MacFarquhar, *Origins of the Cultural Revolution,* 150.

37. Selden, *Political Economy,* 77, 15, 25, 124.

38. Croll, *Women and Rural Development,* 25.

39. Selden, *Political Economy,* 122 (emphasis added).

40. Ibid., 124–25; Victor D. Lippit, *Land Reform and Economic Development in China: A Study of Institutional Change and Development Finance* (White Plains, NY: International Arts and Sciences Press, 1974), 155; Riskin, *China's Political Economy,* 141–42.

41. Franz Schurmann accurately described the Great Leap Forward as "the product of a vision rather than of a plan." Riskin, Ibid., 114.

42. Ibid., 151; T. White, *China's Longest Campaign,* 46. Other scholars use a lower figure, "a total increase of 20 million in the city population during the period 1958–60." Riskin, *China's Political Economy,* 144.

43. Thomas Scharping, *Birth Control in China, 1949–2000: Population Policy and Demographic Development* (London: Routledge, 2003), 48.

44. Lynn T. White III, *Policies of Chaos: The Organizational Causes of Violence in China's Cultural Revolution* (Princeton, NJ: Princeton University Press, 1989), 101, 118, 164.

45. Elizabeth J. Perry, *Challenging the Mandate of Heaven: Social Protest and State Power in China* (Armonk, NY: M. E. Sharpe, 2002), 220.

46. T. White, *China's Longest Campaign,* 46; Scharping, *Birth Control,* 48. Selden argued that the regime introduced the *hukou* system earlier, in 1955, though he says it was not until 1960 that it was "rigorously enforced." Selden, *Political Economy,* 24.

47. T. White, *China's Longest Campaign,* 46.

48. Selden, *Political Economy,* 174–75, 151–52.

49. Riskin, *China's Political Economy,* 126.

50. MacFarquhar, *Origins of the Cultural Revolution,* 327.

51. Ibid, 119; Riskin, *China's Political Economy,* 60.

52. Riskin, Ibid., 270; Andrew G. Walder, "The Remaking of the Chinese Working Class, 1949–1981," *Modern China* 10, no. 1 (January 1984), 15.

53. Riskin, *China's Political Economy,* 98–9; Walder, "Remaking of the Chinese Working Class," 21.

54. Riskin, *China's Political Economy,* 275.

55. Walder, "Remaking the Chinese Working Class," 15.

56. Riskin, *China's Political Economy,* 151, 144, 268–69.

57. Gao Xiaoxian, "China's Modernization and Changes in the Social Status of Rural Women," in *Engendering China: Women, Culture and the State,* ed. Christina K. Gilmartin, Gail Hershatter, Lisa Rofel, and Tyrene White (Cambridge, MA: Harvard University Press, 1994), 83.

58. Xiaoxian, "China's Modernization," 24; Hershatter, *Women in China's Long Twentieth Century,* 60–61.

59. MacFarquhar, *Origins of the Cultural Revolution,* 324.

60. Alice H. Amsden, *The Rise of 'The Rest': Challenges to the West from Late-Industrializing Economies* (Oxford: Oxford University Press, 2001), 83.

61. Kane, *Famine in China,* 60.

62. MacFarquhar, *Origins of the Cultural Revolution,* 327.

63. Ibid.; Selden, *Political Economy,* 16.

64. Riskin, *China's Political Economy,* 133; Likewise, coal production plummeted from 300 million tons in 1959 to 170 million tons in 1961. Selden, *Political Economy,* 16.

65. MacFarquhar, *Origins of the Cultural Revolution,* 126.

66. Kane, *Famine in China,* 54, 58–59; Basil Ashton, Kenneth Hill, Alan Piazza, and Robin Zeitz, "Famine in China, 1958–61," in *The Population of Modern China,* ed. Dudley L. Poston Jr. and David Yaukey (New York: Plenum Press, 1992), 244.

67. MacFarquhar, *Origins of the Cultural Revolution,* 125.

68. Riskin, *China's Political Economy,* 126.

69. MacFarquhar, *Origins of the Cultural Revolution,* 328.

70. Kane, *Famine in China,* 48.

71. Bossen, *Chinese Women,* 45, 43, 73. One feminist scholar has argued that "the connection of foot-binding practices and women's productive labor remains poorly understood. In many regions, foot-binding appears to have been quite compatible with women's participation in agricultural labor." Hershatter, *Women in China's Long Twentieth Century,* 57.

72. Croll, *Women and Rural Development,* 19.
73. Ibid., 34–35; Bossen, *Chinese Women,* 101, 207.
74. Bossen, Ibid., 106, 108.
75. Ibid., 125.
76. Kane, *Famine in China,* 57.
77. Ibid., 59.
78. Ibid., 42.
79. Ibid., 55; MacFarquhar, *Origins of the Cultural Revolution,* 329.
80. Riskin, *China's Political Economy,* 137.
81. Kane, *Famine in China,* 62. The regime gave a somewhat different estimate, reporting that grain exports increased from 2.9 million tons in 1958 to 4.2 million tons in 1959. Ashton, "Famine in China," 237.
82. Kane, *Famine in China,* 116; Selden, *Political Economy,* 24.
83. Kane, *Famine in China,* 77, 134.
84. Ibid., 130.
85. MacFarquhar, *Origins of the Cultural Revolution,* 141.
86. Amartya Sen, *Poverty and Famines: An Essay on Entitlement and Deprivation* (Oxford: Clarendon Press, 1981), 80.
87. Riskin, *China's Political Economy,* 128; Selden, *Political Economy,* 21.
88. Kane, *Famine in China,* 65, 68, 75.
89. Ibid., 82.
90. Ibid., 89–90, 84–87; Riskin, *China's Political Economy,* 147n17.
91. MacFarquhar, *Origins of the Cultural Revolution,* 330; Selden, *Political Economy,* 28.
92. Kane, *Famine in China,* 100, 102.
93. James S. Donnelly, Jr., *The Great Irish Potato Famine* (Phoenix Mill, UK: Sutton, 2001), 171; Sen, *Poverty and Famines,* 52; Marcus Rediker, *The Slave Ship: A Human History* (New York: Viking, 2007), 5; John Keegan, *The Second World War* (New York: Viking, 1989), 289, 284. The demographic collapse of indigenous peoples in North America after the conquest was probably worse, though it occurred over a long period of time and for rather different reasons. Wallerstein argues that "In Mexico, the indigenous population fell from 11 million in 1519 to about 1.5 million in circa 1650. Brazil and Peru seem to have had an equally dramatic decline" Immanuel Wallerstein, *The Modern World-System: Capitalist Agriculture and the Origins of the European World-Economy in the Sixteenth Century* (New York: Academic Press, 1974), 90.
94. MacFarquhar, *Origins of the Cultural Revolution,* 335.
95. Riskin, *China's Political Economy,* 266, 182n5; Walder, "Remaking of the Chinese Working Class," 16.
96. Riskin, *China's Political Economy,* 266; Selden, *Political Economy,* 23.
97. Selden, Ibid., 166.
98. MacFarquhar, *Origins of the Cultural Revolution,* 335.
99. Scharping, *Birth Control,* 29.
100. Ibid., 43; T. White, *China's Longest Campaign,* 22–25, 35.
101. Susan Greenhalgh and Edwin A. Winkler, *Governing China's Population: From Leninist to Neoliberal Biopolitics* (Stanford, CA: Stanford University Press, 2005), 78.
102. T. White, *China's Longest Campaign,* 38–39.
103. MacFarquhar, *Origins of the Cultural Revolution,* 10. According to Leonid Brezhnev, Mao's cynical comments greatly alarmed the Soviet leadership.
104. Scharping, *Birth Control,* 478.

105. Kane, *Famine in China,* 142; T. White, *China's Longest Campaign,* 40–41.

106. MacFarquhar, *Origins of the Cultural Revolution,* 1.

107. Richard R. Nelson, "A Theory of the Low-Level Equilibrium Trap in Underdeveloped Economies," *American Economic Review* 46, no. 5 (December 1956), 894–908.

108. Simon Kuznets, "The Gap: Concept, Measurement, Trends," in *Gap Between Rich and Poor Nations: Proceedings of a Conference Held by the International Economics Association at Bled, Yugoslavia,* ed. Gustav Ranis (London: MacMillan Press, 1972), 21.

109. John Wilson Lewis and Litai Xue, *China Builds the Bomb* (Stanford, CA: Stanford University Press, 1988), 107, 108, 130.

110. Meisner, *Mao's China,* 437.

111. Kane, *Famine in China,* 139.

112. Riskin, *China's Political Economy,* 152, 154, 169, 239; Lippit, *Land Reform,* 179–80.

113. T. White, *China's Longest Campaign,* 49; Selden, *Political Economy,* 21.

114. Selden, Ibid., 20.

115. Ibid.; Riskin, *China's Political Economy,* 149, 261.

116. Selden, *Political Economy,* 21.

117. Riskin, *China's Political Economy,* 263, 264; Walder, "Remaking of the Chinese Working Class," 23, 43. Lippit says that urban wages fell 14 percent in this period. Lippit, *Land Reform,* 150. Although wages fell, women's entry into the urban workforce increased household incomes slightly. Riskin, *China's Political Economy,* 263.

118. Walder, "Remaking of the Chinese Working Class," 24; Riskin, *China's Political Economy,* 242.

119. Wallerstein, *Modern World-System,* 90–103.

120. Ibid., 313, 247–51, 90, 100. The regime in China did not reduce workers to slavery, if only because, historically, slaves are not very useful if they are employed in any job that requires skill.

121. Riskin, *China's Political Economy,* 137.

122. Meisner, *Mao's China,* 109; Selden, *Political Economy,* 128, 127.

123. Meisner, *Mao's China,* 109.

124. Riskin, *China's Political Economy,* 55.

Chapter Three

1. Hong Yung Lee, *The Politics of the Chinese Cultural Revolution* (Berkeley: University of California Press, 1978), 4.

2. Lynn T. White III, *Policies of Chaos: The Organizational Causes of Violence in China's Cultural Revolution* (Princeton, NJ: Princeton University Press, 1989), 28.

3. Jack Grey and Patrick Cavendish, *Chinese Communism in Crisis: Mao and the Cultural Revolution* (New York: Frederick A. Praeger, 1968), 45; Carl Riskin, *China's Political Economy: The Quest for Development Since 1949* (Oxford: Oxford University Press, 1987), 158.

4. Mark Selden, *The Political Economy of Chinese Development* (Armonk, NY: M. E. Sharpe, 1993), 108; Penny Kane, *Famine in China, 1959–61: Demographic and Social Implications* (Houndsmills, UK: MacMillan Press, 1988), 128; Roderick MacFarquhar, *The Origins of the Cultural Revolution: 2 The Great Leap Forward, 1958–1960* (New York: Columbia University Press, 1983), 52.

5. MacFarquhar, *Origins of the Cultural Revolution,* 235.

6. Andrew J. Nathan, *China's Crisis: Dilemmas of Reform and Prospects for Democracy* (New York: Columbia University Press, 1990), 26.

7. MacFarquhar, *Origins of the Cultural Revolution,* 38.

8. Julia Kwong, *The Political Economy of Corruption in China* (Armonk, NY: M. E. Sharpe, 1997), 34.

9. Grey and Cavendish, *Chinese Communism,* 18.

10. Xiaobo Lu, *Cadres and Corruption: The Organizational Involution of the Chinese Communist Party* (Stanford, CA: Stanford University Press, 2000), 31.

11. L. T. White, *Policies of Chaos,* 140.

12. Kwong, *Corruption in China,* 35.

13. Lu, *Cadres and Corruption,* 86.

14. Victor D. Lippit, *Land Reform and Economic Development in China: A Study of Institutional Change and Development Finance* (White Plains, NY: International Arts and Sciences Press, 1974), 8.

15. Lu, *Cadres and Corruption,* 38–40, 36–37, 67, 80, 35, 116, 41, 46–47.

16. Ibid., 50, 138.

17. Ibid., 140.

18. Selden, *Political Economy,* 169, 145, 147–48.

19. L. T. White, *Policies of Chaos,* 200–02; Kwong, *Corruption in China,* 99.

20. MacFarquhar, *Origins of the Cultural Revolution,* 175.

21. Ibid.

22. Lu, *Cadres and Corruption,* 68.

23. Kwong, *Corruption in China,* 58.

24. Lu, *Cadres and Corruption,* 122, 55, 60–61.

25. Yan Sun, *Corruption and Market in Contemporary China* (Ithaca, NY: Cornell University Press, 2004), 27–33; Lu, *Cadres and Corruption,*10–12.

26. Lu, Ibid., 93.

27. Kwong, *Corruption in China,* 7.

28. Joel S. Migdal, *Strong Societies and Weak States: State-Society Relations and State Capabilities in the Third World* (Princeton, NJ: Princeton University Press, 1988), 215–24, 242–43, 260, 204, 208.

29. Tyrene White, *China's Longest Campaign: Birth Planning in the People's Republic, 1949–2005* (Ithaca, NY: Cornell University Press, 2006), 8.

30. Lu, *Cadres and Corruption,* 88, 84, 101–02.

31. Ibid., 104.

32. Ibid., 107, 101.

33. L. T. White, *Policies of Chaos,* 144.

34. MacFarquhar, *Origins of the Cultural Revolution,* 207.

35. Frederick C. Tiewes, *Leadership, Legitimacy, and Conflict in China: From a Charismatic Mao to the Politics of Succession* (Armonk, NY: M. E. Sharpe, 1984), 128.

36. Alain Bouc, *Mao Tse-Tung: A Guide to His Thought* (New York: St. Martins, 1977), 36–37.

37. MacFarquhar, *Origins of the Cultural Revolution,* 54–55.

38. Ibid.

39. Ibid., 296.

40. Selden, *Political Economy,* 70.

41. Lee, *Politics of the Chinese Cultural Revolution,* 327.

42. Riskin, *China's Political Economy,* 130.

43. Robert K. Schaeffer, *Power to the People: Democratization Around the World* (Boulder, CO: Westview Press, 1997), 132–39, 86–90.

44. Robert K. Schaeffer, *Understanding Globalization: The Social Consequences of Political, Economic, and Environmental Change* (Lanham, MD: Rowman and Littlefield, 2009), 2–3.

45. Torry D. Dickinson and Robert K. Schaeffer, *Fast Forward: Work, Gender and Protest in a Changing World* (Lanham, MD: Rowman and Littlefield, 2001), 84–85; Schaeffer, *Power to the People,* 86.

46. Elisabeth Croll, *Chinese Women Since Mao* (London: Zed Books, 1983), 75.

47. Hong Yung Lee, "Historical Reflections on the Cultural Revolution as a Political Revolution," in *The Chinese Cultural Revolution Reconsidered: Beyond Purge and Holocaust,* ed. Kam-yee Law (New York: Palgrave Macmillan, 2003), 100.

48. L. T. White, *Policies of Chaos,* 10–11, 88.

49. Ibid., 88–89.

50. Ibid., 11, 143.

51. Selden, *Political Economy,* 161.

52. Robert Schaeffer, "A Critique of the 'New Class' Theorists: Towards a Theory of Working Class in America," *Social Praxis* 4, no. 1–2 (1978); Robert Schaeffer and James Weinstein, "Between the Lines," in *Between Labor and Capital,* ed. Pat Walker (Boston: South End Press, 1979).

53. Schaeffer, "A Critique," 73–99; Schaeffer and Weinstein, "Between the Lines," 143–72.

54. Andrew Ross, *Nice Work If You Can Get It: Life and Labor in Precarious Times* (New York: New York University Press, 2009), 49, 62, 203, 169, 186, 48.

55. L. T. White, *Policies of Chaos,* 11–12n14; Lippit, *Land Reform,* 6.

56. Dickinson and Schaeffer, *Fast Forward,* 3–48.

57. Shaoguang Wang, "Between Destruction and Construction: The First Year of the Cultural Revolution," in Lee, *Politics of the Cultural Revolution,* 35; "If the father's a hero, the son's a good chap; if the father's a reactionary, the son's a bad egg," was another iteration of this idea. L. T. White, *Policies of Chaos,* 222.

58. Lee, *Politics of the Chinese Cultural Revolution,* 54–55; Riskin, *China's Political Economy,* 356.

59. Erving Goffman, *Stigma: Notes on the Management of Spoiled Identity* (Englewood Cliffs, NJ: Prentice Hall, 1963), 4.

60. L. R. Melvern, *A People Betrayed: The Role of the West in Rwanda's Genocide* (London: Zed, 2000), 10–11; Philip Gourevitch, *"We Wish to Inform You That Tomorrow We Will Be Killed with Our Families"* (New York: Farrar, Straus and Giroux, 1998), 56–57.

61. Gourevitch, *"We wish,"* 48.

62. William I. Thomas and Dorothy Swain Thomas, *The Child in America* (New York: Knopf, 1928), 572.

63. Lee, "Historical Reflections," 98–99; Grey and Cavendish, *Communism in Crisis,* 51.

64. Grey and Cavendish, Ibid., 100.

65. Lee, *Politics of the Chinese Cultural Revolution,* 327.

66. Central Committee of the Chinese Communist Party, "Decision Concerning the GPCR," August 8, 1966.

67. Lee, *Politics of the Chinese Cultural Revolution,* 65.

68. Lee, "Historical Reflections," 100.

69. Arif Dirlik, "The Politics of the Cultural Revolution in Historical Perspective," in Law, *Chinese Cultural Revolution Reconsidered* (see note 47), 175.

70. William A. Gamson, *The Strategy of Social Protest* (Belmont, CA: Wadsworth, 1990), 155, 165–67.

71. Nathan, *China's Crisis,* 35.

72. Lee, "Historical Reflections," 103, 101–02; Lee, *Politics of the Chinese Cultural Revolution,* 342; L. T. White, *Policies of Chaos,* 14.

73. L. T. White, Ibid., 40.

74. Ibid., 48; Mark Lupher, "The Cultural Revolution and the Origins of Post-Mao Reform," in Law, *Chinese Cultural Revolution Reconsidered* (see note 47), 188–89; Lynn T. White III and Kam-yee Law, "Explanations for China's Revolution at its Peak," in Law, Ibid., 10.

75. Lee, *Politics of the Chinese Cultural Revolution,* 80.

76. Ibid., 82; L. T. White, *Policies of Chaos,* 288.

77. Lee, *Politics of the Chinese Cultural Revolution,* 79.

78. Ibid., 77.

79. Ibid., 75, 74.

80. L. T. White, *Policies of Chaos,* 222. In another version she wrote, "If one's father is a revolutionary, his son tries hard to be a hero, and if one's father is a reactionary, his son should rebel." Lee, *Politics of the Chinese Cultural Revolution,* 73.

81. Lee, Ibid., 261, 280.

82. Ibid., 72, 192 (emphasis added).

83. Roderick MacFarquhar and Michael Shoenhals, *Mao's Last Revolution* (Cambridge, MA: Harvard University Press, 2006), 102.

84. Lee, *Politics of the Chinese Cultural Revolution,* 89–90.

85. MacFarquhar and Shoenhals, *Mao's Last Revolution,* 8.

86. L. T. White, *Policies of Chaos,* 276, 277.

87. Ibid., 7n8, 9. Stephen Rosskamm Shalom, *Deaths in China Due to Communism: Propaganda Versus Reality* (Tempe: Center for Asian Studies, Arizona State University, 1984); White and Law, "Explanations," in Law, *Cultural Revolution Reconsidered,* 4.

88. Riskin, *China's Political Economy,* 187; Thomas P. Bernstein, "Introduction," in *The Rustication of Urban Youth in China: A Social Experiment,* ed. Peter J. Seybolt (White Plains, NY: M. E. Sharpe, 1977), xii; T. White, *China's Longest Campaign,* 58.

89. Xiaoxia Gong, "The Logic of Repressive Collective Action: A Case Study of Violence in the Cultural Revolution," in Law, *Chinese Cultural Revolution Reconsidered* (see note 47), 115.

90. Riskin, *China's Political Economy,* 187; T. White, *China's Longest Campaign,* 58.

91. Tiewes, *Leadership, Legitimacy,* 7.

92. Wang, "Between Destruction and Construction," 33; Lee, *Politics of the Chinese Cultural Revolution,* 16; Lu, *Cadres and Corruption,* 15.

93. Lee, *Politics of the Chinese Cultural Revolution,* 3, 59; L. T. White, *Policies of Chaos,* 24.

94. Lu, *Cadres and Corruption,* 86; Maurice Meisner, *Mao's China and After: A History of the People's Republic* (New York: Free Press, 1986), 412; Lee says it grew from seventeen million in 1961 to twenty-three million in 1973, which gives a lower starting figure but arrives at the same number of new members. Lee, *Politics of the Chinese Cultural Revolution,* 324.

95. Immanuel Wallerstein, *The Modern World-System III: The Second Era of Great Expansion of the Capitalist World-Economy, 1730–1840s* (New York: Academic Press, 1989), 47, 100, 45.

96. Immanuel Wallerstein, *The Modern World-System: Capitalist Agriculture and the Origins of the European World-Economy in the Sixteenth Century* (New York: Academic Press, 1974), 351.

97. Lee, *Politics of the Chinese Cultural Revolution,* 287.

98. T. White, *China's Longest Campaign,* 57.

99. White and Law, "Explanations," 14; Wang, "Between Destruction and Construction," 25.

100. Gong, "The Logic of Repressive Collective Action," 128.

101. Lu, *Cadres and Corruption,* 164–65; Lee, "Historical Reflections," 108.

Chapter Four

1. Tony Saich, "The Reform Decade in China: The Limits to Revolution from Above," in *The Reform Decade in China: From Hope to Dismay,* ed. Marta Dassu and Tony Saich (London: Kegan Paul, 1992), 14; Mark Selden, *The Political Economy of Chinese Development* (Armonk, NY: M. E. Sharpe, 1993), 25.

2. "In 1977, the average wage of state employees was 5.5 percent lower than it had been in 1957; that of industrial workers was 8.4 percent lower," and "the peasantry, which comprised 80 percent of the population, experienced a long-term per capita income decline between 1955 and 1978." Saich, "The Reform Decade," 14; Mark Selden, "The Social and Political Consequences of Chinese Reform: The Road to Tiananmen," in *Pacific-Asia and the Future of the World-System,* ed. Ravi Arvind Palat (Westport, CT: Greenwood Press, 1993), 152.

3. Carl Riskin, *China's Political Economy: The Quest for Development Since 1949* (Oxford: Oxford University Press, 1987), 257.

4. Three other highly placed leaders—Tung Pi-wu, K'ang Shen, and Chu The—also died in 1975 and 1976. Maurice Meisner, *Mao's China and After: A History of the People's Republic* (New York: Free Press, 1986), 427.

5. Frederick C. Tiewes, *Leadership, Legitimacy, and Conflict in China: From a Charismatic Mao to the Politics of Succession* (Armonk, NY: M. E. Sharpe, 1984), 119–21.

6. Ibid., 126.

7. Richard Baum, *Burying Mao: Chinese Politics in the Age of Deng Xiaoping* (Princeton, NJ: Princeton University Press, 1994), 8, 30; Tiewes, *Leadership,* 179.

8. Meisner, *Mao's China,* 454.

9. Baum, *Burying Mao,* 10; Tiewes, *Leadership,* 123.

10. Baum, *Burying Mao,* 10; Tiewes, *Leadership,* 122.

11. Meisner, *Mao's China,* 424.

12. Baum, *Burying Mao,* 32–36.

13. Ibid., 30–31, 38.

14. Ibid., 116, 39–42.

15. Ibid., 44–46, 63; Tiewes, *Leadership,* 83.

16. Baum, *Burying Mao,* 54.

17. Meisner, *Mao's China,* 454; Baum, *Burying Mao,* 10.

18. Baum, Ibid., 64, 116.

19. Riskin, *China's Political Economy,* 197.

20. Carl Riskin, Zhao Renwei, and Li Shi, "Introduction," in *China's Retreat from Equality: Income Distribution and Economic Transition*, ed. Carl Riskin, Zhao Renwei, and Li Shi (Armonk, NY: M. E. Sharpe, 2001), 18; John Knight and Lina Song, "Economic Growth, Economic Reform, and Rising Inequality in China," in Riskin, Zhao, and Li, Ibid., 120.

21. Baum, *Burying Mao,* 114.

22. Nicholas D. Kristof, "Suicide of Jiang Qing, Mao's Widow, Is Reported," *New York Times* (June 5, 1991); Fox Butterfield, "Lust, Revenge, and Revolution," *New York Times* (March 4, 1984).

23. Kristof, "Suicide of Jiang Qing."

24. Ibid.

25. Ibid.

26. Schaeffer, *Power to the People: Democratization Around the World* (Boulder, CO: Westview Press, 1997), 78–79, 168–69.

27. Selden, *Political Economy,* 5.

28. Meisner, *Mao's China,* 455.

29. Ibid.

30. Henry Kissinger, *White House Years* (Boston: Little, Brown, 1979), 1058.

31. Margaret MacMillan, "Nixon, Kissinger, and the Opening to China," in *Nixon in the World: American Foreign Relations, 1969–1977,* ed. Fredrik Logevall and Andrew Preston (Oxford: Oxford University Press, 2008), 119.

32. MacMillan, Ibid., 112; Robert Dallek, *Nixon and Kissinger: Partners in Power* (New York: HarperCollins, 2007), 331.

33. Kissinger, *White House Years,* 1049.

34. Riskin, *China's Political Economy,* 193.

35. MacMillan, "Nixon, Kissinger," 120–21; North Korean dictator Kim Il Sung agreed, stating, "Nixon's visit to China is not a march of the victor but a trip of the defeated." This may have been the only accurate observation Kim ever made. Young Whan Kihl, *Politics and Policies in Divided Korea: Regimes in Contrast* (Boulder, CO: Westview Press, 1984), 56.

36. MacMillan, "Nixon, Kissinger," 109.

Chapter Five

1. Richard Baum, *Burying Mao: Chinese Politics in the Age of Deng Xiaoping* (Princeton, NJ: Princeton University Press, 1994), 17.

2. Daniel Kelliher, *Peasant Power in China: The Era of Rural Reform, 1979–1989* (New Haven, CT: Yale University Press, 1992), 11.

3. Thomas Bernstein, "Democratization in China," in *Global Transformation and the Third World,* ed. Robert O. Slater, Barry M. Schutz, and Steven R. Dorr (Boulder, CO: Lynne Rienner, 1993), 114.

4. Mark Selden, "The Social and Political Consequences of Chinese Reform: The Road to Tiananmen," in *Pacific-Asia and the Future of the World-System,* ed. Ravi Arvind Palat (Westport, CT: Greenwood Press, 1993), 152.

5. Sasumu Yabuki, *China's New Political Economy: The Giant Awakes* (Boulder, CO: Westview Press, 1995), 41–43.

6. Mark Selden, *The Political Economy of Chinese Development* (Armonk, NY: M. E. Sharpe, 1993), 196.

7. Carl Riskin, *China's Political Economy: The Quest for Development Since 1949* (Oxford: Oxford University Press, 1987), 294; Claude Aubert, "China's Food Takeoff?" in *Transforming China's Economy in the Eighties, Volume 1, The Rural Sector, Welfare, and Employment,* ed. Stephan Feuchtwang, Athar Hussain, and Thierry Pairault (London: Zed Books, 1988), 107.

8. Kelliher, *Peasant Power,* 89–90; Nicholas R. Lardy, *Agriculture in China's Modern Economic Development* (Cambridge: Cambridge University Press, 1983), 149; Mark Selden and Victor Lippit, *The Transition to Socialism in China* (Armonk, NY: M. E. Sharpe, 1982), 244; Yabuki, *China's New Political Economy,* 92. Per capita food grain consumption reached 1957 levels only in 1979. Lardy, *Agriculture,* 15. Per capita sugar consumption was "only a tenth of the world average. . . ." Ibid., 156.

9. Lardy, Ibid., 176.

10. Kathleen Hartford, "No Way Out? Rural Reforms and Food Policy in China," in *The Reform Decade in China: From Hope to Dismay,* ed. Marta Dassu and Tony Saich (London: Keegan Paul, 1992), 108n22.

11. Hartford, "No Way Out?" 81–82.

12. Kelliher, *Peasant Power,* 52.

13. Ian Jeffries, *Socialist Economies and the Transition to the Market: A Guide* (London: Routledge, 1993), 142; Riskin, *China's Political Economy,* 284–85; Kelliher, *Peasant Power,* 56; Hartford, "No Way Out?" 85–86.

14. Elisabeth Croll, *Women in China's Long Twentieth Century* (Berkeley: University of California Press, 2007), 33–36.

15. Ganesh K. Trichur, "Internal Migration in Mainland China: Regional and World-Systemic Aspects," in *Globalization and Emerging Societies: Development and Inequality,* ed. Jan Nederveen Pieterse and Boike Rehbein (New York: Palgrave MacMillan, 2009), 109.

16. Riskin, *China's Political Economy,* 286.

17. Kelliher, *Peasant Power,* 56.

18. David Zweig, *Freeing China's Farmers: Rural Restructuring in the Reform Era* (Armonk, NY: M. E. Sharpe, 1997), 47.

19. Riskin, *China's Political Economy,* 287.

20. Kelliher, *Peasant Power,* 59–60; Riskin, *China's Political Economy,* 286; Zweig, *Freeing China's Farmers,* 64–66.

21. Kelliher, *Peasant Power,* 79.

22. Trichur, "Internal Migration," 109–110; Kelliher, *Peasant Power,* 58.

23. Kelliher, Ibid., 234, 235, 237, 253.

24. Riskin, *China's Political Economy,* 288, 298.

25. Jean C. Oi, *State and Peasant: The Political Economy of Village Government* (Berkeley: University of California Press, 1989), 185–86.

26. Oi, *State and Peasant,* 206–08; Kelliher, *Peasant Power,* 206.

27. Oi, *State and Peasant,* 227.

28. Jeffries, *Socialist Economies,* 143.

29. There have been, evidently, some gray-market "sales" of land. Kelliher, *Peasant Power,* 183; Jeffries, *Socialist Economies,* 143.

30. Jeffries, Ibid.

31. Kelliher, *Peasant Power,* 139–40; Shujie Yao, *Agricultural Reforms and Grain Production in China* (New York: St. Martin's Press, 1994), 76.

32. Zweig, *Freeing China's Farmers,* 190; Jan S. Prybyla, *Reform in China and Other Socialist Economies* (Washington, DC: American Enterprise Institute, 1990), 174; Selden, *Political Economy,* 201.

33. Jeffries, *Socialist Economies,* 144; Selden, *Political Economy,* 177; Elisabeth J. Croll, "The New Peasant Economy," in Feuchtwang, Hussain, and Pairault, *Transforming China's Economy* (see note 7), 88.

34. Carl Riskin, Zhao Renwei, and Li Shi, "Introduction," in *China's Retreat from Equality: Income Distribution and Economic Transition,* ed. Carl Riskin, Zhao Renwei, and Li Shi (Armonk, NY: M. E. Sharpe, 2001), 16–17.

35. Daniel Southerland, "Gansu Province: 'A Third World' Within China," *Washington Post* (November 18, 1988).

36. Kelliher, *Peasant Power,* 189–90.

37. Hartford, "No Way Out?" 97; Oi, *State and Peasant,* 158.

38. Oi, Ibid., 160.

39. Kelliher, *Peasant Power,* 150.

40. Ibid., 179–80.

41. Zweig, *Freeing China's Farmers,* 332; Terry McKinley, *The Distribution of Wealth in Rural China* (Armonk, NY: M. E. Sharpe, 1996), 68; Kelliher, *Peasant Power,* 193–94.

42. McKinley, *Distribution of Wealth,* 68, 128; Zweig, *Freeing China's Farmers,* 76.

43. Riskin, *China's Political Economy,* 300.

44. Kelliher, *Peasant Power,* 204.

45. During the 1980s "the real rates of return on all forms of financial assets were turning negative." McKinley, *Distribution of Wealth,* 90.

46. Selden, *Political Economy,* 34.

47. McKinley, *Distribution of Wealth,* 19, 70; Selden, *Political Economy,* 310; Jean C. Oi, *Rural China Takes Off: Institutional Foundations of Economic Reform* (Berkeley: University of California Press, 1999), 22.

48. Kelliher, *Peasant Power,* 149.

49. Ibid., 174.

50. Yao, *Reforms,* 69; Kelliher, *Peasant Power,* 124; Aubert, "China's Food Takeoff?" 126.

51. Kelliher, *Peasant Power,* 144.

52. Ibid., 110, 137.

53. Oi, *State and Peasant,* 175; Kelliher, *Peasant Power,* 168; Hartford, "No Way Out?" 98; Yabuki, *China's New Political Economy,* 91.

54. Robert K. Schaeffer, *Power to the People: Democratization Around the World* (Boulder, CO: Westview Press, 1997), 151n164.

55. Zweig, *Freeing China's Farmers,* 333, 340; Yao, *Agricultural Reforms,* 29.

56. Jeffries, *Socialist Economies,* 154; Tony Saich, "The Reform Decade in China: The Limits to Revolution from Above," in Dassu and Saich, *The Reform Decade* (see note 10), 29–30; Harlan W. Jencks, "The Military in China," *Current History* (September 1989), 265–91.

57. Jencks, Ibid., 265.

58. Gerald Segal, "The Challenges to Chinese Foreign Policy," in Dassu and Saich, *The Reform Decade* (see note 10), 182–83; Roberto Bertinelli, "China's Open-Door Policy: Results and Perspectives," in Dassu and Saich, Ibid., 208–09.

59. Schaeffer, *Power to the People,* 84–97, 98–131.

60. Riskin, *China's Political Economy,* 322, 369. In 1984 manufactured goods comprised more than half of all exports from China, agricultural goods about 12 percent, and raw materials about 30 percent. Alice H. Amsden, *The Rise of 'The Rest': Challenges to the West from Late-Industrializing Economies* (Oxford: Oxford University Press, 2001), 178–79.

61. Susan L. Shirk, *The Political Logic of Economic Reform in China* (Berkeley: University of California Press, 1993), 49; Riskin, *China's Political Economy,* 333–34; Gang Xu, "China in the Pacific Rim: Trade and Investment Links," in *Changing China: A Geographical Appraisal,* ed. Chiao-min Hsieh and Max Lu (Boulder, CO: Westview Press, 2004), 175–76; Meredith Woo-Cumings, "The 'New Authoritarianism' in East Asia," *Current History* (December 1994), 283.

62. Shirk, *Political Logic,* 48.

63. Hsin-Huang Michael Hsiao and Alvin So, "Ascent Through National Integration: The Chinese Triangle of Mainland–Taiwan–Hong Kong," in Palat, *Pacific-Asia* (see note 4), 135.

64. Prybyla, *Reform in China,* 241; Jan S. Prybyla, "All That Glitters: The Foreign Investment Boom," *Current History* (September 1995), 275; Schaeffer, *Power to the People,* 150n152. Estimates about the size of foreign direct investment vary considerably. Jan Prybyla says that total FDI between 1979 and 1991 "came to $51 billion contracted and $26 billion actual," whereas other scholars argue for a much lower figure: $3.1 billion between 1979 and 1988. Giovanni Arrighi, Po-Keung Hui, Ho-Fung Hung, and Mark Selden, "Historical Capitalism, East and West," in *The Resurgence of East Asia: 500, 150, and 50 Year Perspectives,* ed. Giovanni Arrighi, Takeshi Hamashita, and Mark Selden (London: Routledge, 2003), 314–15, 317.

65. Meredith Woo-Cumings, "East Asia's America Problem," in *Past as Prelude: History in the Making of a New World Order,* ed. Meredith Woo-Cumings and Michael Loriaux (Boulder, CO: Westview Press, 1993), 155; Arrighi, Hui, Hung, and Selden, "Historical Capitalism," 315, 317; Hsiao and So, "Ascent," 140.

66. Hsiao and So, Ibid., 138.

67. Arrighi, Hui, Hung, and Selden, "Historical Capitalism," 314.

68. Riskin, *China's Political Economy,* 325–26.

69. Schaeffer, *Power to the People,* 131.

70. Yabuki, *China's New Political Economy,* 47; Richard Baum, *Burying Mao,* 68.

71. Joseph Fewsmith, "Elite Politics," in *The Paradox of China's Post-Mao Reforms,* ed. Merle Goldman and Roderick MacFarquhar (Cambridge, MA: Harvard University Press, 1999), 69.

72. Elizabeth J. Perry, "Crime, Corruption, and Contention," in Goldman and MacFarquhar, Ibid., 313.

73. Riskin, *China's Political Economy,* 336.

74. Giovanni Arrighi and Beverly Silver, *Chaos and Governance in the Modern World-System* (Minneapolis: University of Minnesota Press, 1999), 121–22; Sun Sheng Han, "Agricultural Surplus Labor Transfer," in *The Population of Modern China,* ed. Dudley J. Poston Jr. and David Yaukey (New York: Plenum Press, 1992), 78.

75. As Arrighi and Silver have argued, "Large-scale migration to cities and rapid growth of the urban population would have bankrupted the state coffer and must therefore be prevented." Arrighi and Silver, *Chaos,* 44.

76. Kate Merkel-Hess and Jeffrey N. Wasserstrom, "A Country on the Move: China Urbanizes," *Current History* (April 2009), 167.

77. Dorothy J. Solinger, "China's Floating Population," in Goldman and MacFarquhar, *The Paradox* (see note 71), 223.

78. Arrighi and Silver, *Chaos,* 50, 22; Solinger, "China's Floating Population," 223–24.

79. Solinger, Ibid., 234.

80. Ibid., 235–36; Merkel-Hess and Wasserstrom, "A Country on the Move," 170–71.

81. Solinger, "China's Floating Population," 235.

82. George J. Gilboy and Eric Heginbotham, "The Latin Americanization of China?" *Current History* (September 2004), 259.

83. Trichur, "Internal Migration,"104; Jeffries, *Socialist Economies,* 148. The number of migrants is difficult to estimate, and some scholars suggest it could have been two or three times as many. Selden, *Political Economy,* 32; Hartford, "No Way Out?" 101.

84. Kam Wing Chan, "Internal Migration," in Hsieh and Lu, *Changing China* (see note 61), 236–37; C. Cindy Fan, "Gender Differences in Chinese Migration," in Hsieh and Lu, Ibid., 256–57. The US government encouraged this kind of settler colonialism in California and Texas during the mid-nineteenth century.

85. Gail Hershatter, *Women in China's Long Twentieth Century* (Berkeley: University of California Press, 2007), 67.

86. Arrighi and Silver, *Chaos,* 164.

87. Steven Greenhouse and Elizabeth Becker, "A.F.L.-C.I.O. to Press Bush," *New York Times* (March 16, 2004).

88. Eric Eckholm, "How's China Doing? Yardsticks You Never Thought Of," *New York Times* (April, 11, 2004); Robert Schaeffer, "Dilemmas of Sovereignty and Citizenship in the Republican Interstate System," in *The Constitutional and Political Regulation of Ethnic Relations and Conflicts,* ed. Mitja Zagar, Boris Jesih, and Romana Bester (Ljubljana, Slovenia: Institute for Ethnic Studies, 1999), 11–12.

89. C. Cindy Fan, *China on the Move: Migration, the State, and the Household* (London: Routledge, 2008), 53, 4. Trichur, "Internal Migration," 112.

90. Fan, *China on the Move,* 7.

91. Schaeffer, "Dilemmas of Sovereignty and Citizenship," 11–12.

92. Solinger, "China's Floating Population," 232–33, 239.

93. Fan, *China on the Move,* 43, 46.

94. Eric Eckholm, "As Beijing Pretties Up, Migrants Face Expulsion," *New York Times* (April, 18, 1999).

95. Nan Lin, *The Struggle for Tiananmen: Anatomy of the 1989 Mass Movement* (Westport, CT: Praeger, 1992), 38–39.

96. Gilboy and Heginbotham, "The Latin Americanization of China," 260.

97. Fan, *China on the Move,* 107–10, 109.

98. Ibid., 105–06.

99. "Industrial accidents claim more than 30,000 fingers from workers each year," and the "standard payout for such injuries is $60 per finger." Gilboy and Heginbotham, "The Latin Americanization of China?" 260.

100. Fan, *China on the Move,* 108.

101. Ibid., 24, 48; Ann Tyson and James Tyson, "China's Human Avalanche," *Current History* (September 1996), 277; Merkel-Hess and Wasserstrom, "A Country on the Move," 169; Howard W. French, "China Strains to Fit Migrants into Mainstream Classes," *New York Times* (January 25, 2001).

102. Hershatter, *Women in China's Long Twentieth Century,* 70–71, 70.

103. "In some developing countries and poor areas, migration and remittances from migrant work are essential for the subsistence of rural households and households in poverty." Fan, *China on the Move,* 8.

104. C. Cindy Fan, "Out to the City and Back to the Village: The Experiences and Contributions of Rural Women Migrating from Sichuan and Anhui," in *On the Move: Women and Rural-to-Urban Migration in Contemporary China,* ed. Arianne M. Gaetano and Tamara Jacka (New York: Columbia University Press, 2004), 187.

105. Ibid., 188 (emphasis added).

106. Fan, *China on the Move,* 91.

107. Rachel Murphy, "The Impact of Labor Migration on the Well-Being and Agency of Rural Chinese Women: Cultural and Economic Contexts and Life Courses," in Gaetano and Jacka, *On the Move* (see note 104), 256, 262, 270.

108. Fan, *China on the Move,* 89.

109. Ibid., 12–13; Bettina Gransow, "Risk Employment and Social Risk Management—Job Searching Strategies of Rural-to-Urban Migration," in *Labour Mobilization in Urban China,* ed. Michela Baur, Bettina Gransow, Yihong Jin, and Guonqing Shi (Berlin: Lit Verlag, 2006), 91.

110. Torry D. Dickinson and Robert K. Schaeffer, *Fast Forward: Work, Gender and Protest in a Changing World* (Lanham, MD: Rowman and Littlefield, 2001), 32, 168.

111. Fan, *China on the Move,* 9.

112. Susan Greenhalgh and Edwin A. Winckler, *Governing China's Population: From Leninist to Neoliberal Biopolitics* (Stanford, CA: Stanford University Press, 2005), 100; Scharping, *Birth Control,* 61.

113. Greenhalgh and Winckler, *China's Population,* 64, 78–79; Tyrene White, *China's Longest Campaign: Birth Planning in the People's Republic, 1949–2005* (Ithaca, NY: Cornell University Press, 2006), 248.

114. Susan Greenhalgh, *Just One Child: Science and Policy in Deng's China* (Berkeley: University of California Press, 2008), 59.

115. Greenhalgh and Winckler, *China's Population,* 85.

116. Greenhalgh, *Just One Child,* 59.

117. Greenhalgh and Winckler, *China's Population,* 85.

118. Greenhalgh, *Just One Child,* 75, 87.

119. Ibid., 88; Greenhalgh and Winckler, *China's Population,* 95.

120. Greenhalgh, *Just One Child,* 234.

121. Dudley Poston Jr. and Yu Mei-Yu, "The Distribution of Overseas Chinese," in Poston and Yaukey, *Population of Modern China* (see note 74), 1.

122. Greenhalgh and Winckler, *China's Population,* 219; Croll, *Women in China's Long Twentieth Century,* 89.

123. Greenhalgh and Winckler, *China's Population,* 250.

124. White, *China's Longest Campaign,* 2.

125. Scharping, *Birth Control,* 101.

126. White, *China's Longest Campaign,* 90–91.

127. Ibid., 86; Greenhalgh and Winckler, *China's Population,* 233; Karin Evans, *The Lost Daughters of China* (New York: Tarcher/Putnam, 2000), 105–06.

128. White, *China's Longest Campaign,* 89, 107.

129. Scharping, *Birth Control,* 179.

130. Delia Davin, "The Single-Child Family Policy in the Countryside," in *China's One-Child Family Policy,* ed. Elisabeth Croll, Delia Davin, and Penny Kane (New York:

St. Martin's Press, 1985), 98–99; Scharping, *Birth Control,* 129. Over time the value of economic incentives declined because the regime failed to adjust them for inflation, which grew rapidly during the 1980s. Scharping, Ibid., 142.

131. Scharping, Ibid., 147.

132. Davin, "Single-Child Family Policy," 50.

133. Ibid.; Margery Wolf, *Revolution Postponed: Women in Contemporary China* (Stanford, CA: Stanford University Press, 1985), 118; White, *China's Longest Campaign,* 105, 120.

134. White, Ibid., 97; Scharping, *Birth Control,* 136–37, 141, 145, 149.

135. White, *China's Longest Campaign,* 30; Davin, "Single-Child Family Policy," 50.

136. Scharping, *Birth Control,* 141.

137. White, *China's Longest Campaign,* 170; Greenhalgh and Winckler, *China's Population,* 129.

138. Greenhalgh and Winckler, Ibid., 139.

139. Tyson and Tyson, "China's Human Avalanche," 277.

140. Evans, *Lost Daughters,* 105, 114.

141. Scharping, *Birth Control,* 107.

142. White, *China's Longest Campaign,* 109, 110.

143. Greenhalgh and Winckler, *China's Population,* 223.

144. White, *China's Longest Campaign,* 136; Scharping, *Birth Control,* 123.

145. White, *China's Longest Campaign,* 134; Scharping, *Birth Control,* 108.

146. White, *China's Longest Campaign,* 134; Scharping, *Birth Control,* 57.

147. White, *China's Longest Campaign,* 136, 141.

148. Evans, *Lost Daughters,* 111 (emphasis in the original).

149. Greenhalgh and Winckler, *China's Population,* 256–57.

150. Scharping, *Birth Control,* 57.

151. Greenhalgh, *Just One Child,* 1; Greenhalgh and Winckler, *China's Population,* 112, 319.

152. Greenhalgh and Winckler, Ibid., 259, 261, 252, 272; Evans, *Lost Daughters,* 111.

153. Davin, "Single-Child Family Policy," 38, 68.

154. Scharping, *Birth Control,* 224.

155. Greenhalgh and Winckler, *China's Population,* 262.

156. Scharping, *Birth Control,* 225; Riskin, *China's Political Economy,* 304.

157. Greenhalgh and Winckler, *China's Population,* 231.

158. Greenhalgh and Winckler, *China's Population,* 263. Cartier said that the suicide rate for women is "40 percent higher than among men." Carolyn Cartier, "Engendering Industrialization in China Under Reform," in Hsieh and Lu, *Changing China* (see note 61), 282.

159. Cartier, Ibid.

160. Emile Durkheim, *Suicide* (New York: The Free Press, 1989), 71.

161. World Health Organization, "Suicide Rates Per 100,000 by Country, Year, and Sex, 2008," www.who/int/mental-health/prevention/suicide_rates/en/print/html.

162. Evans, *Lost Daughters,* 114; White, *China's Longest Campaign,* 202.

163. White, Ibid., 148, 200–04.

164. Evans, *Lost Daughters,* 113.

165. White, *China's Longest Campaign,* 203.

166. Kay Ann Johnson, *Wanting a Daughter, Needing a Son: Abandonment, Adoption, and Orphanage Care in China* (St. Paul, MN: Young and Young, 2004), 60; Greenhalgh and Winckler, *China's Population,* 226.

167. Rita J. Simon and Howard Altstein, *Adoption Across Borders: Serving the Children in Transracial and Intercountry Adoptions* (Lanham, MD: Rowman and Littlefield, 2000), 11.

168. Scharping, *Birth Control,* 228–29.

169. Greenhalgh and Winckler, *China's Population,* 269; Johnson, *Wanting a Daughter,* 22, 38, 70.

170. Simon and Altstein, *Adoption Across Borders,* 8, 10.

171. Greenhalgh and Winckler, *China's Population,* 266–67.

172. Ibid., 267, 275.

173. Cartier, "Engendering Industrialization," 279.

174. White, *China's Longest Campaign,* 172–99; Scharping, *Birth Control,* 230–31.

175. Scharping, Ibid., 227; Cartier, "Engendering Industrialization," 16; Greenhalgh and Winckler, *China's Population,* 278.

176. Greenhalgh and Winckler, Ibid., 278–79.

177. Greenhalgh, *Just One Child,* 151.

178. Scharping, *Birth Control,* 68.

179. White, *China's Longest Campaign,* xii.

180. Greenhalgh, *Just One Child,* 34.

181. Davin, "Single-Child Family Policy," 74.

182. Greenhalgh and Winckler, *China's Population,* 19; Greenhalgh, *Just One Child,* 42.

183. White, *China's Longest Campaign,* 233, 200.

184. Greenhalgh and Winckler, *China's Population,* 249, 250.

185. Greenhalgh, *Just One Child,* 237 (emphasis added), 245, 258. See the critique of the science behind the number, 237–59.

186. Greenhalgh and Winckler, *China's Population,* 3.

187. Riskin, *China's Political Economy,* 303; Davin, "Single-Child Family Policy," 42. Scharping says that total fertility rates for urban and rural women declined from 6.57 in 1964 to 2.97 in 1978. *Birth Control,* 240, 253, 271.

188. White, *China's Longest Campaign,* 75.

189. Greenhalgh and Winckler, *China's Population,* 313; Scharping, *Birth Control,* 259.

190. White, *China's Longest Campaign,* 75.

191. Dickinson and Schaeffer, *Fast Forward,* 40n42, n43.

192. Scharping, *Birth Control,* 311.

193. My colleague, the demographer Laszlo Kulcsar, suggested this as a possible reason for the dramatic decline in fertility rates in China during the 1960s.

194. Yao, *Agricultural Reforms,* 41, 78, 41, 42.

195. Scharping, *Birth Control,* 335.

196. Robert K. Schaeffer, *Understanding Globalization: The Social Consequences of Political, Economic, and Environmental Change* (Lanham, MD: Rowman and Littlefield, 1997), 222–25, 225–26.

197. Amartya Sen, "Population: Delusion and Reality," *New York Review of Books* (September 22, 1994), 68, 70.

198. Greenhalgh and Winckler, *China's Population,* 317.

199. Sen, "Population," 69, 71.

Chapter Six

1. Robert Devlin, Antoni Estevadeordal, and Andres Rodriquez-Clare, eds., *The Emergence of China: Opportunities and Challenges for Latin America and the Caribbean* (New York: Inter-American Development Bank; David Rockefeller Center for Latin American Studies, Harvard University, 2006), xxv, xxi.

2. Robert K. Schaeffer, *Understanding Globalization: The Social Consequences of Political, Economic and Environmental Change* (Lanham, MD: Rowman and Littlefield, 2009), 181n4.

3. Torry D. Dickinson and Robert K. Schaeffer, *Fast Forward: Work, Gender and Protest in a Changing World* (Lanham, MD: Rowman and Littlefield, 2001), 124n70.

4. Ibid.

5. Robert K. Schaeffer, *Power to the People: Democratization Around the World* (Boulder, CO: Westview Press, 1997), 134n8, 134n13.

6. Ibid., 137n37, n38, n39; 137n37, n38, n39; 137n36.

7. Ibid., 137n42, n43; 137n40, n41.

8. Prior to this, US Secretary of State Dean Acheson had placed them outside the "defensive perimeter" of the United States and argued that "it must be clear that no person can guarantee these areas against military attack." Schaeffer, Ibid., 134n15. But the war quickly changed US policy, and the Truman administration moved to protect both South Korea and Taiwan. Ibid., 135n19, n20.

9. Schaeffer, *Understanding Globalization,* 158n38.

10. Schaeffer, *Power to the People,* 135, 236n26, 136n27.

11. Ibid., 136n30, 136.

12. Dickinson and Schaeffer, *Fast Forward,* 125n74, 126.

13. Schaeffer, *Understanding Globalization,* 42n18, 44n26, 42–43, see also 35–60.

14. Schaeffer, *Power to the People,* 140n61.

15. You-tien Hsing, *Making Capitalism in China: The Taiwan Connection* (New York: Oxford University Press, 1998), 14.

16. Schaeffer, *Power to the People,* 141, 141n65.

17. Hsing, *Making Capitalism,* 14.

18. Schaeffer, *Power to the People,* 143n84.

19. Hsing, *Making Capitalism,* 14; Schaeffer, *Power to the People,* 144n95.

20. Schaeffer, Ibid., 145n104.

21. Hsing, *Making Capitalism,* 50, 13, 50.

22. Schaeffer, *Power to the People,* 142n77, n78.

23. Hsing, *Making Capitalism,* 15; Dickinson and Schaeffer, *Fast Forward,* 127n77.

24. Schaeffer, *Power to the People,* 147n125.

25. Ibid., 145n107, 145n108, 145n109.

26. Ibid., 147n127, 147n128.

27. Ibid., 147n129, 147n130; Tun-Jen Cheng, "The Economic Significance of Taiwan's Democratization," in *Taiwan's Economic Success Since 1990,* ed. Chao-Cheng Mai and Chien-Sheng Shih (Cheltenham, UK: Edward Elgar, 2001), 127.

28. Schaeffer, *Power to the People,* 147–48n131, n132, n133.

29. Ibid., 141; Clark L. Clifford, *Troubled Tiger: Businessmen, Bureaucrats, and Generals in South Korea* (Armonk, NY: M. E. Sharpe, 1998), 239.

30. Clifford, Ibid.

31. Schaeffer, *Power to the People,* 159n41.

32. Ibid., 144n96, n97, n98, n99.

33. Ibid., 143n91, n88, n89, n90.

34. Ibid., 144n100, n101, n102; Clifford, *Troubled Tiger*, 276.

35. John Kie-chiang Oh, *Korean Politics: The Quest for Democratization and Economic Development* (Ithaca, NY: Cornell University Press, 1999), 112–13; Young Whan Kihl, *Transforming Korean Politics: Democracy, Reform, and Culture* (Armonk, NY: M. E. Sharpe, 2005), 81.

36. Schaeffer, *Power to the People*, 144n92, n93, n94; Oh, *Korean Politics*, 90.

37. Oh, Ibid., 88.

38. Carl J. Saxer, *From Transition to Power Alternation: Democracy in South Korea, 1987–1997* (New York: Routledge, 2002), 57, 59; Oh, *Korean Politics*, 87.

39. Schaeffer, *Understanding Globalization*, 161n48; Clifford, *Troubled Tiger*, 233.

40. Schaeffer, *Understanding Globalization*, 156.

41. Saxer, *From Transition*, 58–59.

42. Schaeffer, *Understanding Globalization*, 161n49.

43. Oh, *Korean Politics*, 116–19.

44. Tun-Jen Cheng, "The Economic Significance of Taiwan's Democratization," in Mai and Shih, *Taiwan's Economic Success* (see note 27), 145–46; Oh, *Korean Politics*, 136.

45. Jiann-Chyuan Wang and Chao-Cheng Mai, "Industrial Development Strategy and Structural Transformation," in Mai and Shih, *Taiwan's Economic Success* (see note 27), 214.

46. Gang Xu, "China in the Pacific Rim: Trade and Investment Links," in *Changing China: A Geographical Appraisal*, ed. Chiao-min Hsieh and Max Lu (Boulder, CO: Westview Press, 2004), 177.

47. Andrew J. Nathan, *China's Crisis: Dilemmas of Reform and Prospects for Democracy* (New York: Columbia University Press, 1990), 100.

48. Xu, "China in the Pacific Rim," 177.

49. Hsing, *Making Capitalism*, 79.

50. Ganesh K. Trichur, "Internal Migration in Mainland China: Regional and World-Systemic Aspects," in *Globalization and Emerging Societies: Development and Inequality*, ed. Jan Nederveen Pieterse and Boike Rehbein (New York: Palgrave MacMillan, 2009), 117–18.

51. Hsing, *Making Capitalism*, 91.

52. Hsin-Huang Michael Hsiao and Alvin So, "Ascent Through National Integration: The Chinese Triangle of Mainland–Taiwan–Hong Kong," in *Pacific-Asia and the Future of the World-System*, ed. Ravi Arvind Palat (Westport, CT: Greenwood Press, 1993), 138.

53. Hsing, *Making Capitalism*, 1.

54. Oh, *Korean Politics*, 114.

55. Nicholas R. Lardy, *Integrating China into the Global Economy* (Washington, DC: Brookings Institution Press, 2002), 160–61.

56. Hsing, *Making Capitalism*, 51.

57. Lardy, *Integrating China*, 52.

58. Nicholas D. Kristof, "How the Hardliners Won," *New York Times Magazine* (November 12, 1989); Richard Baum, *Burying Mao: Chinese Politics in the Age of Deng Xiaoping* (Princeton, NJ: Princeton University Press, 1994), 253.

59. Kristof, "How the Hardliners Won," 41; Baum, *Burying Mao*, 253–54.

60. Schaeffer, *Power to the People*, 178–79, 179n40, 180–81.

61. Mark Selden, "The Social and Political Consequences of Chinese Reform: The Road to Tiananmen," in Palat, *Pacific-Asia* (see note 52), 159–60.

62. Jay Matthews, "Whuan Wakes to *Minzhu:* Democracy a Hazy Concept in Industrial City," *Washington Post* (May 29, 1989).

63. Selden, "Social and Political Consequences," 160.

64. Rensselaer W. Lee, III, "Issues in Chinese Economic Reform," in *Economic Reform in Three Giants,* ed. John Echeverri-Gent and Friedemann Muller (Washington, DC: Overseas Development Council, 1990), 84 (emphasis added).

65. Elizabeth J. Perry, "Crime, Corruption, and Contention," in *The Paradox of China's Post-Mao Reforms,* ed. Merle Goldman and Roderick MacFarquhar (Cambridge, MA: Harvard University Press, 1999), 314.

66. Lee, "Issues in Chinese Economic Reform," 84.

67. Mark Selden, *The Political Economy of Chinese Development* (Armonk, NY: M. E. Sharpe, 1993), 211; Nathan, *China's Crisis,* 113.

68. Nathan, Ibid., 110.

69. Barry Naughton, "Inflation and Economic Reform in China," *Current History* (September 1989), 270.

70. Nathan, *China's Crisis,* 108.

71. Naughton, "Inflation," 270–71.

72. Schaeffer, *Power to the People,* 151n167, n168.

73. Kathleen Hartford, "The Political Economy Behind Beijing Spring," in *The Chinese People's Movement: Perspectives on Spring 1989,* ed. Tony Saich (Armonk, NY: M. E. Sharpe, 1990), 64; Jan S. Prybyla, *Reform in China and Other Socialist Economies* (Washington, DC: American Enterprise Institute, 1990), 176.

74. Prybyla, Ibid.

75. Schaeffer, *Power to the People,* 151n166; Selden, *Political Economy,* 220; Sasumu Yabuki, *China's New Political Economy: The Giant Awakes* (Boulder, CO: Westview Press, 1995), 124.

76. Prybyla, *Reform in China,* 176. "For a few months in the summer of 1988 prices were actually rising at an annual rate of about 80 percent," Naughton observed. Naughton, "Inflation," 270.

77. Schaeffer, *Power to the People,* 151–52n169.

78. Lee, "Issues in Chinese Economic Reform," 80.

79. Selden, "Social and Political Consequences," 157.

80. Naughton, "Inflation," 270.

81. Baum, *Burying Mao,* 192.

82. Prybyla, *Reform in China,* 177.

83. Hartford, "Beijing Spring," 72.

84. Schaeffer, *Power to the People,* 152n171.

85. Marie-Claire Bergere, "Tiananmen 1989: Background and Consequences," in *The Reform Decade in China: From Hope to Dismay,* ed. Marta Dassu and Tony Saich (London: Kegan Paul, 1992), 134, 144; Lee, "Issues in Chinese Economic Reform," 82.

86. Selden, "Social and Political Consequences," 158.

87. Ibid., 161, 162.

88. Schaeffer, *Power to the People,* 152n178.

89. Selden, "Social and Political Consequences," 163.

90. During his visit Gorbachev dismissed the protestors as "hotheads." As he told Zhao Ziyang, "We are struggling with a similar phenomena. We also have hotheads who, in most

cases, favor the renewal of socialism, but who are more intent on that than on the leadership of the party which began the process. They want it all done in one night. This is not the way it happens in life. This only happens in fairy tales." Sheryl WuDunn, "Gorbachev Backs Away from Protest 'Hotheads,'" *New York Times* (May 17, 1989).

91. Kristof, "How the Hardliners Won," 66; see also "It Is Necessary to Take a Clear-Cut Stand Against Disturbances," *Renmin ribao (People's Daily)*, April 26, 1989.

92. Melanie Manion, "Introduction: Reluctant Duelists," in *Beijing Spring: Confrontation and Conflict: The Basic Documents,* ed. Michel Oksenberg, Lawrence R. Sullivan, and Marc Lambert (Armonk, NY: M. E. Sharpe, 1990), xvii.

93. Schaeffer, *Power to the People,* 152n179.

94. Baum, *Burying Mao,* 263, 264–65, 268–69; Schaeffer, *Power to the People,* 152n181.

95. Baum, *Burying Mao,* 276.

96. Selden, "Social and Political Consequences," 167.

97. Schaeffer, *Power to the People,* 153n185, n186, n187.

98. Selden has argued that there were significant divisions: "Political divisions at the highest level became manifest in the public conflict between Party Secretary Zhao Ziyang and Premier Li Peng over official response to the movement in the usurpation of power of the Politburo Standing Committee by Deng Xiaoping . . . and in the refusal of the Thirty-eighth Army leadership to follow orders to crush the demonstrations." Selden, *Political Economy,* 224.

99. Kristof, "How the Hardliners Won," 66.

100. Nicholas D. Kristof, "China Erupts," *New York Times Magazine* (June 4, 1989), 90; Kristof, "How the Hardliners Won," 65–66.

101. Nathan, *China's Crisis,* 205.

102. Zhao Ziyang, *Prisoner of the State: The Secret Journal of Zhao Ziyang* (New York: Simon and Schuster, 2009), 10.

103. Kristof, "How the Hardliners Won," 67, 68.

104. Deng Xiaoping, "Deng's June 9 Speech: 'We Found a Rebellious Clique' and 'Dregs of Society,'" *New York Times* (June 30, 1989).

105. Ibid.

Chapter Seven

1. You-tien Hsing, *Making Capitalism in China: The Taiwan Connection* (New York: Oxford University Press, 1998), 83.

2. John Kie-chiang Oh, *Korean Politics: The Quest for Democratization and Economic Development* (Ithaca, NY: Cornell University Press, 1999), 197, 198.

3. Yan Zhu, "The Role of the Overseas Chinese in the Sino-Japanese Economic Relationship," in *Japan and China: Cooperation, Competition, and Conflict,* ed. Hanns Gunther-Hilpert and Rene Haak (New York: Palgrave, 2002), 198, 200, 196–97.

4. Robert K. Schaeffer, *Understanding Globalization: The Social Consequences of Political, Economic and Environmental Change* (Lanham, MD: Rowman and Littlefield, 2009), 35–60.

5. Satoshi Ikeda, *The Trifurcating Miracle: Corporations, Workers, Bureaucrats, and the Erosion of Japan's National Economy* (New York: Routledge, 2002), 59, 81.

6. Ibid., 59.

7. Jiann-Chyuan Wang and Chao-Cheng Mai, "Industrial Development Strategy and Structural Transformation," in *Taiwan's Economic Success Since 1990*, ed. Chao-Cheng Mai and Chien-Sheng Shih (Cheltenham, UK: Edward Elger, 2001), 211. For instance, "the registered capital of Japanese firms in Thailand rose from 2.8 billion baht in 1986 to 38 billion baht in 1991." Pasuk Phongpaichit and Chris Baker, *Thailand's Crisis* (Chiang, Mai, Thailand: Silkworm Books, 2000), 33.

8. T. J. Pempel, "Japan's Search for a New Path," *Current History* (December 1998), 433.

9. Ibid., 434; Richard Katz, *Japan: The System That Soured: The Rise and Fall of the Japanese Economic Miracle* (Armonk, NY: M. E. Sharpe, 1998), 5.

10. Katz, Ibid., 230; Wang and Mai, "Industrial Development," 213; Schaeffer, *Understanding Globalization*, 52.

11. Schaeffer, Ibid., 53n55, n56.

12. Greg Austin and Stuart Harris, *Japan and Greater China: Political Economy and Military Power in the Asian Century* (London: Hurst and Co., 2001), 227, 213; Zhu, "Overseas Chinese," 194; Katsuji Nakagane, "Japanese Direct Investment in China: Its Effects on China's Economic Development," in Gunther-Hilpert and Haak, *Japan and China* (see note 3), 54.

13. Katz, *Japan*, 10.

14. David Barboza, "Some Assembly Needed: China as Asia Factory," *New York Times* (February 9, 2006).

15. Jorge G. Casteneda, "The Clouding Political Horizon," *Current History* (February 1993), 64; Nora Lustig, *Mexico: The Remaking of an Economy* (Washington, DC: Brookings Institution Press, 1998), 125, 148–49, 155–56; Paul Krugman, *The Return of Depression Economics* (New York: W. W. Norton, 1999), 45.

16. Casteneda, "Political Horizon," 64.

17. Lustig, *Mexico,* 155–56.

18. Krugman, *Depression Economics*, 50.

19. Lustig, *Mexico*, 144–45, 148–49; Krugman, *Depression Economics*, 49.

20. Schaeffer, *Understanding Globalization*, 44–46.

21. Peter H. Smith, "Political Dimensions of the Peso Crisis," in *Mexico 1994: Anatomy of an Emerging-Market Crash*, ed. Sebastian Edwards and Moises Naim (Washington, DC: Carnegie Endowment for International Peace, 1997), 39–40.

22. Suzanne Bilello, "Mexico: The Rise of Civil Society," *Current History* (February 1996), 85.

23. Smith, "Peso Crisis," 42, 40; Lustig, *Mexico*, 158.

24. Sebastian Edwards, "Bad Luck or Bad Policies: An Economic Analysis of the Mexican Crisis," in Edwards and Naim, *Mexico 1994* (see note 21), 114.

25. Lustig, *Mexico*, 158; Smith, "Peso Crisis," 41.

26. Edwards, "Bad Luck," 111–12; Lustig, *Mexico*, 158.

27. Smith, "Peso Crisis," 40–41.

28. Lustig, *Mexico,* 158; Edwards, "Bad Luck," 117.

29. Edwards, Ibid., 116; Lustig, *Mexico*, 160, 162.

30. Lustig, Ibid., 162.

31. Krugman, *Depression Economics*, 56; Lustig, *Mexico*, 170.

32. Smith, "Peso Crisis," 45; Krugman, *Depression Economics*, 54.

33. Krugman, Ibid., 54–56.

34. Lustig, *Mexico*, 194.

35. Paul Fischer, *Foreign Direct Investment in Russia: A Strategy for Industrial Recovery* (New York: St. Martin's Press, 2000), 249–50; Jorge G. Casteneda, "NAFTA at 10: A Plus or a Minus?" *Current History* (February 2004).

36. Casteneda, "NAFTA at 10," 53–54.

37. The manufacturing firms located in "maquiladoras" along the US-Mexico border had long been exempt from tariffs. NAFTA essentially reduced tariffs for export-oriented firms in the rest of Mexico.

38. Oded Shenkar, *The Chinese Century: The Rising Chinese Economy and Its Impact on the Global Economy, the Balance of Power, and Your Job* (Upper Saddle River, NJ: Wharton School, 2006), 110.

39. Schaeffer, *Understanding Globalization*, 195.

40. Marcos Ancelovici and Sara Jane McCaffrey, "From NAFTA to China? Production Shifts and their Implications for Taiwanese Firms," in *Global Taiwan: Building Competitive Strengths in a New International Economy*, ed. Suzanne Berger and Richard K. Lester (Armonk, NY: M. E. Sharpe, 2005), 183.

41. Elisabeth Malkin, "Manufacturing Jobs Are Exiting Mexico: Business Leaders Try to Stop the Exodus of Factories to China," *New York Times* (November 5, 2002); Ancelovici and McCaffrey, "NAFTA to China?" 187.

42. Ancelovici and McCaffrey, Ibid., 172.

43. Shenkar, *Chinese Century*, 111.

44. Ancelovici and McCaffrey, "NAFTA to China?" 176, 166.

45. Malkin, "Manufacturing Jobs Are Exiting."

46. Krugman, *Depression Economics*, 85.

47. "The biggest capital importers between 1990 and 1995 were, in descending order, China, Mexico, Brazil, South Korea, Malaysia, Argentina, Thailand, and Indonesia." Barry Eichengreen, "The Tyranny of Financial Markets," *Current History* (November 1997), 377.

48. Torry D. Dickinson and Robert K. Schaeffer, *Fast Forward: Work, Gender and Protest in a Changing World* (Lanham, MD: Rowman and Littlefield, 2001), 128n85.

49. "The real exchange rate appreciated in all five of the most affected countries in 1995 and 1996, choking exports." Robert Wade, "The Asian Crisis and the Global Economy: Causes, Consequences, and Cure," *Current History* (November 1999), 364. "The real exchange rate [of the Thai baht] appreciated by 10 percent" between 1990 and 1997." Ejaz Nabi and Jayankar Shivakuman, *Back from the Brink: Thailand's Response to the 1997 Economic Crisis* (Washington, DC: The World Bank, 2001), 10. The South Korean won "appreciated in real terms about 12 percent between 1990 and 1997." Hyun-Hoon Lee, "A 'Stroke' Hypothesis of Korea's 1997 Financial Crisis," in *The Korean Economy at the Crossroads*, ed. Moon Joong Tcha and Chung-Sok Suh (London: Routledge-Curzon, 2003), 62.

50. Wade, "The Asian Crisis," 364.

51. Lee, "A 'Stroke' Hypothesis," 57. Massive investment also created excess capacity and falling profits for export businesses. Phongpaichit and Baker, *Thailand's Crisis*, 2; Krugman, *Depression Economics*, 98.

52. Wade, "The Asian Crisis," 364; Eric Van Wincoop and Kie-Mu Yi, "Asia Crisis Postmortem: Where Did the Money Go and Did the U.S. Benefit?" in Tcha and Suh, *Korean Economy at the Crossroads* (see note 49), 259; Ha-Joon Chang, "South Korea: Anatomy of a Crisis," *Current History* (December 1998), 439.

53. Krugman, *Depression Economics*, 89.

54. Moonjoong Tcha, Minsoo Lee, and Chung-sok Suh, "The Korean Economy: Triumphs, Difficulties, and Triumphs Again?" in Tcha and Suh, *Korean Economy at the Crossroads* (see note 49), 8; Phongpaichit and Baker, *Thailand's Crisis*, 43.

55. Wade, "Asian Crisis," 362, 364; Wincoop and Yi, "Asia Crisis Postmortem," 259; Chang, *South Korea*, 439.

56. Ibid., 365.

57. Ibid.; Lee, "A 'Stroke' Hypothesis," 65; Krugman, *Depression Economics*, 97.

58. Chang, *South Korea*, 437.

59. Taiwan escaped the crisis more or less unscathed. See Dickinson and Schaeffer, *Fast Forward*, 129–30; Wade, "Asian Crisis," 368; Ji Chou, "Taiwan's Economic Performance Since 1980," in Mai and Shih, *Taiwan's Economic Success* (see note 7), 55–56, 59.

60. Tcha, Lee, and Suh, "Korean Economy," 13.

61. Dickinson and Schaeffer, *Fast Forward*, 130n95.

62. Wade, "Asian Crisis," 361.

63. Jung-Soo Seo, "Real Exchange Rate and Inward FDI in Crisis-ridden Korea," in Tcha and Suh, *Korean Economy at the Crossroads* (see note 49), 154; Oh, *Korean Politics*, 225.

64. Phongpaichit and Baker, *Thailand's Crisis*, 218.

65. As one US official explained, "Most of these countries are going through a deep and dark tunnel ... but on the other end there is going to be a significantly different Asia in which Americans have achieved much deeper market penetration, much greater access." Phongpaichit and Baker, Ibid., 6. Seo, "Real Exchange Rate," 154.

66. Phongpaichit and Baker, *Thailand's Crisis*, 219.

67. The estimated figure ranges from $80 to $105 billion. Wincoop and Yi, *Asia Crisis*, 247–48; Wade, "Asian Crisis," 362.

68. C. H. Kwan, "The Rise of China as an Economic Power: Implications for Asia and Japan," in Gunther-Hilpert and Haak, *Japan and China* (see note 3), 21.

69. Gang Xu, "China in the Pacific Rim: Trade and Investment Links," in *Changing China: A Geographical Appraisal*, ed. Chiao-min Hsieh and Max Lu (Boulder, CO: Westview Press, 2004), 176.

70. Krugman, *Depression Economics*, 144.

71. Dickinson and Schaeffer, *Fast Forward*, 102n117; Eric Eckholm, "Joblessness: A Perilous Curve on China's Capitalist Road," *New York Times* (January 20, 1998).

72. Seth Faison, "Major Shift for Communist China: Big State Industries Will Be Sold," *New York Times* (September 12, 1997).

73. Seth Faison, "Messy Free-Market Plunge Rattling China's Businesses," *New York Times* (October 5, 1997).

74. Eckholm, "Joblessness."

75. Sheryl WuDunn, "The Layoff Introduced to Chinese," *New York Times* (May 11, 1993).

76. WuDunn, "The Layoff."

77. Elizabeth J. Perry, "Crime, Corruption, and Contention," in *The Paradox of China's Post-Mao Reforms*, ed. Merle Goldman and Roderick MacFarquhar (Cambridge, MA: Harvard University Press, 1999), 318; Patrick E. Tyler, "Discontent Mounts in China, Shaking the Leaders," *New York Times* (April 10, 1994).

78. Arindam Banik and Pradip K. Bhaumik, *Foreign Capital Inflows to China, India, and the Caribbean: Trends, Assessments and Determinants* (New York: Palgrave MacMillan, 2006), 31.

79. Sheryl WuDunn, "The Tail That Wags the Dragon," *New York Times* (June 27, 1997); Edward A. Gargan, "China Already Capitalizing on Hong Kong's Wealth," *New York Times* (December 5, 1996).

80. Schaeffer, *Understanding Globalization*, 195.

81. "China's official FDI figures may be an exaggeration. A large amount of China's FDI has been earned in mainland China but then booked to accounts in Hong Kong for tax purposes, and subsequently comes back to the mainland as FDI, in a process of 'round tripping.'" Banik and Bhaumik, *Foreign Capital*, 189n3; Fischer, *Foreign Direct Investment*, 112–13; Matt Pottinger and Phelim Kyne, "Beijing Restrains Growth in Loans But Raises Risks," *Wall Street Journal* (July 14, 2004); Mark Selden, *The Political Economy of Chinese Development* (Armonk, NY: M. E. Sharpe, 1993), 35–6.

82. Robert Devlin, Antoni Estevadeordal, and Andres Rodriguez-Clare, eds., *The Emergence of China: Opportunities and Challenges for Latin America and the Caribbean* (New York: Inter-American Development Bank; David Rockefeller Center for Latin American Studies, Harvard University, 2006), xxv.

83. Eric Eckholm, "Not (Yet) Gone the Way of All Asia," *New York Times* (November 15, 1998).

84. Banik and Bhaumik, Foreign Capital, 28; Alwyn Young, "A Tale of Two Cities: Factor Accumulation and Technical Change in Hong Kong and Singapore," *NBER Macroeconomic Annual*, 1992, MIT Press.

85. Eckholm, "Not (Yet) Gone."

86. Dickinson and Schaeffer, *Fast Forward*, 105.

87. Ibid., 105, 105n134; Fischer, *Foreign Direct Investment*, 112.

88. B. Sudhakara Reddy, "Introduction," in *Economic Reforms in India and China: Emerging Issues and Challenges*, ed. B. Sudhakara Reddy (New Delhi: SAGE, 2009), 20.

89. Shelendra D. Sharma, "India's Economic Liberalization: The Elephant Comes of Age," *Current History* (December 1996), 416; Amy Waldman, "Sikh Who Saved India's Economy is Named Premier," *New York Times* (May 20, 2004); Pankaj Mishra, "India: The Neglected Majority Wins," *New York Review of Books* (August 12, 2004), 30–31; Alan Heston, "India's Economic Reforms: The Real Thing?" *Current History* (March 1992), 113–16; Robert L. Hardgrave Jr., "After the Dynasty: Politics in India," *Current History* (March 1992), 111.

90. Gautam Adhikari, "India: A New Test Begins," *Current History* (December 1997), 410.

91. Saritha Rai, "India Sees Backlash Fading over Boom in Outsourcing," *New York Times* (July 14, 2004).

92. Reddy, "Introduction," 19; Fischer, *Foreign Direct Investment*, 224; D. Krishnamoorthy, "FDI Flows in India and China," in Reddy, *Economic Reforms* (see note 88), 214–15, 217–18.

93. Schaeffer, *Understanding Globalization*, 192–93n46; Noam Scheiber, "As a Center for Outsourcing, India Could Be Losing Its Edge," *New York Times* (May 9, 2004).

94. Schaeffer, *Understanding Globalization*, 193n47; Saritha Rai, "Indian Voters Turn a Cold Shoulder to High Technology," *New York Times* (May 12, 2004).

95. Saritha Rai, "India Budget Raises Taxes to Finance Aid to Poor," *New York Times* (July 9, 2004).

96. Saritha Rai, "India Market Falls on Jitters After Election," *New York Times* (May 15, 2004); Amy Waldman, "What India's Upset Vote Reveals: That High Tech Is Skin Deep," *New York Times* (May 15, 2004); Saritha Rai, "India's Economic Growth Is Expected to

Slow," *New York Times* (August 6, 2004); Saritha Rai, "Shares Plunge 11% in India on Jitters Over Election," *New York Times* (May 18, 2004).

97. Keith Bradsher, "Bangladesh Is Surviving to Export Another Day," *New York Times* (December 14, 2004).

98. Vikas Bajaj, "India Is Awash in Foreign Investment," *New York Times* (October 14, 2009).

Chapter Eight

1. Steven R. Weisman, "In Major Shift, U.S. Is Imposing Tariffs on China," *New York Times* (March 31, 2007).

2. In 2006 U.S. officials agreed to enhance the regime's power in the International Monetary Fund and give it a greater voice in decision making. Steven R. Weisman, "I.M.F. Votes to Enhance Power of China and Others," *New York Times* (September 19, 2006); Paul Krugman, "Taking On China," *New York Times* (October 1, 2010).

3. Rebecca Buckman, "Navigating China's Textile Trade," *Wall Street Journal* (September 10, 2004); Saritha Rai, "India Hopes for Growth in Textile Exports," *New York Times* (July 30, 2004); Doug Guthrie, *China and Globalization: The Social, Economic and Political Transformation of Chinese Society* (New York: Routledge, 2006), 103–06.

4. Steven R. Weisman, "$14 Billion in Deals Precede Trade Talks," *New York Times* (June 17, 2008). Secretary of State Hillary Clinton used her fundraising skills to raise $54 million from US firms to finance construction of the US pavilion at the upcoming World Fair in Shanghai. "[The Chinese] have an expo, which is a kind of rite of passage that countries like to do to show they have arrived. [If] we're not there, what does that say? I mean, it would be a terrible message," Clinton explained. Mark Landler and David Barboza, "For Shanghai Expo, World Famous Fund-Raiser Comes Through" *New York Times* (January 3, 2010).

5. Weisman, "$14 Billion"; Nicholas R. Lardy, *Integrating China into the Global Economy* (Washington, DC: Brookings Institution Press, 2002), 4; Peter Morici, "Barring Entry? China and the WTO," *Current History* (September 1997), 274.

6. David Barboza, "Seeking to Tap Olympic Pride, Western Ads Cheerlead for China," *New York Times* (July 20, 2008).

7. Stephen G. Bunker and Paul S. Ciccantel, *East Asia and the Global Economy: Japan's Ascent, with Implications for China's Future* (Baltimore, MD: Johns Hopkins University Press, 2007), 210; Warren I. Cohen, *America's Response to China: A History of Sino-American Relations,* 4th ed. (New York: Columbia University Press, 2000), passim.

8. Robert K. Schaeffer, *Power to the People: Democratization Around the World* (Boulder, CO: Westview Press, 1997), 159–201.

9. Lardy, *Integrating China,* 4.

10. Ibid.

11. Winston Lord, "A Sweet and Sour Relationship: An Interview with Winston Lord, U.S. Assistant Secretary of State for East Asian and Pacific Affairs," *Current History* (September 1995), 248; Joseph Fewsmith, "America and China: A New Cold War?" *Current History* (September 1995), 250; Nancy Bernkopf Tucker, "A Precarious Balance: Clinton and China," *Current History* (September 1998), 244; Elizabeth Economy, "Changing Course on China," *Current History* (September 2003), 247.

12. Robert Schaeffer, "Dictatorship and Development in China: Their Impact on the Workers of the World," in *The Rise of Asia and the Transformation of the World-System,* ed. Ganesh K. Trichur (Boulder, CO: Paradigm Press, 2009), 89–90; Sheryl Gay Stolberg and Somini Sengupta, "Bush Silent, But Others Speak Out on Tibet Crackdown," *New York Times* (March 22, 2008); Mark Landler, "Clinton Seeks Shift on China and Stresses Engagement" *New York Times* (February 14, 2009); Edward Wong, "U.S. and China Celebrate 30 Years of Diplomatic Ties," *New York Times* (January 13, 2009).

13. Keith Bradsher, "Made in U.S., Shunned in China," *New York Times* (November 18, 2005).

14. Weisman, "In Major Shift"; The United States registered its first trade deficit with China in 1983, when it recorded a $300 million deficit. Robert K. Schaeffer, *Understanding Globalization: The Social Consequences of Political, Economic and Environmental Change* (Lanham, MD: Rowman and Littlefield, 2009), 198n63. This deficit grew to $83 billion in 2001, $125 billion in 2004, and $268 in 2008. Ibid., 198n64. It then declined to $208 billion in 2009 as a result of the recession in the United States.

15. Elizabeth Becker, "Staring into the Mouth of the Trade Deficit," *New York Times* (February 21, 2004).

16. Lardy, *Integrating China,* 6–7.

17. Robert Schaeffer, "The Entelechies of Mercantilism," *Scandinavian Economic History Review* XXIX, no. 2 (1981), 81–96.

18. Ibid., 84–85.

19. Keynes's insight was that when consumers stopped spending and hoarded their wealth, the state needed to step in and spend money on their behalf so that businesses could thrive and workers could stay employed until consumer spending recovered.

20. Lardy, *Integrating China,* 1.

21. Keith Bradsher and David Barboza, "The Chinese Disconnection: Google Is Not Alone in Discontent, But Its Threat Stands Out," *New York Times* (January 14, 2010).

22. Cai Youngshun, "Managing Social Unrest," in *China into the Hu-Wen Era: Policy Initiatives and Challenges,* ed. John Wong and Lai Hongyi (Singapore: World Scientific, 2006), 399–400.

23. Howard W. French, "China Covers Up Violent Suppression of Village Protest," *New York Times* (June 27, 2006); Howard W. French, "Beijing Casts Net of Silence over Protest," *New York Times* (December 14, 2005); Youngshun, "Managing Social Unrest," 397.

24. Keith Bradsher, "Not Coming Soon to a Lot Near You: Chinese Cars," *New York Times* (October 18, 2006).

25. Schaeffer, "Dictatorship and Development," 90.

26. Ted C. Fishman, "The Chinese Century," *New York Times Magazine* (June 4, 2004), 28.

27. Bradsher, "Not Coming Soon."

28. Lardy, *Integrating China,* 89.

29. Keith Bradsher, "China's Squeeze on Credit Shows Signs of Success as Economy Slows," *New York Times* (June 12, 2004).

30. Reuters, "Taming Inflation as Chinese Spend," *New York Times* (January, 22, 2010); Keith Bradsher, "Informal Lenders in China Pose Risks to Banking System," *New York Times* (November 9, 2004).

31. Edward S. Steinfeld, "Beyond the Transition: China's Economy at Century's End," *Current History* (September 1999), 275; John Frisbie and Michael Overmyer, "U.S.-China Economic Relations: The Next Stage," *Current History* (September 2006), 245.

32. Keith Bradsher, "Cutting Back? Not in China," *New York Times* (December 10, 2009); Richard Katz, "Does China Face a 'Lost Decade?'" *Current History* (September 2008), 271–72.

33. Lardy, *Integrating China,* 15.

34. Minxin Pei, *China's Trapped Transition: The Limits of Developmental Autocracy* (Cambridge, MA: Harvard University Press, 2006), 116.

35. Keith Bradsher, "In China, Troubling Signs of an Overheating Economy," *New York Times* (April, 14, 2004).

36. Keith Bradsher, "Made in India vs. Made in China," *New York Times* (June 12, 2004).

37. Bradsher, "In China, Troubling Signs"; Pei, *China's Trapped Transition,* 117; Morici, "Barring Entry?" 276; Larry Diamond, "The Rule of Law as Transition to Democracy in China," in *Debating Political Reform in China: Rule of Law vs. Democratization,* ed. Suisheng Zhao (Armonk, NY: M. E. Sharpe, 2006), 80; Robert J. Suettinger, *Beyond Tiananmen: The Politics of U.S.-China Relations, 1989–2000* (Washington, DC: Brookings Institution Press, 2003), 338.

38. Dali L. Yang, *Remaking the Chinese Leviathan: Market Choices and the Politics of Governance in China* (Stanford, CA: Stanford University Press, 2004), 82.

39. Lardy, *Integrating China,* 89.

40. Keith Bradsher, "Another Leap by China, With Steel Leading Again," *New York Times* (May 1, 2004).

41. Keith Bradsher, "Green Power Takes Root in China," *New York Times* (July 3, 2009).

42. Lardy, *Integrating China,* 15, 14.

43. Keith Bradsher, "Chinese Solar Firm Revises Price Record," *New York Times* (August 27, 2009).

44. James Shinn, "Emerging China: Exploiting the Fissures in the Façade," *Current History* (September 1996), 243; Morici, "Barring Entry?" 276.

45. Bradsher and Barboza, "The Chinese Disconnection."

46. Kevin O'Brien, "Upstart Chinese Telecom Company Rattles Industry as It Rises to No. 2," *New York Times* (November 30, 2009); Christopher Rhoads and Charles Hutzler, "China's Telecom Forays Squeeze Struggling Rivals," *Wall Street Journal* (September 8, 2004).

47. Bradsher and Barboza, "The Chinese Disconnection."

48. Guthrie, *China and Globalization,* 81, 86.

49. Ibid., 82, 85; Martin K. Dimitrov, *Piracy and the State: The Politics of Intellectual Property Rights in China* (Cambridge: Cambridge University Press, 2009), 196–204.

50. David Barboza, "IPhone Maker in China Is Under Fire After a Suicide," *New York Times* (July 27, 2009); David Barboza, "Where False Rings True," *New York Times* (April 28, 2009).

51. Guthrie, *China and Globalization,* 90.

52. David Barboza, "Danone Exits China Venture after Years of Legal Dispute," *New York Times* (August 31, 2009).

53. David Lague, "Next Step for Counterfeiters: Faking the Whole Company," *New York Times* (May 1, 2006).

54. David Barboza, "Chinese Court Convicts 11 in Microsoft Piracy Case," *New York Times* (January 12, 2009); Dimitrov, *Piracy and the State,* 16.

55. Walt Bogdanich, "Heparin Discovery May Point to Chinese Counterfeiting," *New York Times* (March 20, 2008).

56. Barboza, "Where False Rings True."

57. David Barboza, "China Finds Poor Quality in Its Stores," *New York Times* (July 5, 2007).

58. David Barboza and Brad Stone, "A Nation That Trips Up Many: Google Wasn't the First to Find Barriers to Business in China," *New York Times* (January 16, 2010).

59. Andrew Jacobs and Miguel Helft, "Google May End China Operation Over Censorship," *New York Times* (January 13, 2010).

60. Miguel Helft and John Markoff, "In Google's Rebuke of China, Focus Falls on Cybersecurity," *New York Times* (January 14, 2010).

61. Barboza and Stone, "A Nation That Trips Up Many; Bradsher and Barboza, "The Chinese Disconnection."

62. John F. Burns, "Britain Warned Businesses of Threat of Chinese Spying," *New York Times* (February 1, 2010).

63. Dimitrov, *Piracy and the State,* 4.

64. Barboza, "Where False Rings True."

65. Barboza and Stone, "A Nation That Trips Up Many"; Keith Bradsher, "China Looms as the World's Next Leading Auto Exporter," *New York Times* (April 22, 2005).

66. Jeff Segal and Rob Cox, "China Should Explain," *New York Times* (March 19, 2009); Cyrus Sanati," China's New Era," *New York Times* (August 1, 2008); John Markoff, "Chinese Law Could Impede Microsoft Deal for Yahoo," *New York Times* (March 28, 2008).

67. Keith Bradsher, "As China Stirs Economy, Some See Protectionism, *New York Times* (June 24, 2009).

68. Bradsher and Barboza, "The Chinese Disconnection."

69. Keith Bradsher, "Drawing Critics, China Seeks to Dominate in Renewable Energy," *New York Times* (July 14, 2009).

70. Schaeffer, "Dictatorship and Development," 90–91.

71. Lyric Hughs Hale, "Beijing Eyes a Bear Market," *Current History* (September 2008).

72. James Surowiecki, "The Frugal Republic," *New Yorker* (December 7, 2009), 35.

73. Sharon LaFraniere, "Chinese City Bolsters Scant Consumer Spending with Free Vouchers," *New York Times* (March 19, 2009); Andrew Jacobs, "China's Economy, In Need of Jump Start, Wants for Citizens' Fists to Loosen," *New York Times* (December 3, 2008).

74. Surowiecki, "The Frugal Republic," 35.

75. Hale, Beijing Eyes a Bear Market," 285.

76. Keith Bradsher, "In Downturn, China Exploits Path to Growth," *New York Times* (March 17, 2009).

77. Hale, "Beijing Eyes a Bear Market, 283; Bradsher, "Informal Lenders."

78. Keith Bradsher, "Shifting Buyer Trends Set Back Western Carmakers in China," *New York Times* (April 1, 2005).

79. Surowiecki, "The Frugal Republic," 35.

80. Keith Bradsher, "Consumer Demand at Home Keeps China's Factories Humming and Hiring," *New York Times* (October 21, 2005).

81. Lardy, *Integrating China,* 49; Gang Xu, "China in the Pacific Rim: Trade and Investment Links," in *Changing China: A Geographical Appraisal,* ed. Chiao-min Hsieh and Max Lu (Boulder, CO: Westview Press, 2004), 177.

82. Lardy, *Integrating China,* 48.

83. Keith Bradsher, "In Step to Enhance Currency, China Allows Its Use in Some Foreign Payments," *New York Times* (July 7, 2009).

84. Schaeffer, "The Entelechies of Mercantilism," 81–82.

85. Victor Zhikai Gao, "Heart of Gold," *New York Times* (May 14, 2009).

86. Ibid.

87. Barry Naughton, "The Dangers of Economic Complacency," *Current History* (September 1996), 262.

88. Keith Bradsher, "China Grows More Picky About Debt," *New York Times* (May 21, 2009). Krugman, "Taking On China."

89. Gao, "Heart of Gold"; Bradsher, "China Grows More Picky." Japan also earned dollars from trade with the United States and then used them to purchase $644 billion worth of US treasuries by 2006. Floyd Norris, "Accessory for a U.S. Border Fence: A Welcome Mat for Foreign Loans," *New York Times* (November 4, 2006); Hal Varian, "Economic Scene," *New York Times* (June 3, 2004).

90. Schaeffer, "Entelechies of Mercantilism," 82n3.

91. Ibid., 83.

92. Immanuel Wallerstein, *The Modern World-System: Capitalist Agriculture and the Origins of the European World-Economy in the Sixteenth Century* (New York: Academic Press, 1974), 77.

93. Immanuel Wallerstein, *The Modern World-System II: Mercantilism and the Consolidation of the European World-Economy, 1600–1750* (New York: Academic Press, 1980), 58–59.

94. Keith Bradsher, "China Losing Taste for Debt from the U.S.," *New York Times* (January 8, 2009).

95. Eduardo Porter, "Hoping the Yen, If Not the Yuan, Will Show Muscle," *New York Times* (March 18, 2004).

96. Mark Landler, "China Jittery About Obama Amid Signs of Harder Line," *New York Times* (January 24, 2009); Edward Wong, "China Rejects Accusations of Currency Manipulation," *New York Times* (January 25, 2009). Both Snow and Geithner subsequently retreated from their positions and softened their rhetoric toward the regime. Keith Bradsher, "China Cuts Bond Buys from U.S. and Others," *New York Times* (April 13, 2009); David Barboza, "Geithner Softens Tone in Approach to Beijing," *New York Times* (June 2, 2009).

97. Chris Buckley, "China Is Said to Consider Revaluing Its Currency," *New York Times* (February 10, 2004); David Lague, "China to Let Market Forces Weigh on Value of Yuan," *New York Times* (November 29, 2009).

98. Bradsher, "China Cuts Bond Buys"; Floyd Norris, "Debt Burden Now Rests More on U.S. Shoulders," *New York Times* (January 23, 2010). They have also used their seat on the UN Security Council to block U.S. efforts to prevent Iran from obtaining nuclear weapons, threatening to side with Iran as a way to win U.S. concessions on other issues, particularly on exchange rates. Alan Cowell, "China Renews Its Opposition to Tougher Sanctions on Iran," *New York Times* (February 5, 2010).

99. Paul Krugman, "Chinese New Year," *New York Times* (January 1, 2010); Paul Krugman, "China's Dollar Trap," *New York Times* (April, 3, 2009); Paul Krugman, "The

Chinese Disconnect," *New York Times* (October 23, 2009); Paul Krugman, "World Out of Balance," *New York Times* (November 16, 2009).

100. David Barboza, "For Foreign Companies in China, A Rising Yuan Is hard to Swallow, Exported Products Would Cost More," *New York Times* (October 15, 2005).

101. Mark Landler and David E. Sanger, "China Seeks Assurances That U.S. Will Cut Its Deficit," *New York Times* (July 29, 2009); Michael Wines, Keith Bradsher, Mark Landler, "China's Premier Seeks Guarantee from U.S. on Debt," *New York Times* (July 7, 2009).

102. Jim Yardley and David Barboza, "China Is Forming Agency to Invest Foreign Reserves," *New York Times* (March 10, 2007); Keith Bradsher, "Dollars to Spare in China's Trove," *New York Times* (March 6, 2007).

103. Bradsher, Ibid.

104. Keith Bradsher, "Has Irrational Exuberance Hit China?" *New York Times* (December 14, 2003).

105. Joseph Kahn, "Investment Bubble Builds New China," *New York Times* (March 23, 2005).

106. Alan Greenspan, head of the U.S. Federal Reserve, first warned of a possible bubble in China in 2003. Bradsher, "Has Irrational Exuberance Hit China?"

107. David Barboza, "China Builds Its Dreams and Some Fear a Bubble," *New York Times* (October 18, 2005).

108. Charles Hughes Smith, "Global Economy's Next Threat: China's Real Estate Bubble," *Daily Finance* (January 10, 2010).

109. Katz, "Does China Face," 269.

110. Andrew Jacobs, "A County in China Sees Its Fortunes in Tea Leaves Until a Bubble Bursts," *New York Times* (January 17, 2009).

111. Paul Krugman, personal conversation with author, March 16, 2007.

112. Diamond, "The Rule of Law," 80.

113. Keith Bradsher, "In a Tidal Shift, Chinese Are Spending More Money Overseas," *New York Times* (February 3, 2009); Keith Bradsher, "In China, Signs of Softening," *New York Times* (August 5, 2008).

114. David Barboza, "Shorting China," *New York Times* (January 8, 2010).

115. David Barboza, "Chinese President Sees Threat to Growth from Slowdown," *New York Times* (December 1, 2008).

116. Barboza, "Shorting China."

117. Paul Krugman, personal conversation. He attributed this maxim to Herb Stein.

118. Guthrie, *China and Globalization,* 12.

119. Ibid., 150.

120. Tracie Rozhou, "A Tangle in Textiles," *New York Times* (April, 21, 2005).

121. Matt Richtel, "Outsourced All the Way: Small Ventures Top Giants in Trend: No Factory, Warehouse or Store," *New York Times* (June 21, 2005).

122. Katie Zezima, "Headstones Too Go Global, and One City Pays the Price," *New York Times* (October 25, 2006).

123. Guthrie, China and Globalization, 22.

124. Elizabeth Becker, "U.S. Moves to Limit Imports of Clothing," *New York Times* (May 14, 2005); Elizabeth Becker, "Textile Quotas to End, Punishing Carolina Towns," *New York Times* (November 2, 2004).

125. Eduardo Porter, "Market Place," *New York Times* (February 11, 2004).

126. David Barboza and Keith Bradsher, "China Lists U.S. Shares for S.E.C.," *New York Times* (February 10, 2010).

127. Elizabeth Becker, "Industry and Labor Step Up Fight over China's Currency," *New York Times* (September 10, 2004).

128. Louis Uchitelle, "Spending Stalls and Businesses Slash U.S. Jobs," *New York Times* (September 26, 2008).

129. Neil King Jr. and Michael Schroeder, "China Is Talk of Campaigns," *Wall Street Journal* (July 20, 2004); Oded Shenkar, *The Chinese Century: The Rising Chinese Economy and Its Impact on the Global Economy, the Balance of Power, and Your Job* (Upper Saddle River, NJ: Wharton School, 2006), 122, 133; Steven Greenhouse, "A Unified Voice Argues the Case for U.S. Manufacturing," *New York Times* (April 26, 2007).

130. Katherine Boo, "The Best Job in Town: The Americanization of Chennai," *New Yorker* (July 5, 2004), 59.

131. Steven Greenhouse, "Falling Fortunes of the Wage Earner," *New York Times* (April 12, 2005).

132. Schaeffer, *Understanding Globalization,* 15, 13–21, 16–17; Hal R. Varian, "American Companies Show an Edge in Putting Information to Work," *New York Times* (January 12, 2006).

133. Schaeffer, *Understanding Globalization,* 17.

134. Ibid. The percentage of unionized workers in private industry—9.4 percent—is about what it was in 1929. Ibid., 18.

135. Eduardo Porter, "After Years of Growth, What About Workers' Share?" *New York Times* (October 15, 2006); Mark Trahant, "Borrowing on All Levels Is What Is Driving Our Economy," *Manhattan Mercury* (April 4, 2005).

136. Eduardo Porter, "How Long Can Workers Tread Water? Income Gains Go Mostly to the Affluent," *New York Times* (July 14, 2005).

137. Steve Lohr, "An Elder Challenges Outsourcing's Orthodoxy," *New York Times* (September 9, 2004).

138. Kyle Hutzler, "Unhealthy Wages," *New Yorker* (February 8, 2010), 5; Schaeffer, *Understanding Globalization,* 26.

139. Schaeffer, Ibid., 25; Robert Frank, "Economic Scene," *New York Times* (March 17, 2005).

140. Schaeffer, *Understanding Globalization,* 26; Eduardo Porter, "Inherit the Wind; There's Little Else Left," *New York Times* (March 26, 2006).

141. John Cassidy, "After the Blowup," *New Yorker* (January 11, 2010), 33.

142. Gretchen Morgenson, "Another Day Older and Deeper in Debt," *New York Times* (July 20, 2008). By contrast, Japanese households save on average about 12 percent of their income and have $100,000 deposited in the bank. Schaeffer, *Understanding Globalization,* 26.

Chapter Nine

1. Kellee S. Tsai, *Capitalism Without Democracy: The Private Sector in Contemporary China* (Ithaca, NY: Cornell University Press, 2007), 1, 2, 3.

2. Robert Schaeffer, "Dictatorship and Development in China: Their Impact on the Workers of the World," in *The Rise of Asia and the Transformation of the World-System,* ed. Ganesh K. Trichur (Boulder, CO: Paradigm Press, 2009), 91 (emphasis added).

3. Doug Guthrie, *China and Globalization: The Social, Economic and Political Transformation of Chinese Society* (New York: Routledge, 2006), 303.

4. Steven I. Levine, "China and America: The Resilient Relationship," *Current History* (September 1992), 252.

5. Merle Goldman, "Is Democracy Possible?" *Current History* (September 1995), 259.

6. Bruce J. Dickson, *Red Capitalists in China: The Party, Private Entrepreneurs, and Prospects for Political Change* (Cambridge: Cambridge University Press, 2003), 167, 167–68.

7. Andrew Jacobs, "In Sentence of Activist, China Gives West a Chill," *New York Times* (December 26, 2009).

8. Joseph Kahn, "For China, One Party Is Enough, Leader Says," *New York Times* (September 16, 2004); Joseph Kahn, "China's Leader Vows to Uphold One-Party Rule," *New York Times* (June 27, 2007).

9. Michael Wines, "In China, No Plans to Emulate West's Way," *New York Times* (March 10, 2009); Joseph Kahn, "In China, Talk of Democracy Is Simply That," *New York Times* (April 20, 2007); Joseph Fewsmith, "America and China: Back from the Brink," *Current History* (September 1994), 254.

10. Yan Sun, *Corruption and Market in Contemporary China* (Ithaca, NY: Cornell University Press, 2004), 119.

11. Ibid., 39.

12. Minxin Pei, *China's Trapped Transition: The Limits of Developmental Autocracy* (Cambridge, MA: Harvard University Press, 2006), 39.

13. Sun, *Corruption and Market,* 210.

14. Martin Dimitrov, "The Resilient Authoritarians," *Current History* (January 2008), 27–28.

15. Michael Johnston, "The Vices—and Virtues—of Corruption," *Current History* (September 1997), 273; Sun, *Corruption and Market,* 200.

16. You-tien Hsing, *Making Capitalism in China: The Taiwan Connection* (New York: Oxford University Press, 1998), 118–19.

17. Sun, *Corruption and Market,* 66.

18. Tsai, *Capitalism Without Democracy,* 58.

19. Sun, *Corruption and Market,* 202; Tsai, *Capitalism Without Democracy,* 7.

20. Tsai, Ibid., 118, 58.

21. Yan Sun, "Corruption, Growth, and Reform: The Chinese Enigma," *Current History* (September 2005), 261.

22. Hsing, *Making Capitalism in China,* 140, 137.

23. Barry Naughton, "China's Left Tilt; Pendulum Swing or Midcourse Correction?" in *China's Changing Political Landscape: Prospects for Democracy,* ed. Cheng Li (Washington, DC: Brookings Institution Press, 2008), 154.

24. Sun, *Corruption and Market,* 69.

25. David Barboza, "The Corruptibles," *New York Times* (September 4, 2009).

26. Johnston, "The Vices," 272.

27. Sun, *Corruption and Market,* 198.

28. David Barboza, "National Audit in China Finds $35 Billion in Fraud Among Government Officials," *New York Times* (December 30, 2009); David Barboza, "Report Accuses Officials in China of Embezzlement," *New York Times* (August 29, 2008); Yanzhong Huang, "Is the Chinese State Being Revamped?" in *China Under Hu Jintao: Opportunities, Dangers, and Dilemmas,* ed. Tun-jen Cheng, Jacques DeLisle, and Deborah Brown (Singapore: World Scientific, 2006), 55.

29. Sun, *Corruption and Market,* 115; George T. Crane, "Greater China: The Ties That Don't Bind," *Current History* (September 1995), 278.

30. One economist argued that in 2000, illegal capital exports of $8 billion may have exceeded capital imports of $41 billion. Huang, "Is the Chinese State Being Revamped?" 56; Crane, "Greater China," 278.

31. Sun, *Corruption and Market,* 200; Johnston, "The Vices," 273.

32. Sun, *Corruption and Market,* 101, 102.

33. Seth Faison, "China's Chief Tells Army to Give Up Its Commerce," *New York Times* (July 23, 1998); Dali L. Yang, *Remaking the Chinese Leviathan: Market Choices and the Politics of Governance in China* (Stanford, CA: Stanford University Press, 2004), 128–29; Peter Morici, "Barring Entry? China and the WTO," *Current History* (September 1997), 275.

34. Yang, *Remaking the Chinese Leviathan,* 133.

35. Hsing, *Making Capitalism in China,* 139.

36. Sun, *Corruption and Market,* 258; Hsing, *Making Capitalism in China,* 135.

37. Stanley Rosen, "The State of Youth/Youth and the State in Early 21st Century China: The Triumph of the Urban Rich?" in Cheng, DeLisle, and Brown, *China Under Hu Jintao* (see note 28), 166.

38. Sun, *Corruption and Market,* 180; Rosen, "The State of Youth," 165.

39. Dickson, *Red Capitalists,* 126n7; Sun, *Corruption and Market,* 159.

40. Xiaobo Lu, *Cadres and Corruption: The Organizational Involution of the Chinese Communist Party* (Stanford, CA: Stanford University Press, 2000), 222.

41. Huang, "Is the Chinese State Being Revamped?" 55.

42. Pei, China's Trapped Transition, 153; Mark McDonald, "Chinese Officials Gamble and Their Luck Runs Out," *New York Times* (January 15, 2009); Andrew Jacobs, "Chinese Trial Reveals Vast Web of Corruption and Fuels a Political Career," *New York Times* (November 4, 2009).

43. Lu, *Cadres and Corruption,* 222. Pei argues that the number of party members disciplined by the regime was smaller—between 97,260 and 174,580—during the 2000s, but that the percentage of those who were criminally prosecuted was higher—2.9 to 13.1 percent. Minxin Pei, "Fighting Corruption: A Difficult Challenge for Chinese Leaders," in Li, *China's Changing Political Landscape* (see note 23), 231.

44. Pei, *China's Trapped Transition,* 153.

45. John Frisbie and Michael Overmyer, "U.S.-China Economic Relations: The Next Stage," *Current History* (September 2006), 247; Li Yuan and Paul Glader, "Looming Battle: As China's Largest Steelmaker Gathers Steam, Western Competitors Scramble to Come Up with a Game Plan," *Wall Street Journal* (September 27, 2004); Jialin Zhang, "Guiding China's Market Economy," *Current History* (September 1994), 280; Merle Goldman, "Is Democracy Possible?" 262.

46. Frisbie and Overmyer, "U.S.-China Economic Relations," 247.

47. Michael A. Santoro, "Global Capitalism and the Road to Chinese Capitalism," *Current History* (September 2000), 264.

48. Goldman, "Is Democracy Possible?" 262.

49. Alvin So, *Social Change and Development* (Newbury Park, CA: SAGE, 1990), 50–53; Dickson, *Red Capitalists,* 10–13.

50. Dickson, Ibid., 11–12.

51. Lu, *Cadres and Corruption,* 86; Susumu Yabuki, *China's New Political Economy: The Giant Awakes* (Boulder, CO: Westview Press, 1995), 73; Dickson, *Red Capitalists,* 31.

52. Lu, *Cadres and Corruption,* 86; Dali L. Yang, "Forced Harmony: China's Olympic Rollercoaster," *Current History* (September 2008); 244; Dickson, *Red Capitalists,* 34.

53. Bruce J. Dickson, "Dilemmas of Party Adaptation: The CCP's Strategies for Survival," in Cheng, DeLisle, Brown, *China Under Hu Jintao* (see note 28), 145–47; Bruce J. Dickson, "Beijing's Ambivalent Reformers," *Current History* (September 2004), 250, 252–53.

54. Dickson, *Red Capitalists,* 36.

55. Dickson, "Dilemmas of Party Adaptation," 151.

56. Hsing, *Making Capitalism,* 152.

57. Bruce J. Dickson, "The Party Is Far from Over," *Current History* (September 2007), 244; Eduardo Porter, "Study Finds Wealthy Inequality Is Worldwide," *New York Times* (December 6, 2006).

58. Porter, Ibid.

59. Dorothy J. Solinger, "The Political Implications of China's Social Future: Complacency, Scorn, and the Forlorn," in Li, *China's Changing Political Landscape* (see note 23), 260; Dickson, *Red Capitalists,* 22.

60. David S. Goodman, "The New Middle Class," in *The Paradox of China's Post-Mao Reforms,* ed. Merle Goldman and Roderick MacFarquhar (Cambridge, MA: Harvard University Press, 1999), 260–61.

61. Maurice Meisner, "The Other China," *Current History* (September 1997), 269.

62. Tsai, *Capitalism Without Democracy,* 4–5; Margaret M. Pearson, "China's Emerging Business Class: Democracy's Harbinger," *Current History* (September 1998), 271–72.

63. David Brooks, "The Dictatorship of Talent," *New York Times* (December 4, 2007).

64. Immanuel Wallerstein, *The Modern World-System: Capitalist Agriculture and the Origins of the European World-Economy in the Sixteenth Century* (New York: Academic Press, 1974), 246n.

65. Ibid., 244, 242n81.

66. James Shinn, "Emerging China: Exploiting the Fissures in the Façade," *Current History* (September 1996), 242.

67. Jim Yardley, "In a Tidal Wave, China's Masses Pour from Farm to City," *New York Times* (September 12, 2004); George J. Gilboy and Eric Heginbotham, "The Latin Americanization of China?" *Current History* (September 2004), 259.

68. Gilboy and Heginbotham, Ibid., 260.

69. Wang Feng, *Boundaries and Categories: Rising Inequality in Post-Socialist Urban China* (Stanford, CA: Stanford University Press, 2008), 118–19.

70. Carl Riskin, Zhao Renwei, and Li Shi, "Introduction," in *China's Retreat from Equality: Income Distribution and Economic Transition,* ed. Carl Riskin, Zhao Renwei, and Li Shi (Armonk, NY: M. E. Sharpe, 2001), 12–13.

71. Zhao Litao, "Labor Market Reforms under the Hu-Wen Administration," in *China into the Hu-Wen Era: Policy Initiatives and Challenges,* ed. John Wong and Lai Honyi (Singapore: World Scientific, 2006), 377; Feng, *Boundaries and Categories,* 95.

72. Jim Yardley, "Farmers Being Moved Aside by China Real Estate Boom," *New York Times* (December 8, 2004). "According to official statistics, some 34 million farmers have

either lost their land entirely [between 1987 and 2004] or own less than 0.3 mu, and the new surge in land transfers almost certainly indicates a new acceleration of that process." Gilboy and Heginbotham, "The Latin Americanization of China?" 258.

73. Keith Bradsher, "Newest Export Out of China: Inflation Fears," *New York Times* (April 16, 2004).

74. Howard W. French, "Wealth Grows, But Health Care Withers in China," *New York Times* (January 14, 2006).

75. Pei, *China's Trapped Transition,* 173.

76. Naughton, "China's Left Tilt," 146; Feng, *Boundaries and Categories,* 27.

77. Dorothy J. Solinger, "The New Crowd of the Dispossessed: The Shift of the Urban Proletariat from Master to Mendicant," in *State and Society in 21st Century China: Crisis, Contention, and Legitimation,* ed. Peter Hayes Gries and Stanley Rosen (London: Routledge, 2004), 50; Nicholas R. Lardy, *Integrating China into the Global Economy* (Washington, DC: Brookings Institution Press, 2002), 23.

78. Naughton, "China's Left Tilt," 147.

79. Solinger, "The New Crowd of the Dispossessed," 50.

80. Louis Uchitelle, "When the Chinese Consumer Is King," *New York Times* (December 14, 2003); Bloomberg News, "Cracks in U.S.-China Relations Are Widening Again in Crisis," *New York Times* (December 29, 2008).

81. Jim Yardley, "Jobs Here and in China a White House Topic," *New York Times* (December 9, 2003).

82. Elisabeth Rosenthal, "Poverty Spreads, and Deepens, in China's Cities," *New York Times* (October 4, 1999); Riskin, Renwei, and Shi, "Introduction," 3.

83. Genesh K. Trichur, "Internal Migration in Mainland China: Regional and World-Systemic Aspects," in *Globalization and Emerging Societies: Development and Inequality,* ed. Jan Nederveen Pieterse and Boike Rehbein (New York: Palgrave MacMillan, 2009), 126; Feng, *Boundaries and Categories,* 6.

84. Feng, *Boundaries and Categories,* 5–6.

85. Yongnian Zheng, *Globalization and the State: Transformation in China* (Cambridge: Cambridge University Press, 2004), 145.

86. Feng, *Boundaries and Categories,* 10; Riskin, Renwei, and Shi, "Introduction," 8.

87. Schaeffer, "Dictatorship and Development," 96.

88. Ching Kwan Lee, "Is Labor a Political Force in China?" in *Grass Roots Political Reform in Contemporary China,* ed. Elizabeth J. Perry and Merle Goldman (Cambridge, MA: Harvard University Press, 2007), 230.

89. Edward Wong, "After Deadly Clashes, Many Chinese Ask, Where Were Police?" *New York Times* (July 18, 2009); Lee, "Is Labor a Political Force in China?" 231.

90. Lee, Ibid.; Pei, *China's Trapped Transition,* 189; Dimitrov, "The Resilient Authoritarians," 26; Zheng, *Globalization and State,* 156.

91. Joseph Kahn and Jim Yardley, "Amid China's Boom, No Helping Hand for Young Qingming," *New York Times* (August 1, 2004).

92. Howard W. French, "Visit to Chinese Anytown Shows a Dark Side of Progress" *New York Times* (January 19, 2006).

93. Joseph Kahn, "Harsh Birth Control Steps Fuel Violence in China," *New York Times* (May 22, 2007).

94. Associated Press, "Lead Poisoning of Children in China Leads to Disturbance," *New York Times* (August 18, 2009).

95. Wines, "Smelter in China."

96. Edward Wong, "China Presses Grieving Parents to Take Hush Money on Quake," *New York Times* (July 24, 2008).

97. Jim Yardley, "Chinese Forces Say They've Secured Tibet's Capital," *New York Times* (March 16, 2008); Edward Wong, "Report Says Valid Grievances at Root of Tibet Unrest," *New York Times* (June 6, 2009).

98. Edward Wong, "For Poor Migrants, Grief in China's Ethnic Strife," *New York Times* (July 9, 2009).

99. Howard W. French, "Beijing Casts Net of Silence Over Protest," *New York Times* (December 14, 2005); Howard W. French, "China Covers Up Violent Suppression of Village Protest," *New York Times* (June 27, 2006).

100. Lee, "Is Labor a Political Force in China?" 225.

101. Eric J. Hobsbawm, *Primitive Rebels: Studies in Archaic Forms of Social Movements in the 19th and 20th Centuries* (New York: W. W. Norton, 1959).

102. Merle Goldman, *From Comrade to Citizen: The Struggle for Political Rights in China* (Cambridge, MA: Harvard University Press, 2005), 19.

103. Jonathan Ansfield, "China Starts to Lift Region's Web Blackout," *New York Times* (December 30, 2009); Andrew Jacobs, "Experts Say Chinese Filter Would Make PCs Vulnerable to Intrusion," *New York Times* (June 13, 2009).

104. Peter Hays Gries, "Chinese Nationalism: Challenging the State?" *Current History* (September 2005), 252; Keith Bradsher, "Beijing Adds Curbs on Access to Internet," *New York Times* (June 26, 2009); Andrew Jacobs, "Uproar over China's Rule on Software Filter for PCs," *New York Times* (June 11, 2009).

105. Lee, "Is Labor a Political Force in China?" 296.

106. Wong, "China Presses Grieving Parents"; Edward Wong, "A Year After China's Quake, New Lives Can't Heal Old Wounds," *New York Times* (May 6, 2009); Andrew Jacobs, "One-Child Policy Lifted for Parents of China Quake Victims," *New York Times* (May 27, 2008); Edward Wong, "China Concedes Possible Flaws in Schools That Collapsed in May Earthquake," *New York Times* (September 5, 2008); Andrew Jacobs, "Parents of Quake Victims Protest at Ruined Schools," *New York Times* (June 2, 2008).

107. Keith Bradsher, "Bowing to Protests, China Halts Sale of Steel Mill," *New York Times* (August 17, 2009); Reuters, "China Steel Executive Killed as Workers and Police Clash," *New York Times* (July 27, 2009).

108. Keith Bradsher, "2 Lose Posts over Deaths near Mine," *New York Times* (September 15, 2008).

109. Sharon LaFraniere, "Graft in China Covers Up Toll of Coal Miners," *New York Times* (April 11, 2009).

110. Dimitrov, "Resilient Authoritarians," 26.

111. Yardley, "Farmers Being Moved Aside."

112. Howard W. French, "Fast-Growing China Says Little of Child Slavery's Role," *New York Times* (June 21, 2007); Edward Wong, "Chinese Stifle Grieving Parents' Protest of Shoddy School Construction," *New York Times* (June 4, 2008); Andrew Jacobs, "Parents' Grief Turns to Rage at Chinese Officials," *New York Times* (May 28, 2008).

113. Andrew Jacobs, "Seeking Justice, Chinese Land in Secret Jails," *New York Times* (March 9, 2009).

114. US Department of State, "China: Country Reports on Human Rights Practices," 2007 (Bureau of Democracy, Human Rights and Labor, March 11, 2008), 3, www.state.gov/g/drl/rls/hrrpt/2007/100518.htm. Lianjiang Li, "Driven to Protest: China's Rural Unrest," *Current History* (September 2006), 251.

115. US Department of State, "China," 3; Joseph Kahn, "Chinese Abused for Complaints, Study Concludes," *New York Times* (December 9, 2005).

116. Matt Pottinger, "China Takes Hard Line on Protesters," *Wall Street Journal* (September 10, 2004).

117. Keith Bradsher, "China Is Accused of Abuses in Secret Jails," *New York Times* (November 13, 2009); Kahn, "Chinese Abused."

118. Jacobs, "Seeking Justice."

119. Andrew Jacobs, "A Rare Look at Secret Detentions," *New York Times* (November 27, 2009); Edward Wong, "China Sentences Women Held After Protest Attempt," *New York Times* (July 31, 2009).

120. Kahn, "Chinese Abused"; Jacobs, "Seeking Justice"; Bradsher, "China Is Accused"; Li, "Driven to Protest," 253.

121. Jacobs, "Seeking Justice."

122. Howard W. French, "Survivor's Stories from China," *New York Times* (August 25, 2009).

123. Andrew Jacobs, "No Voice Is Too Small for a China Still Nervous About Dissent," *New York Times* (August 30, 2008); US Department of State, "China," 4; Keith Bradsher, "China Issues 2-Year Plan To Protect Civil Liberties," *New York Times* (April 14, 2009).

124. Charles Hutzler, "In Rural China, Religious Groups Face Suppression," *Wall Street Journal* (July 27, 2004).

125. Andrew Jacobs, "After 10 Years and 2,000 Deaths, China Still Presses Its Crusade Against Falun Gong," *New York Times* (April 28, 2009).

126. Murray Scot Tanner, "Cracks in the Wall: China's Eroding Coercive State," *Current History* (September 2001), 244–45.

127. Andrew Jacobs, "China Fears Ethnic Strive Could Agitate Uighur Oasis," *New York Times* (July 23, 2009).

128. US Department of State, "China," 9.

129. Yardley, "Chinese Forces Say They've Secured Tibet's Capital."

130. Nicholas D. Kristof, "Riddle of China: Repression as Standard of Living Soars," *New York Times* (September 7, 1993).

131. Edward S. Steinfeld, "Beyond the Transition: China's Economy at Century's End," *Current History* (September 1999), 283.

132. Michael Wines, "China Is Said to Hinder Human Rights Lawyers," *New York Times* (May 28, 2009); Andrew Jacobs, "China's Defiance on Human Rights Stirs Fears for Missing Dissident," *New York Times* (February 3, 2010).

133. US Department of State, "China," 5.

134. Pei, *China's Trapped Transition,* 71.

135. US Department of State, "China," 4.

136. James D. Seymour, "Human Rights in China," *Current History* (September 1994), 258.

137. US Department of State, "China," 5 (emphasis added).

138. Ibid., 6.

139. Andrew Jacobs, "China Limits the Crimes Punishable by Death," *New York Times* (July 30, 2009); Andrew Jacobs, "Effort Made to Save Man China Convicted of Spying," *New York Times* (November 27, 2008); US Department of State, "China," 6.

140. David Lague, "China Moves to Lessen Broad Use of Death Sentences," *New York Times* (November 1, 2006); Mark McDonald and Michael Wines, "Report Says Executions

Doubled Worldwide," *New York Times* (March 25, 2009); Jim Yardley, "In Worker's Death, View of China's Harsh Justice," *New York Times* (December 31, 2005).

141. Seymour, "Human Rights in China," 258; Jacobs, "China Limits the Crimes."

142. Andrew Jacobs, "Britain Fights for the Life of One of Its Citizens in China," *New York Times* (October 14, 2009).

143. Joseph Kahn, "Deep Flaws, and Little Justice in China's Court System," *New York Times* (September 21, 2005); Joseph Kahn, "China Quick to Execute Drug Official," *New York Times* (July 11, 2007).

144. Andrew J. Nathan, "China and the International Human Rights Regime," in *China Joins the World: Progress and Prospects,* ed. Elizabeth Economy and Michel Oksenberg (New York: Council on Foreign Relations Press, 1999), 143–44; David Shambaugh, "The United States and China: A New Cold War?" *Current History* (September 1995), 243.

145. Michael Wines, "China Announces a System for Voluntary Organ Donors," *New York Times* (August 27, 2009).

146. In 2009 the regime announced that it would reform the system of organ donation, but the thrust of the reform was to ban the use of organ transplants for foreigners. Wines, Ibid.; Mark McDonald, "Beijing Investigates Transplants for Tourists," *New York Times* (February 18, 2009); US Department of State, "China," 3.

147. Kahn, "China Quick to Execute."

148. Sharon LaFraniere, "2 Executed in China for Selling Tainted Milk," *New York Times* (November 25, 2009); David Barboza, "China Plans to Execute 2 in Scandal over Milk," *New York Times* (January 23, 2009).

149. Sarah Lyall, "The Winner's Chair Remains Empty at Nobel Event," *New York Times* (December 11, 2010).

150. David Barboza, "Foreign News Sites Appear to Be Blocked in China," *New York Times* (December 10, 2010).

151. Benjamin Haas and David Wong, "In Beijing, as in Oslo, an Honoree Is Absent," *New York Times* (December 10, 2010).

152. Thomas L. Friedman, "We've Only Got America A," *New York Times* (December 15, 2010).

153. Lyall, "The Winner's Chair."

Conclusion

1. Miguel Helft and David Barboza, "Google Closes Search Service in China," *New York Times* (March 23, 2010).

2. Keith Bradsher, "Green Power Takes Root in China," *New York Times* (July 3, 2009).

3. David Barboza, "As China Raises Wages, Export Prices Could Follow," *New York Times* (June 8, 2010).

4. David Barboza and Hiroko Tabuchi, "Labor Strife Signals Shift in China," *New York Times* (June 9, 2010).

5. Vikas Bajaj, "From China, a Hint That Its Currency May Rise," *New York Times* (April 2, 2010).

6. Sewell Chan, "Senators Losing Patience with U.S. Policy on China," *New York Times* (June 11, 2010).

Index

About the Author

Robert K. Schaeffer is Professor of Global Sociology at Kansas State University. He is the author of *Warpaths: The Politics of Partition* (Hill and Wang, 1990), *Power to the People: Democratization Around the World* (Westview Press, 1997), *Understanding Globalization* (Rowman & Littlefield, 1997, 2003, 2005, 2009), *Severed States: Dilemmas of Democracy in a Divided World* (Rowman & Littlefield, 1999), and with Torry D. Dickinson, coauthor of *Fast Forward: Work, Gender, and Protest in a Changing World* (Rowman & Littlefield, 2001) and *Transformations: Feminist Pathways to Global Change* (Paradigm Publishers, 2008).